ALMOST A REAL DOCTOR

ONE VETERINARIAN'S STRUGGLE TO SURVIVE IN A DOG-EAT-DOG WORLD

By

Dr. Robert G. Cimer, D.V.M.

This book is a work of creative nonfiction. I portray the events to the best of my memory with minimal dramatic license. While the stories in this book are true the names, dates, and specific details have been changed to protect the parties and pets described in this book.

Copyright © 2019 by Robert G. Cimer

All rights reserved. No part of this book may be reproduced or used in any manner without written permission of the copyright owner except for the use of quotations in a book review.

ALMOST A REAL DOCTOR

First Paperback Edition July 2019

Cover/Book Design by Aaron Lightbody-Cimer

ISBN: 9781079725216

I dedicate this book to:

    My mother for a childhood rich in pets,
    My brother for a life lesson rich in honor,
    My wife for a marriage rich in love,
    My children for a family rich in innocence,
    My God for a lifetime full of riches.

"Far better it is to dare mighty things, to win glorious triumphs, even though checkered by failure... then to rank with those poor spirits who neither enjoy much nor suffer much, because they live in the great twilight that knows not victory nor defeat."

- Theodore Roosevelt at the Hamilton Club 1899
Announcing his resignation from his job in Phoenix, Arizona to start his private law practice in Tulsa, Oklahoma.

ALMOST

A REAL

DOCTOR

CONTENTS

Preface..i
Veterinarian's Oath...v
Prologue..vii

Chapter 1: Left Out in the Cold..............................1

Chapter 2: A Boy's Strife..19

Chapter 3: Welcome to the Jungle........................47

Chapter 4: Descent into the Abyss........................71

Chapter 5: Last Picked for the Big Dance..........103

Chapter 6: A Rude Awakening............................127

Chapter 7: You Can't Cure Crazy.......................153

Chapter 8: Warlock's Apprentice........................185

Chapter 9: The Stinky Kid on the Block............215

Chapter 10: Time to Wear the Big Boy Pants...241

Chapter 11: Madame, You Have Cats in Your Mattress..275

Chapter 12: Defending the Innocent...................307

Chapter 13: Knocking on Heaven's Door..........329

Chapter 14: The Worst-Case Scenario...............347

Chapter 15: Shattered Dreams............................379

Bibliography..413

PREFACE

In thirty years as a veterinarian I have often heard my colleagues repeat a familiar mantra, "I wish our clients knew what we deal with every day, they have no idea. The stories we could tell." In this plea from weary and underpaid professionals lies the first reason for writing this book. I intend to dispel those common misconceptions that permeate the public view of this profession. I call this common false narrative, "fluff." The idea that veterinarians are nothing more than over-educated animal lovers, spending their days squeezing puppies and petting pretty ponies-their intense passion overriding any desire to have a private life or earn a decent living. I believe it has subjugated veterinary medicine to a less important discipline than our counterparts in the human medical profession. In my stories, I illuminate the heart from which still beats my passion, I reveal the root of my mounting frustration, and I show the growing malignancy which threatens this profession.

Secondly, this book is at its heart a memoir; the story of my life from a naïve adolescent to a hopeful student, to a successful and somewhat disillusioned professional. By recreating the acts of my life, compassionately and humorously, I hope to instill the empathy needed to accept my opinions and appreciate my critical conclusions on this cherished profession. This an honest, unfiltered portrayal of my life's avocation. The hippies of the seventies used to ask this question: "Do you know where I'm coming from?" I hope by the end of this book the reader knows "where I'm coming from."

Thirdly, I wrote this book to show the forces behind the changes in the field of veterinary medicine, or more precisely the business of veterinary medicine. The traditional small-town veterinarians are quickly disappearing; they are being replaced by the fiscally efficient acumen and deep pockets of corporate America. This change in veterinary medicine, like the pharmacists a generation before, is disturbing to those of us who fantasized about retiring under our own eternally respected and weather-worn shingle.

In writing this book, I revisited memories which spanned twenty-five years and traveled the emotional spectrum from painful agony to victorious exhilaration. The dialogue, the characters, and the cases gleaned from memory and record. The names have been changed to protect the innocent and to convict the guilty. (Just Kidding).

I have had essential mentors who by fates hand lead me to become a better veterinarian. These were veterinary school instructors and practicing clinicians. These were men and women who taught me to treat the patient while considering the owner instead of only treating the pet while ignoring the client. I learned that points memorized in four years of veterinary school are useless without the logic and common sense to use these facts to treat the patient. It is akin to having a large truck full of paving blocks, and you have a road map. Your medical knowledge is a load of bricks and the road map the logical path to lay those bricks. This map directs the veterinarian down a smooth, solid path to diagnose and cure the pet. If you can't follow a route, your road goes nowhere, destined to be bogged down in a murky swamp. There are good, and there are bad veterinarians. In many cases, the pet owner chooses their veterinarian based on bedside manner, alone; which is not a reliable gauge to determine their pet's doctor. A better gauge would be how smoothly that veterinarian travels down that magical yellow brick road.

Today, even more than when I was young, there is a plethora of books, reality shows and failed sitcoms which glamorize and trivialize veterinarians. They tend to ignore some of the harsher realities of the practice and business of veterinary medicine. This book is more than just heartfelt fluffy stories of rescued puppies and mischievous kittens, although I have included my fair share of "Fluff" in this memoir. It also speaks to the daily trials of the practicing veterinarian; how we deal with impossible clients and accept our unescapable failures. Veterinarians are human; they make mistakes, they get frustrated with owners, they burn out, and they yearn for more respect. I may be more human and infinitely more flawed than most.

Finally, I am by nature a man who prefers a day spent with his beautiful wife and three children over a morning dodging a biting dog or debating an irate client. Therefore, in a profession which offers as much agony as ecstasy, I must admit that often it is the people with whom I spend my day which makes coming to work enjoyable. (After all, I met my wife while working in a veterinary hospital). The technicians, receptionists, and "some" doctors make the workday tolerable; we are soldiers in the same foxhole. Like the players in a *M*A*S*H* episode their humor, sarcasm, and empathy allow me to survive those problematic and disappointing days. Veterinary medicine has at its heart a love for animals which helps us to smile in the face of daily adversity; there's where the fluff comes in.

VETERINARIAN'S OATH

Being admitted to the profession of veterinary medicine, I solemnly swear to use my scientific knowledge and skills for the benefit of society through the protection of animal health and welfare, the prevention and relief of animal suffering, the conservation of animal resources, the promotion of public health, and the advancement of medical knowledge.

I will practice my profession conscientiously, with dignity, and in keeping with the principles of veterinary medical ethics.

I accept as a lifelong obligation the continual improvement of my professional knowledge and competence.

PROLOGUE

The third bead of sweat trickled, slowly down my glasses, blurring the scarlet numbers on the pulse oximeter. Was that a thirty or a ninety? I couldn't tell, but I could see he still wasn't breathing.

"Breathe for him, Robin," I ordered. "Put your mouth over his face. We've got to get air into him. Get him on a heating pad!" My hand was starting to cramp as I struggled to mimic the heartbeat of the eight-pound animal; holding the fragile chest in my clenched palms, I squeezed the ribs like I was pressing a ripe lemon-twice every second; my compressions were firm but guarded. I was starting to panic as this animal was dying.

"Any heartbeats on that thing, or is that me?" I asked. When I stopped my compressions, it took only seconds for the beeping pulse to slow down and quickly grow silent.

"No, that's me. Get me another dose of epi. Hurray! Yes, dilute one to ten." I inserted the syringe deep between two ribs and drew the hub back. As a thin line of blood swirled toward me, I injected a milliliter of diluted epinephrine directly into the heart. Seconds later I detected a heartbeat. "I got it again," I announced. "Keep breathing. Try to get a tube in him. We've got to get him on oxygen!"

Thirty seconds passed as the head technician made a futile attempt to place an endotracheal tube in the deep, pen size opening. "Forget it," I said, flipping him on his other side. "Start mouth to mouth again. Robin, try to get a butterfly in the back leg." She failed twice before I could hear the heart rate slowing; one hundred and twenty, ninety, thirty…

"Stop!" I yelled as I started to compress his ribs again. "Inject a couple of tenths of Doxapram under the tongue. Keep breathing. Again!" His pupils were fixed and dilated, and he wasn't breathing. "Damn, why isn't he breathing?" Shit! In all my years of practice, I had never lost one like this. 'God, not this one, not this one,' I thought. "I lost it again. Get me another dose of epi. What? No, I've never had this happen before. Not twenty minutes after surgery. Never!"

I responded to one of the concerned voices fluttering around me. That was true; in twenty-five years of practice and over a hundred procedures, this had never happened. I never suspected there was a chance this pet could die; this was not a thought when I scheduled the surgery, this was not a thought when I left my home one hour before with that grey pet carrier nestled in my back seat, this was not a thought when I injected the tranquilizer into this animal's thigh muscle, like I had done countless times before. However, now one thought did flood my mind; how would I explain this to the three children who adored him and their mother who trusted her husband to perform this simple surgery and bring their family's pet home-alive.

"Get me another dose. Now! Keep breathing for him. Keep breathing. Again…

CHAPTER 1

LEFT OUT IN THE COLD

"That'll do, pig. That'll do."

- The Movie: "Babe" (1995)

I never liked pigs. I couldn't respect an animal whose bucket list consisted of foraging in compost and sunbathing in the mud. Coming from New Jersey, I just had no intention of seeing one outside of a butcher shop. In fact, in vet school, I would often joke that the only pork I would ever treat was with a Kansas City pork marinade before one of my back-yard barbecues. So, it wasn't ironic that an early December night had turned frigid and snowy–Missouri winters tended to rush the season a bit. Neither was it ironic that another Missouri sow was about to farrow another litter of piglets–that's how they stayed off Denny's breakfast menu. What was truly ironic was that it was midnight and I, among all people, would be lying on an old wooden door propped up over a muddy pigpen dangling head first over an angry, pregnant 800-pound sow, one arm wrist deep up to her cervix the other holding on to the doorknob to prevent me from falling into the cold mud and feces. This entire macabre drama was illuminated by the high beams of an old Ford pickup which sliced through the flurries like an iconic scene from a bad horror movie. I only hoped the irony was not wasted on the farmer and my inexperience wasted on the pig.

I had earned my degree of Doctor of Veterinary Medicine (DVM) from the University of Missouri -College of Veterinary Medicine precisely seven months before in the hot sun of a bright day in early May with even brighter hopes for the future. I had spent the last eight years in school memorizing every anatomic and physiologic fact of every domestic species from the field mouse to the quarter horse. I endured thousands of hours of lecture, tens of thousands of questions on everything from the blood flow of a bull's penis to the embryologic origin of the ventricles of the canine brain.

I, like every veterinary school graduate, was proficient in all domestic species. Specialization while in vet school, at least in the eighties, was not an option within the DVM program at Missouri. You were free to choose after graduation; most of us were either specializing in Equine medicine, farm animal medicine, small animal medicine, or a combination of all three called mixed animal medicine, a common practice in mostly rural settings. Some rare veterinarians specialized in zoo animal medicine, avian medicine such as commercial chicken production, marine animal medicine, or swine medicine. Ironically, at that time some of the highest paid veterinarians were in the aromatic field of pig production.

Most of the veterinary class becomes somewhat polarized along the lines of these specialized interests. In the mid-eighties, the veterinary student at the University of Missouri-College of Veterinary Medicine could not opt out of those disciplines he or she felt trivial, so like it or not this Jersey boy had to take eight weeks of farm animal medicine and eight weeks of equine medicine. Lucky for us, the more urbanistic students, these clinical rotations tended to be conducted by laid back country doctors while the small animal medical and surgical rotations were more intense taught by uptight residents and minor deities called attending clinicians. It wasn't the large animal medicine was any less challenging; it was the relaxed attitude of the professors was a pleasant respite from the searing spot-light of small animal rotations. Most of the small animal students learned large animal subjects for two reasons; to pass the class and nailing the questions on the future board exams we would take just before graduation-then we would never need this minutia again.

Consequently, in my cavalier approach, I regarded these rotations as technical courses filled with fun animals and cool field trips to dairy farms and hen houses. Didactic or lectures were handled in the clinical blocks with much more ease and made these courses enjoyable. I was confident I would never need their practical applications as I was a small animal all the way. Book smarts and practical skills are two separate traits. Thus, when circumstances brought me upside down with my hand in the opposite end of a sow's ear, I started to regret not being more focused on those farm trips. As a child, I had thought the closest I would get to a pig was a hot dog stand at a Phillies game. However, like one of my professors loved to say, "Never say never."

I knew when I graduated, I would have to endure another blast furnace summer and flash frozen winter in Missouri. Circumstances would keep me in the college town of Columbia, Missouri for another year. I needed a job. The problem was Columbia was a town of 60,000 people, six small animal veterinary clinics and about seventy-five graduates every year. That created a rather small window of opportunity for a herd of hungry Missouri good old boys and girls in a limited job pool. I didn't have a chance. I had to compromise my goals.

Thus, about a month after graduation I obtained a position in a mixed animal practice in a rural town, 30 miles west of Columbia called Booneville; a quaint village along the Missouri River. It was a living cliché out of a Mark Twain novel complete with a pot-bellied sheriff and a bloodhound named Bufford. The practice was owned by Dr. Gary Lister a fellow Missouri graduate, who grew up in a family of mid-Missouri dairy farmers. He was a quiet, mild-tempered man, in his thirties with a slight Midwestern draw. He practiced out of a prefabricated freestanding metal building with a three-room small animal facility in the front and large animal pens and stanchions in the back. He serviced the surrounding countryside dairy, horse and pig farms, as well, as the dog and cat population-hence a mixed animal practice.

His primary interest was in the emerging science of embryo transfer in dairy cows. This veterinarian was kind enough to hire me to be a small animal practitioner with the assumption I would treat the small animals, and he would cover the farm calls, but if needed I could muddle through a corral or two-after all I was a veterinary school graduate-I knew everything.

This concept was great in theory. It was a perfect practice to start my career. The workload was mild, and the hours were reasonable. When I first graduated, I was cautious about everything. Every injection I gave, every medication I prescribed, and every surgery I performed I went to sleep that night worrying about the consequences. I read every drug insert, and I prayed before and after every operation. I was both surprised and exhilarated to see a pet bouncing in his cage the morning after surgery. "Great, she is still alive!" In between my 2 or 3 appointments each morning I would read professional journals and textbooks to hone my skills and increase my confidence. Dr. Lister would leave in the morning on farm calls, and I would hold down the fort with dogs and cats. I hadn't seen a farm animal in a month and was content to keep it that way.

Then in mid–July things got more serious; we got a call. I had to vaccinate two dozen calves in a nearby farm. The problem was Dr. Lister was going down south for the day to a cattle auction and was unable to handle the job.

"No problem," I said. "I got this." A monkey could vaccinate a couple of calves.

"Take the truck and head on over there." Dr. Lister said, pointing to the specially modified Chevy pickup I had seen him drive out on farm calls every day for the last month. This truck had a specialized cover in the truck bed with multiple drawers and a small refrigerator for cooled medications. It was a small truck that surprisingly kept everything you would need on the average farm call.

"You got it," I said as I caught the keys and headed for the door. "Besides it would be nice to be outside for the afternoon."

So, I was going out on my first farm call. The Jersey boy was taking the pickup and headed out to spend the day with the cows. I was excited. This case was the first solo farm call of my career. I couldn't wait until I could call my mom that night and tell her what I did at work today.

"How cute were those cows, honey?" I knew she would be proud!

I might even like farm life. Like Green Acres: "Booneville might be the place to be." I dressed in my blue overalls, put on my boots and headed out. I sat in the truck closed the door, started the engine and grabbed the stick.

"Stick! Son of a dairy cow, I can't drive a stick!" The desperation of my voice echoed off the searing windshield of the small truck as searing waves of frustration slapped me in the face. I punched the dashboard. What was I going to tell my mom tonight? So much for my first farm call.

Finally, after he stopped laughing Dr. Lister quipped "What, they don't have pickups in New Jersey?"

I didn't know how to answer without sounding sarcastic. It was 1988 only NASCAR drivers knew the secrets of the manual transmission.

Left Out in the Cold

Luckily, Dr. Lister was an understanding man. I spent the rest of the day practicing driving a stick shift in the farmland adjacent to his practice. It took all day and probably cost him a good clutch, but I mastered the most critical attribute of the farm animal veterinarian; to be able to drive out to the farm.

My mother had a great love for animals; she was especially fond of puppies and kittens, but she thought cows were the cutest (perhaps because she was born and raised in Philadelphia, where cattle drives down Market Street were rare). So, when she first heard I was working with farm animals she was beaming. I am sure it was the talk of her Wednesday morning Presbyterian prayer group gossip hour. "Your daughter's a lawyer, that's nice. Your son is an engineer, that's great. "My son put his whole arm up a cow's rear, and now she's pregnant." I am sure all those pretentious church ladies were truly impressed-or maybe not.

Fortunately, for my mother, I would have plenty of attempts to make her proud. Because as the summer wore on, Dr. Lister would be on a separate call, or periodically travel on vacation, and leave me the exclusive responsibility of attending to the farm calls-sometimes for a week at a time. It was trial by fire. To some extent it was what all new graduates had to experience—you take all that "fancy book learning" and try to put it to practical use. However, unlike human medicine the day you get your license is the day you can practice. An internship or residency is not required. In most cases, you will be alone in appointments, alone in surgery, alone on farm calls; whether small animal or large the pressure and responsibility was yours.

In my case, I was familiar with small animal medicine and surgery as I had worked in pet animal hospitals for four years, but I had little "real world experience" handling large animals. I had become much more comfortable driving the hospital truck than in being a farm animal veterinarian. Each day I would drive to work in my little hatchback which became a mobile veterinary library housing all my large animal class notes, textbooks, and a medical formulary. I would even bring some of them along in the truck on each call. I would research the information when I got the call in a futile attempt to elevate my confidence level and gain the farmer's trust. Increasing my confidence was much easier than impressing the farmers. They were neither ignorant nor stupid- especially about their animals. They knew a fake when they saw it. If it was not my Jersey accent that tipped them off, it was my trepidation treating animals as big as my hatchback. I was as nervous about being run over by a 2,000-pound bull on a Missouri pasture as I was getting rear-ended by a truck on a New Jersey Turnpike.

I also became acutely aware of a profound difference in the psychology between a small animal and farm animal practice which makes a considerable difference in the approach one takes in practice. Farm animals are a commodity, each animal is a source of income, and the herd is the farmer's whole livelihood. This premise I learned to appreciate watching to the 6 A.M. farm livestock market reports leading the morning news. The farm report gave the daily prices of livestock; calves, cows, steer, barrows and sows. The rates were based on the weight of the animal and its intended use, such as those sold for slaughter and those sold for breeding. It even had the cost for cow and calves sold in pairs. It changed weekly. The Missouri farmers viewed these reports as essential information as vital as the daily weather report. They bought and sold based on daily prices. It was their Dow Jones stock market report.

The farm animal logic is also one of herd mentality — the sacrifice of the one or few for the good of the many. If a dog or cat is ill, the logical small animal solution would be to diagnose, treat and cure the individual. A small animal practitioner would never think of euthanizing a sick house cat to try and save the other cats in the house. However, in farm animal medicine one hopes to treat the sick animal but sometimes has no alternative but to sacrifice that animal to diagnose a disease. The primary goal to diagnose the animal as quickly as possible, may in some cases, require the farmer to cull or sacrifice the animal to prevent spread to additional livestock. The culling of a diseased herd member can lead to the cause or "etiology" of the illness. This proven methodology can potentially save the entire herd. Epidemiology is the study of the spread of disease. In farm animal medicine this science took a close second to preventative medicine. Necropsy or the autopsy on another animal species is one extremely vital skill taught in the veterinary curriculum. It is with these culled herd members or animals who have already died that one finds the identity of the disease and the methods to contain it.

This was a new environment for me to learn, digest and put into practice quickly; as different as the anatomy of the digestive tract of the carnivorous tabby and the farm animal ruminants I was asked to treat.

However, I was up for it. I had come from a family with a European blue-collar mentality which dictated one did what one had to do to succeed-don't rely on anyone else. So, I welcomed the first call after learning how to drive a stick in the afternoon on a broiling mid-July day. My boss was on vacation in the Bahamas, and the responsibility of the entire practice was mine for a week, just my mobile library and me. This was the era long before cell phones and internet veterinary websites, so I was, for the first time, a farm animal veterinarian entirely on my own.

This call was something I could handle. A cow had died at a nearby dairy farm, and it was my job to find out why. I liked performing necropsies; it was not easy to screw up, the cow was already dead, you cut them open and took samples. It was more physically demanding than intellectually challenging. When I arrived at the barn, the farmer informed me the cow was not in the cool shade of the barn by a half a mile away in the south pasture.

"She's that way. You can't miss-er." The farmer said, pointing south in the general direction of the late afternoon sun.

So, my pickup and I bounced along the rough dirt road leading through the pasture. I couldn't see the cow at first, and all I kept thinking was how foolish I would look returning to the barn with the news that I couldn't find a 1500-pound animal lying in an open pasture in the middle of the day. Finally, I spotted her over a small ridge and stopped about twenty feet from the bloated corpse of a dead Holstein. I exited into the 100-degree heat and immediately learned which way the wind was blowing; straight from the cow into my face.

10

Left Out in the Cold

Anyone who has driven past roadkill will know how fast a corpse starts to smell; a dead animal will degrade very quickly. The intestinal bacteria and internal body fluids start a nuclear-like reaction that hydrolyzes the body's tissue within 30 minutes. Bake a cow for three hours in the hot summer sun, and the final dish is an aromatic bloated corpse-a smell which wilts your nasal hairs for days. By this time rigor mortis has set in, the purple tongue stiffly protrudes from the locked jaw, the barrel-shaped abdomen bloats to twice normal size and the only thing moving is the swarms of horse flies which seem to pan out six feet away from their rotting prize.

After I performed a quick external examination, I readied the delicate medical tools required to complete the internal necropsy-an ax, bolt cutters and a twelve-inch necropsy knife. Wearing latex gloves, plastic goggles and fully covered in dark overalls (I had forgotten the latex apron we had used in vet school). I cut open the abdominal cavity, slicing through the leather wall, the cut released much of the odorous gas like a punctured football. Immediately the intestines toppled down as I remembered another forgotten accessory–rubber boots. Now ankle deep in gastric fluid I used the knife to open each of the four compartmentalized stomachs and the small and large intestine. I took small samples from each, and quarter size wedge resections of the primary organs; liver, kidney, spleen, and bladder and moved on to the chest. Here is where the ax and bolt cutters came in handy. I would stand over the body, my left foot on her chest like a deranged Captain Morgan add and swing the ax to break the ribs on each side of the sternum. It was just like chopping wood except it splattered blood onto your overalls and into your face, hence the purpose of the goggles. Then when I broke the ribs, I would cut each with the bolt cutters and fold the sternum up exposing the heart and lungs; then I took samples of each organ. Finally, I would use the necropsy knife to follow the esophagus and trachea through the thoracic inlet and up through the neck and pull them out like a bloody pool noodle; and if done by the book the tongue would still be attached. I did not open the skull in the field so in my necropsy no brain samples were taken-I did have my limits.

    I then stood there in the empty field, sweat pouring down my back, body and face spattered with blood, socks drenched in abdomen fluid, arms shaking, fatigued from breaking ribs the size of broomsticks, alongside a fifteen-hundred-pound cow split almost in two open from head to tail. All I could think was the famous Harrison Ford line from Star Wars: "And I thought they smelled bad on the outside."

    Just one week later I had what I thought was a similar call: A six- month old calf was missing at the Gleason farm the next town south, and there was a high suspicion the calf was down. I guess I had so impressed Dr. Lister with the first necropsy I was the perfect choice for today's job. Either that or Dr. Lister found someone else to do the dirty work; namely me. However, if I were to see another dead cow this time, I would be ready. I made sure I had my apron and my boots. Upon leaving the office, I ask Dr. Lister, "If there was any possibility the calf could have run away"?

Left Out in the Cold

"Runaway?" He shot back as he adjusted his cap down lower over his eyes, as he so often did; I think to hide his scow. "Damn boy, it's not a stray cat"!

Fifteen minutes later I drove over a cattle guard and along the uneven path which meandered through the high pasture grass of farm very different from the last. This farm wasn't a pasture it was a jungle-it was even impossible to delineate its respective borders. I parked alongside two thirty-year-old Fords on cinder blocks. They were blocking the driveway which led up to a dilapidated ranch house which I feared would produce at any moment a chainsaw-wielding mutant in overalls.

Instead, I was met at a tattered screen door by a white-haired old woman in a housedress and slippers who, between puffs of her homemade cigarette, told me the story of the lost calf. "I might have seen her last week, somewhere before the last storm. My boy Earl was supposed to go looking for her, but he don't listen to me no-more. Thirty years old you would think he would have more common sense. It like these damn cars-he was supposed to get them running again." She said sarcastically, as she flicked the cigarette butt onto the rusted car hood.

I then started on my quest to find the calf. I walked on a narrow dirt path to the pasture where Mrs. Gleason had last seen the calf. The trail ended, as I trail blazed through waist-high fescue grass down to the wood line to the south. A one point I must have startled a giant snake which leaped above the grass and fell to the ground slithering away. "This is great. Eight years of school," I thought, "and I'm dodging snakes, and hunting stray cows in the woods." Thirty minutes later I meandered through the fields and entered a

13

break in the tree line and walked down to a dry stream bed. Finally, there she was or more appropriately used to be.

Lying on the bottom of the dry stream bed was a mere outline of an animal. It was like a police chalk outline of a small calf. A slithering white mass the size of a baby pool. It was the dead carcass, or precisely at this point maybe some leather covered three inches deep in thousands of maggots. This poor thing died a while ago. How long would it take maggots to eat a four-hundred-pound calf? I couldn't even guess, but it was a sure bet it was longer than a week. One thing I knew I would not need my apron and boots today.

Upon returning to the house, I informed Mrs. Gleason of the bad news that her calf was long gone. However, there was good news; now Earl could focus on fixing those damn cars. I refrained from telling her that the poor calf was nothing more than a maggot stain on the side of a ravine. My sympathy waned a bit when she asked, "What do you think killed her?" Through the thick smoke of that nasty cigarette blowing in my face.

"Suicide!" Which is what I wanted to say. However, those words never left my mouth. I tried to be a compassionate professional and invented a story about how the calf probably went to the river bed to get a drink after the rain, broke her leg and died of exposure. Who would have proven me wrong? At that point, there were barely any bones left?

Summer passed, and through the fall I had an occasional farm visit for routine vaccinations and sick livestock. Mostly, I was hospital bound treating the local dog and cat population. I had very few real opportunities to make my mother proud. Thus, in

14

Left Out in the Cold

December, when Dr. Lister left for a seminar, I leaped at the chance to do something exciting on a live farm animal in a muddy pigpen on a frigid Missouri night.

I was packing up for the night when the call came. A two-year-old sow was in dystocia; which is an abnormal or prolonged labor to deliver piglets. It was exciting and a perfect opportunity to bring new life into the world. On the drive, over to the farm, I ran the scenario over in my head. I would enter the farrowing barn, administer oxytocin to stimulate the first uterine contractions and the first Chihuahua size piglet would slide on out-and then another and another. If they still weren't coming, I would administer additional oxytocin until I could deliver all the piglets. I would methodically clean up each piglet, removing the placenta, aspirate the mucous from the nose, roll them in a towel to warm them and swing them like a pendulum to clear their nostrils until they were breathing clearly. If they still were not breathing, I would administer oral Doxapram, a respiratory stimulant. They would spring to life as each little piglet would be pinker and cuter than the last.

Upon pulling up to the swine farm, I was greeted by the unmistakable odor, well, of pigs. Unfortunately, there was not a farrowing barn in sight, for a far as I could see through the twilight was pen after pen made of three feet high wire fencing. Each eight by ten pen was covered on a side by a plywood cover the pigs used as a shelter. I was startled by a two yellow Labradors who bounded over to greet me as I exited the truck. Behind them strolled a middle- age farmer in overalls. "I'm Dr. Cimer from---."

"She's right over there, Doc," interrupted the farmer, pointing to a pen about 30 yards away,

Almost A Real Doctor

partially lite by the lights of an old Ford truck-its engine running, smoke billowing from the exhaust.

"How long has she been in labor?" I asked as I walked my bag over to the pen and started to climb in.

"Whoa! I wouldn't do that Doc; she can be real ornery! Especially now." He added as he tugged my arm back from the top of the fence. "I think you're gonna have to do everything you need to do from outside the pen."

My question went unanswered. Before my eyes was a 400-pound sow laying on its side halfway under an old wooden door with its rear facing into the muddy pen, I could make out her snout puffing a warm breath every few seconds through the cold air. I couldn't put my arms through the fence its openings were too, small-so I had to devise a plan from above, and I don't mean God.

I placed my equipment on the door and climbed aboard. The door was getting slippery as the snow had just started to fall; with one hand holding on to the icy glass doorknob I suspended my body down to her level and placed my other gloved hand into her vaginal canal to evaluate the situation. I immediately felt the small bony front legs of the first piglet. I added some KY lube, twisted to the fetus 180 degrees and slowly withdrew the piglet. I briefly tried to resuscitate the lifeless purple form, but I knew immediately, it was dead. The soft, limp feel of a dead fetus became very easy to identify even with my limited experience. There was nothing I could do to save this one.

"This first one's dead," I screamed to the farmer as I sat upright on the door.

Left Out in the Cold

"Throw it over there," came the reply, as he pointed towards the front of the pickup.

I was sure he would retrieve the body and dispose of it. Like a beanbag, I tossed the piglet over the fence through the beams of the headlights and into the leaping jowls of one of the waiting dogs. In great revelry, he ran off into the dark with his catch. I was both shocked and nauseated as I stared jaw agape into the dark face of the farmer.

"Don't worry," he said, "Cooter will be back for more if you got em."

Shaking my head, I went back to work. I gave an injection of oxytocin and pulled the next dead fetus out of the canal. This one too was lifeless and limp. One by one I pulled dead piglets from the sow and one by one upon direction from the farmer threw each into the waiting jaws of one of the family dogs. The reality quenched my pride in delivering the piglets in a truly severe situation knowing their fate was nothing more than lifeless dog toys. Finally, the sixth and last one was pulled and tossed into the snowy car lights.

"What a minute, this one's alive." Yelled the farmer as he wrestled the prize piglet from one of the Labradors like an old shoe.

To our surprise, this one was wiggling and let out a squeal. Then the farmer then rubbed it clean and put it in his coat. The dogs were looking at him like they had been teased out of a juicy steak bone- saliva dripping from their lips. "Get outta here, go up to the house!" he chided as the dogs ran into the darkness.

The grateful farmer walked back to his truck, content. I think he may have been satisfied with one live piglet-at least it would ultimately pay for my visit to his farm that evening. The thirty-minute drive back to the hospital allowed my hands and feet to thaw after lying on that cold wooden door for what seemed like an eternity. I had some degree of satisfaction that out of a trying night I had been responsible for the life of a warm pink addition to the world. Of course, I knew that the piglet's future would be at best as a breeding sow in a muddy eight by ten world, or at worst as a main course in next year's pig roast. However, tonight, I was content that I had made a small difference in the life of a pig. That night planted a new seed of respect for the species and a new love for a tiny, pink, squealing piglet. This story would certainly make my mother proud. I would, of course, skip the part with the piggy beanbag toss.

    This scene would be the subject of my next call home. I'm sure my mother beamed with pride as she spoke of it at the next weekly prayer meeting. However, she would say later that upon hearing the tale the pious cackling hens of her prayer group would follow up with the same mindless question that often followed such stories-a question which would leave her speechless and me irritated.

"A veterinarian," they would ask," isn't that almost a real doctor?" I have been asked this question numerous times by innocent children and clueless adults. "A veterinarian. Isn't that almost a real doctor?" In a sow's ear, or should I say cervix.

CHAPTER 2

A BOY'S STRIFE

"The Road is Long, With Many a Winding Turn"

- The song: He Ain't Heavy, He's My Brother

My mother died on Tuesday, August 29, 2011. In her memorial on the following Saturday, I gave her praise for two founding principles of my life: my faith in God and my love for animals. She was a lifelong Presbyterian, Sunday school teacher, and church deacon who fostered our Christian faith. Secondly, my mother introduced me to a world filled with stray dogs and cats, cultivated my compassion for suffering wildlife, and nurtured my dream to become a veterinarian. My mother attended my veterinary school graduation on a scalding day in May of 1988. She flew halfway across the country, divorced, alone, with the money she earned as a live-in nanny, to witness the ceremony - the only family member in attendance. Twenty-three years later, I thought it vital to include her philosophy in a thirty-minute memorial covering seventy-nine years of my mother's life.

    I grew up in a German-Yugoslavian home in a middle-class, rural community in Southern New Jersey during the 1960s. We had many dogs; some lived outdoors; some were house dogs, most never saw a vet. My absolute favorite was Samantha, a stray who landed on our doorstep when I was ten. She lived through my adolescence and into my first year of vet school. Her puppy picture still decorates my office wall. She is the pet who most influenced my path to become a veterinarian. My Slavic grandfather had a small farm next store where he raised chickens who laid eggs, which he handed out to the family. We also had a plethora of stray cats who were very adept at breeding, each popping out two to three litters every year. Our house was a cinder block, stucco ranch with sunken basement windows. In cold winter months, my mother would line the window wells with old linens and my father would cover the windows with plywood. There the queens would have their kittens, and through the window, I could watch the miracle of life from the warmth of my basement. These cats multiplied because of my mother's generosity-which conflicted with my father's frugality. My memory still echoes with his rant, "Bev, stop feeding those damn cats! The more you feed them, the more they'll come back." She ran a cat rescue before there were rescues. Sometimes, these feral cats would be cute enough to

20

finagle their way into our home in winter and have a litter before spring. Some of my fondest memories are of waking up in a bed filled with four-week-old kittens; immersed in the simplicity of the moment, oblivious to the fact that my father would soon exile these kittens outside with the spring thaw. I would pray for a long winter, hoping to keep them in my room for another few weeks.

I grew up two doors away from a boy named Joe who was ten years my senior. Joe owned a colossal Newfoundland dog which lived in his garage. On occasion, he would let me play with the gentle giant whose coat that was as thick as the purple shag rug that carpeted my brother's bedroom. In the early seventies, in the era of Vietnam and Watergate, Joe attended Rutgers University and then was accepted into the College of Veterinary Medicine at Cornell University in Ithaca, New York. He was later to become a very successful, well-respected veterinarian. At the time, I remember thinking how lucky he was to achieve such a lofty goal; like a high school baseball infielder becoming a major league third baseman. At the same time, it was a profoundly inspiring accomplishment which planted a budding seed; if a kid that grew up on my block in my dull, middle-class town could become a veterinarian than maybe I had a chance.

When I was twelve, we had a first-time queen in dystocia; my mother called one of the local veterinary hospitals for assistance. A veterinarian then gave me instructions on freeing the kittens, cutting the cords, and separating the placentas. I used the edge of sterile gardening scissor to cut the umbilical cords and then cleaned and warmed the kittens-all three survived, wrapped in warm towels on our bathroom floor. Even at twelve, I was impressed by a doctor who would take time out of his day to advise a stranger on how to save the lives of three kittens. My mother's OB-GYN would never have offered free advice over the phone, to help her squeeze my oversized head out onto our cheap linoleum floor. My mom must have seen a spark because the following Christmas I received *The Merck Veterinary Manual*, the professional "bible" for veterinary medicine. I would read it like most boys at that time would read the baseball encyclopedia. It would be many years before I had the medical knowledge to comprehend its content fully, but I could pretend.

Growing up on a busy country road I experienced almost as much death as life. Many of my mother's dearest companions had their lives end as common roadkill on that rural highway. Decades before Steven King invented the plot for his book, Pet Cemetery; our yard was seeded with old bones of pets once cherished. My father had an archaic belief that cats should live outside; this taught my mother a heartbreaking lesson: that outdoor cats live shorter lives. I learned that death was a part of life. This valuable lesson was a guidepost for the philosophy I would develop over the years of practice. I believe it gave me the ability to help pet owners make the most difficult decision of when to end their pet's life.

Before New Jersey became nationally infamous for Superfund sites and superhighways, it was well known for thoroughbred horses, dairy, and swine farms. We would stop roadside, along lush pastures lined with wooden fences, and feed apples to Standardbred horses. We would pass fields marked by silos and count the black and white Holstein cows lying in the green fields, chewing their cud. We would pass by swine farms on Sunday drives when the pungent odor was so thick my brother, and I would scream for my dad to drive faster. These Sunday drives convinced me that the pig was the one animal I never wanted to be around. Never!

New Jersey also had its share of wildlife. Ignoring the threat of rabies, I nurtured baby squirrels, feeding them formula until they were strong enough to run away. Before we knew of disease caused by salmonella, I raised and kept a wild box turtle in a homemade wooden cage in my basement. I fed it lettuce and carrots for six months until I felt such guilt for its cruel imprisonment that I released it back into a nearby swamp. Despite the superstitious fear of warts, I kept a toad, feeding it dead flies and ground beef with tweezers until it made a brave hop for freedom and escaped over a year later. Before we ever heard of bird droppings transmitting chlamydia, I rehabilitated an injured starling I named Charlie, whom I fed and kept in a spare bathroom for over a month - scrubbing the bird droppings off the tile walls and hand feeding it wild bird seed. When it flew away four weeks later, I cried-I had lost a friend, but I'm not sure the feeling was mutual. These experiences may not have been unique, but for me, such memories amplified my dream to devote my life to animals.

It was with this youthful idealism that twenty-one sophomore students and I walked into a small high school classroom on career day to be enlightened and energized by the profession of veterinary medicine. Unfortunately, this was not the generous Doctor who gave me such valuable advice when I was twelve. On this day, the guest speaker was

Almost A Real Doctor

Dr. Benjamin Rankin V.M.D. (Veterinary Medical Doctor is the degree only awarded by the University of Pennsylvania School of Veterinary Medicine, the oldest vet school in the country). He owned a pet animal practice in the center of town. His office was tiny. The waiting room was no larger than an elevator, the exam room the size of a phone booth. He would have the owner muzzle all dogs before he came into the room. Then he would appear briefly through a door on the opposite side of a stainless-steel table. He would then mumble a few words, vaccinate the pet, then disappear out the back door like a magician in a magic show. When it was time to pay the bill and exit the "elevator," you always felt like asking the same question - Is that all there is? I don't think he was a people-person-I know the dogs didn't trust him-I guess that is why he needed to muzzle his adoring patients.

    He was a bitter man. Maybe he was resentful because he spent eight years in school to enter a profession which he regarded as banal and demeaning, or perhaps he resented the long hours and mediocre pay, or just maybe he had claustrophobia from spending twelve hours a day practicing in a small brick box. Regardless, and because he had the bedside manner of Dr. Hannibal Lecter, he was not the prudent choice to light the fire in the young minds of those of us aspiring to dedicate our lives to be veterinarians.

    He stood at the podium, an impassive man with a tragic face. He wore wide, black rim glasses, black twisted hair, and was short-his shoulders barely clearing the podium. He had one visual aid in his hand- a pamphlet published by the University of

Pennsylvania illustrating their program, requirements, and prerequisites which he handed to twenty-two anxious students before his talk. His lecture was as depressing as his countenance. Through the years, I have tried to forget the exact text of his fifteen-minute speech, but I will always remember the high points: "The life of a veterinarian is hard. Your grades must be impeccable to get into a veterinary college. If you're lucky enough to do get into a school, it is four long years of sacrifice and hard work. You will graduate in debt and start a job with long hours, high pressure, and meager wages. Let me repeat; the life of a veterinarian is hard!" His final gem of inspiration was, "…think about another profession - like engineering." I proceeded to my next career choice lecture disillusioned and heartbroken. I carried my pamphlet home and placed it in the pages of my "Merck Veterinary Manual" and put it on a shelf along with my dream to become a veterinarian.

Through the two years following Dr. Rankin's uninspired testimonial I had to be realistic, especially when I considered my mediocre scholastic career and an abysmal financial portfolio (I was a penniless "B" student). I certainly wasn't going to spend eight years in school on a career that would transform me into an angry dwarf peeking over a podium destroying the dreams of teenagers at a local high school. It was obvious I had to search for an alternative career. I knew my second choice during career day; a professional baseball player was not an option. Thus, my pure crystalline logic, which would serve me so well through the years, spoke to me: "Bob, you like science, you enjoy cloud animals, and Willard Scott seems pretty cool. Why not become a weatherman?" Meteorology, of course, is the study of weather; contrary to what my friends would quip, it is not the study of meteors. I enrolled in one of two state colleges that offered this major. So, I left veterinary medicine behind as I packed my books and moved into the dorm on the first step on the path to be the next Willard Scott.

Eight weeks later, on a Saturday afternoon in early November, I sat at my desk like a petrified bust. Listening to Bruce Springsteen's Hungry Heart on my old transistor radio, I started drawing a stationary front on a map of the Northeastern United States (this was before computer programs would draw them faster and with greater accuracy). I was truly bored. I felt "Like a river that don't know where it's flowing, I took a wrong turn and just kept going." I had honestly tried to fit in, even going the extra mile and joining the Meteorology Club. Their monthly meetings consisted of a group of dweebs in short sleeve Arrow shirts watching footage of natural disasters like tornadoes. Amazingly, they would cheer for the twisters as they destroyed some unsuspecting Midwestern town. However, in my opinion, the club's greatest disappointment was that not one member had a pair of breasts. I knew two things I didn't want to live in the Midwest, and I didn't want to be a meteorologist. So, whether it was boredom, hormones, or a combination of both, I started to realize my logical voice had been flawed.

I sat with my number two pencil tapping on the map of the Northeastern seaboard and started to scan my desk for any distraction from this monotonous task. There it was - *The Merck Veterinary Manual*. I had brought it to college more out of pride than practicality; the symbol of a dream long ago surrendered to reality. I was still in high school the last time I had opened its pages. I started leafing through the chapters. Out fell the University of Pennsylvania brochure I had taken over two years before. On the cover was a veterinary surgeon dressed in a blue mask and surgical gown performing surgery in a high-tech surgical suite. Whether it was the flashy brochure that dazzled me or the fact that my life had become like that stagnant stationary front over North Jersey, I gathered the courage to dispel the doubts of adolescence and made a life-changing decision. I made a quick call to my mom announcing, "I have decided to change my major to pre-veterinary medicine. I know it's a long shot. I don't even know how to start. However, what the hell? What's the worst that can happen?"

"That's great, luv," my mother replied. "Listen, you won't know if you can make it until you try." Then she added the best words of advice ever uttered from my mother's lips, "Honey, you better like what you do for a living. You are going to be doing it for a long time."

All I needed was my mother's blessing. I knew my father's approval would be much more tenuous. Six months later I presented my new academic price schedule to my dad. He immediately shot his scornful remark, "That's ridiculous. I don't know how you're going to pay for that. I don't have that kind of money! I think you're crazy." My dad was always afraid we were going to ask him for money like we were going to stiff him for the bill at the local Diner. It wasn't that he was just cheap; his genes were spliced with European frugality and minimalist practicality. College was as alien a concept to my father as television to a Buddhist monk. At eighteen, my brother and I were much like my mother's stray kittens who, at three months, were exiled, alone, destined to dodge cars on life's dangerous highway.

I remember reading a Bob Hope biography in which he described his early days as a stand-up comedian. He recalled an incident in which he had proudly invited his family to see one of his shows. His father gave his critical review of the show by shaking his head in disapproval and concluding, "He just doesn't have it." My mother recalled a similar incident around the time I changed my career path. During their conversation, my father said he did not think I had what it took to become a doctor. He didn't think I could do it. He thought I was wasting my time. Now, it is easy to understand why I didn't seek nor want my father's approval.

By the end of the fall semester, I had switched my major to biology, rescheduled my spring schedule, and had plans to transfer to the University of Delaware, which offered a well-respected, pre-veterinary curriculum. Now I needed practical experience. Vet schools required 400 hours of documented experience in any sphere of veterinary medicine. In the early 80's weak economy, most pre-veterinary students had to volunteer to gain this experience.

I arranged for a volunteer position to start the first Sunday of my winter break at a local veterinary emergency service owned by a gentleman named Dr. Jeffrey Goldblatt. I was very uncomfortable in new environments and extremely anxious. I slept little the night before. I didn't know what to expect. Most freshman pre-vet students already had solid contacts in local veterinary hospitals. I knew little about the field I was about to enter.

I arrived at 10 A.M. on a cold Sunday morning with sweaty palms and a sour stomach. The office was an unimpressive strip mall space with a simple sign and bland storefront. The interior consisted of small rooms, blank walls, and stained tile floors. The air hung heavy with the smell of urine. Dr. Goldblatt was in surgery when I arrived, so his technician gave me a quick tour of the hospital and introduced me to the staff. The doctor barely raised an eyebrow in response and continued his procedure without acknowledgment. The surgery suite was sparse-only a table and a small anesthetic machine. A tall, skinny, goblin of a man sat on a lab bench in street clothes wearing only a scrub top, but no mask or gown. I remember thinking this picture didn't live up to the one on my brochure. I started to think I had no reason to be intimidated. They certainly were making no effort to make a good first impression. After the first hour, I was comfortable, shadowing the technicians, and observing the doctor. I was starting to relax, my confidence just beginning to build, when I entered the room at the start of a procedure on a fractious cat. I stood motionless in the doorway watching as the doctor gave an injection that sent the cat into a frenzied alligator roll, leaping off the table, through my legs and into the hall.

"What's wrong with you?" Dr. Goldblatt screamed, his jet-black eyes burning a hole through my chest. "Think, use your head! What are you an idiot? When a cat freaks out you shut the door!"

I backed away and as one of the technicians lassoed the cat with a leash and pulled it back into the room. Dr. Goldblatt slammed the door in my face leaving me standing alone in the hall. I crept back to the break room and sat down. In a few minutes, the door opened, and the doctor and technician exited the room with the cat alongside in its carrier. I honestly expected the doctor to offer a thinly masked explanation or maybe a brief, shallow apology. He offered neither. Instead, his technicians explained, "Sometimes when he's stressed, he loses it and lashes out, and he takes it out on us. He may seem insensitive, but he does care. Don't take it personally." Then, as a final insult to my ego, Dr. Goldblatt asked me to go pick up lunch at the pizzeria across the street. Apparently, I possessed little additional benefit to his practice, except as an errand boy. I left the building and drove home never to return. I often wonder how long it was before they realized lunch was cold. I regret not taking the pizza home for myself that cold Sunday afternoon-maybe it would have settled my sour stomach.

My first foray into my new vocation was a monumental failure. I did not speak of it for weeks; it was just too painful. Through the years, I have always regarded my brief encounter with Dr. Goldblatt as one of the lows of my budding career. The fact that he treated a volunteer in that manner was indeed cruel. However, to abuse a nineteen-year-old kid with a sincere professional goal, who was looking to him for guidance, who was searching for validation, who was craving acceptance into his chosen profession, is despicable. In my twenty-seven years of practice, I have entertained a myriad of aspiring young pre-vet students, some who have spent months observing and learning this profession. Because of Dr. Goldblatt, I do my best to temper my impatience and refrain from any undue criticism which could sour their dream. Fortunately, that day I was too young and stubborn to allow him to do that to me.

I have often imagined at least once during the thousands of dog castrations I have performed that it was not the testicles of someone's dog, tied spread eagle on the table, I was removing, but the balls of good old Dr. Jeffrey Goldblatt. The cold, pale testicles would sit soft and lifeless in my hands as I would skillfully toss them, like a simple free throw, into the stainless-steel waste can. What can I say-nothing but net.

I was not disillusioned with veterinary medicine; however, I was disenchanted with veterinarians. The irony was that I had to rely on one of them to get the practical experience I needed to get into vet school. The following summer, I narrowed down my search by scanning the phone book (for those growing up on Google, the phone book was a massive book with private phone numbers in white pages and business phone numbers in yellow pages-all in a convenient, alphabetical order). I called down the list of thirty veterinarians telling the receptionist I was a pre-vet student looking for work experience. They all had a similar response, "We don't have an opening now, but if you leave your resume, we will keep it on file. Of course, you can always come in and observe the doctor." Each time my memory shot back to my last day of volunteering-I was not going to let that happen again.

I had one remaining, very obscure listing; only the name Dr. Kim Doo Park DVM with an address. There were two things I will always remember from my first call that June day in 1981: Dr. Park personally answered the phone in a strong Korean accent and bold broken English, and he immediately offered me an interview for a paid position as a veterinary assistant. One phone call introduced me to a man who would change my life.

The next day, I entered an ample-sized ranch house that Dr. Park had converted to a modest-sized veterinary hospital. I was immediately impressed by the comfortable size of the waiting room, the spacious reception area, and the appealing scent of bleach and Roccal-D (an antiseptic liquid cleanser commonly used in veterinary hospitals). He greeted me with a broad smile and a warm handshake. Dr. Park was a pleasant, middle-aged Korean man who dressed in suit pants, crisp white shirt and matching tie. He had opened this second practice location just two months before. His original practice was in an economically depressed suburb of Philadelphia. He planned to build this New Jersey practice to sustain a level which would allow him to close his Philadelphia practice permanently. Currently, he employed a part-time receptionist, and he needed a veterinary assistant to help him during appointments and in surgery.

Dr. Park was a friendly man who controlled the direction of a conversation. He always wanted me to get to the crux of the matter, not talk around a point. I did not have experience, and that fact alone gave him understandable concern. I strongly wanted to be a veterinarian, and he was my last resort; a point that gave him pause. "Well Bob, you don't have experience, and I might be looking for somebody with experience. You would have to learn a lot." He paused, placed his palm on my knee like a sensitive father and with a smile asked, "How bad do you want to do this?"

"I will do anything to be...what you are," I replied with a conviction that still shocks me to this day.

"Well, OK, I'll give you a try. After all, someone has to take over my practice when I retire."

I started the following Monday. My duties included a bit of everything; lab testing, taking x-rays, holding patients, making up medications, bathing animals, answering the phone, discharging patients, and assisting in surgery. That first night, Dr. Park performed a lateral ear ablation on a basset hound. An ear ablation is a corrective procedure for severe, chronic ear infections usually in floppy-eared dogs. The surgeon opens the entire ear canal to the air, thereby improving ventilation and drainage, which prevents reinfection. I was swimming elbow deep in this bloody plastic surgery. I drove home that night after a twelve-hour day in a bloody scrub top and a glowing halo of satisfaction; I knew this was what I wanted to do the rest of my life.

I cannot overstate Dr. Park's impact on my career. During the college breaks, I would continue to work in some capacity gaining practical experience in every aspect of veterinary medicine and surgery. I was also propelled headfirst into the enigmatic sphere of veterinary medicine vet students would rather ignore - client relations. This time gave me ample experience hours, well exceeding the minimum vet school requirements. Without this documented practical experience and his strong recommendation, my acceptance into a college of veterinary medicine would have been impossible, regardless of how exceptional my grades were through my undergraduate career.

By the middle of my sophomore year at the University of Delaware, I had achieved the high Deans list for three straight semesters. I even became breed proficient in farm animals like pigs, sheep, goats and chickens-a species I thought only came in white. Even my grandfather would have been proud. I was in the top five in my pre-vet class and truly enjoyed my academic experience in a quality institution. I had received accolades from my animal science professors and letters of recognition from the Dean. I, for the first time, truly believed everything was coming together and this dream had legs. However, my legs were shakier than a newborn hatchling.

By December, the expenses of the fall semester had drained my federal financial aid for the academic year. My spring semester tuition was due, and I was penniless. The only option I had was to obtain a $3,000 college loan, but I needed an adult cosigner (in today's dollars, this would not cover room and board let alone tuition and books. But in 1982, it paid an entire semester's expenses). I had only one option; my father had to cosign the loan. In true Yugoslavian fashion, he refused. I had no alternative. On January 30, 1982, I withdrew from the college where I had become so inspired. I filed the paperwork and walked over the marble floors of the administration complex for the last time. I drove home on dark, winding roads of a crisp winter night through the farmlands of rural Southern New Jersey. I took several wrong turns before finding the main expressway that brought me back home — a fitting end to the day.

    I dove deep into a frigid sea of self-pity, regret, and embarrassment that defined the following winter. I had dropped out of college. I hesitated to tell my friends and certainly didn't inform Dr. Park. It appeared that all my ambitions and professional aspirations might have, after all, been a mere daydream on a mundane Saturday afternoon over a year before. There may have been a slim hope of returning to college-I didn't know how or when that could happen. In the meantime, I had to get a full-time job in the worst economy of my lifetime.

    I landed a job a world apart from veterinary medicine, a skeleton shift janitor in a local middle school. I swept the gym, scrubbed dirty locker rooms, and cleaned the library. My partner was a friendly, but crusty, old man who seemed like he had been a janitor for a hundred years, slowly passing the time until his retirement. I rarely saw him. I was alone with my transistor radio in my half of the sprawling school. This time of my life was a lesson in true humility. Six months before, in surgical gloves and mask, I was swabbing blood from the surgical field in a dog. Today, I used latex gloves to scrub the rim of a locker room toilet. Three months ago, I was memorizing the bones of the cat skeleton. Today, I stacked textbooks on a shelf labeled "Health" one was titled: "Calcium - Essential for Growing Bones." One month ago, I was receiving letters of praise from the dean of a major university. Today, I received a compliment from the gym teacher on how well I was cleaning the showers.

    If it wasn't the pure monotony of the job, it was the overnight hours that started to drive me to psychosis. To maintain my sanity, I would attempt to console my damaged ego by escaping to the teachers' lounge and reading my anatomy and physiology textbooks. If I stayed focused on my original goal, I would not be swallowed up by this living nightmare that tortured me each night. During those early morning hours, I also returned my attention to a novel I had on my shelf since high school-a famous biography written by a Scottish veterinarian in the early '70s; the one book, above all other books, that can be credited for encouraging more young men and women to enter the veterinary profession in the last half-century.

Dr. James Herriot wrote, *All Creatures Great and Small*, a memoir about a country veterinarian who practiced rural animal medicine in Yorkshire, England, beginning in the 1940s and '50s. It detailed his experiences in farm and companion animal medicine. He followed this immensely successful book with three sequels, all titles based on lines from a poem by Cecil Francis Alexander. It became a PBS series in the 1980s and two full-length films. It was a story, rich in English country flavor, with *Monty Python*-like accents and eccentric personalities. His occasional successes and personal triumphs tempered his trials and mishaps. He sometimes was offered livestock in payment for his services, other times he didn't get paid at all. The attraction for young, aspiring vets was the focus on a profession full of variety and professional achievement. It didn't focus on public fame or fortune. It did present the life of a veterinarian as one of strong personal commitment and professional respect. Sometimes, he portrayed the farmers as ignorant, cheap, and desperate and James Herriot would come to their rescue. Sometimes, he would be frustrated by the same farmers who thought they knew more than he. In the '70s and '80s, it did for veterinary medicine what *E.R.* did for emergency medicine, or *L.A.* Law did for corporate law; it introduced thousands to their future vocation.

  It was time for me to remember the adage, "When God shuts one door, he always opens another." I now had to choose door number two. Behind the second door was Rutgers University, a nationally respected institution, but like the biblical prophet, "…is without respect in his own land." New Jersey college-bound students considered Rutgers University a fall back school, as in, "Oh God, I hope I get accepted to my first choice, or I'll be stuck going to Rutgers!" However, not only is Rutgers the alma mater of Nobel Prize winners, politicians, and celebrities, it is an internationally well-respected institution. It was a state college, offering greater financial assistance than out of state universities, and therefore more affordable. Five long months deep into my career as a nocturnal sanitation engineer, I received my acceptance as a transfer to Rutgers University to start in the fall as a pre-vet major. I just needed to endure another five months as a janitor. The thought alone made my head spin like the electric floor buffer I used to polish the hallways. Again, the man with the Korean accent saved the day. In the first week of June, Dr. Park gave me a call. He was in dire need of a full-time technician. I had a way out.

  My decision was not easy. Even after all the suffering of the last five months, the technician position, like most jobs in veterinary medicine, paid significantly less than an average janitor. So, how could

I leave? Who would scrape the gum off the bleachers in the gym? My father surprisingly offered constructive encouragement saying, "Well, go back to the vet. After all, you're not going to be a janitor for the rest of your life." I finally took my father's advice; no more lonely nights in a boy's locker room (I hope that isn't taken out of context).

Two years later, after a thousand exams, after hundreds of lecture hours, after endless laboratory reports, after sacrificing a sex life for a cubicle in the Cook-Douglas Library, I was granted a personal interview at the University of Missouri College of Veterinary Medicine in Columbia, Missouri. I had only seven days before I had to appear for the interview of my life. I had one problem-TWA was not UNICEF. They asked for money to book a seat to Saint Louis. I had a severe problem, so I jumped headfirst into an eruptive volcano and asked my father for help; which created a tragic scene between my mother, my father, and me.

"Dad, I have great news. I have an interview for the vet school in Missouri." I continued, as my dad sat speechlessly. "But the bad news is I need $250 for the plane flight."

"How are you going to get that?" My dad said, as his voice cheapened.

"Tony, why don't you give him the money!" Mom quickly interrupted.

"I don't have that kind of money!"

"Oh, you've got the money."

"No, I don't."

"If you don't, then your girlfriend does," Mom said, exposing the elephant in the room.

"That's a lot of money for just an interview," Dad said, ignoring Mom's stab in the back. "Halfway across the country for just an interview. That's crazy. I wouldn't do it."

"It's the only way to get into the school," I snapped back. "They won't accept you unless they interview you in person. I have to be out there in a week!"

"Sorry, I can't help you," He finished as left slamming the front door on the way out. Two months later he moved out forever to be with his fifty-year-old girlfriend.

I petitioned the college for a delay and, in an incredible act of generosity, they granted a new interview date one week later. However, three days before the interview I still didn't have the money. Then, by a stroke of divine providence, I learned through a college secretary about a program at Cook that provided emergency short-term cash loans for funerals and other emergencies. This was one of those emergencies. Two days before my interview, I received the cash from an unlocked filing cabinet in the animal science office. I was on a flight twenty-four hours later. To this day, I still credit that secretary with saving my career.

My academic advisor, on the contrary, was an aged codger. Dr. Eugene Allan looked more like Walter Matthau's older brother than a professor. He was the pre-veterinary advisor and taught microscopic anatomy to senior, pre-veterinary students. When Dr. Allan wasn't lecturing, he would slither back to his windowless basement office in the catacombs of the century-old animal science building on the Cook College campus. There, he was free to chain smoke his cheap filtered cigarettes and escape the hustle and bustle of academic life. While I stood in his doorway, holding my breath, I was given priceless advice from this wise, academic sage, "Cook's pre-vet department has a good reputation out there. They seem to like our students," he paused, flicking ashes onto the concrete floor. Then added, "So, when you go out for your interview, just don't screw it up for someone else."

Thus, three days later, on a bright February Saturday morning with the memory of the "Allan directive" weighing heavy on my mind, I sat, terrified, in front of six representatives from the College of Veterinary Medicine. One was the Assistant Dean of Student Affairs, the others were heads of their respective departments, and they all had more degrees than a summer weather report.

During the sixty-minute interview, I was grilled on the specifics of my practical experience, my academic achievements, my two veterinary essays, and even current affairs. I had only two weeks to prepare; reviewing my job, technical data, and even my biography. Current veterinary students prepped us before the interview, one encouraging us to read the newspaper for the inevitable current events question. It was good advice. My specific question pertained to the presidential candidate Gary Hart and his affair with Donna Rice. The photo of her sitting on his lap made national headlines for weeks. I only remembered the story because she was hot. I still don't know how this issue related to veterinary school, but I knew the answer to the current events question - thanks hormones, they came through again. I hoped I had made a good impression, but the panel was impossible to read. The demographics of the 1984 entering class was seventy Missouri residents and only seven out-of-state students who would come from a pool of candidates from the other forty-nine states and Puerto Rico. I am glad I didn't know that little fact before going into the interview-I may have had better odds of having my own affair with Donna Rice. These six academics would decide the fate of every candidate based on two essays, their GPA, and a sixty-minute interview. The next four years and my career in veterinary medicine were in God's hands and the hands of six strangers with whom I would either become very familiar or would never meet again.

I had applied to three schools of veterinary medicine. I applied to Cornell in November of the previous year. It took their Ivy League hit men three months to decide my fate. The denial letter stated, "Your qualifications were significantly below those of other qualified applicants for the entering class of veterinary medicine." They concluded, "If you would like to discuss the decision with the Dean of Student Affairs, please feel free to call." Yes, maybe I should also call Maria, my high school crush, and discuss her decision to not show up at my prom. I didn't apply to The University of Pennsylvania. In the '80s, the University of Pennsylvania was the Nirvana of veterinary schools (the Buddhist heaven, not the rock band). Pennsylvania was extremely expensive and intensely competitive (acceptance rate was a fraction the overall national vet school acceptance rate of 19%)-it just wasn't worth the slap in the face. The third school was the Ohio State School of Veterinary Medicine. Two weeks after my interview in Missouri, I had an interview in Columbus, Ohio.

Almost from the start, the omens for this trip were portending of something terrible. I left for the airport at six in the morning on a sunny Thursday when I turned the key in my old Chevy Nova to hear only the clicking sound of a dead battery. On closer observation, I noticed that someone had broken the driver's side corner window had turned the headlights on. Someone had sabotaged my battery the night before my trip to the airport. This odd coincidence raised my suspicions; the primary suspects had to be my competition.

However, without proof, I could only get a quick jump from another student and race for the Newark airport. My flight was on the now-defunct airline, Peoples Express. They were a no-frills, economy airline that flew to Columbus, Ohio, for about ninety-six bucks. They didn't have baggage check-in, or provide snacks, or even a gate-boarding was done directly on the tarmac. They also conducted a first come, first serve boarding ticket policy. If you didn't check in two hours before, they bumped you to the next flight. I wasn't even close-I was bounced to the next fight. Four hours later, they did it again. However, as the jet's engines on the 727 fired up, the stewardess motioned for one more passenger. I leaped out of my seat, jumping in front of an old woman with a walker, as I sprinted onto the tarmac and up the ramp onto the plane. By this time, I would have sat in the baggage compartment, if they had one.

Compared to the interview in Missouri, the Ohio state interview was a quick, lonely, empty experience. I had little personal contact and no instruction from fellow students. In the twenty-four-hour visit, I spent most of the time alone in an empty dorm room. I was interviewed by only two attending veterinarians who spent a total of thirty minutes focusing on my mediocre grades (I had a cumulative GPA of only 3.59). The first interviewer admitted in a rather blunt manner that, among this year's applicants, I was somewhat handicapped by my grades.

"Tell me," he stated, "What were your accomplishments outside the realm of academia that would encourage us to consider your candidacy above other, more qualified students?" Accomplishments outside of school! I thought he was kidding. I just spent the last four years sucking the information from every textbook and kissing the ass of every professor to get into vet school. In the interim, I was working nights to keep my kitchen stocked with gourmet Kraft macaroni and cheese and generic hot dogs. What did they want me to say? I was perfecting a cure for cancer, struggling to end world hunger, or maybe I was working with Mother Theresa ministering to the poor in India? What was this, the Miss America Pageant? It wasn't going well. In retrospect, global warming would have been a terrific answer; I would have been ahead of my time. However, I knew the date was over when the second interviewer blindsided me like a 300-pound linebacker. One of my recommendations was one of my brother's highly successful, politically active friends. His letter was submitted directly to the college, so I never read it. In it he had lauded my primary role in his most recent political campaign; now that's fake news.

"What part did you play in his political run?"

"What run was that?" I asked. I had run cross-country races while in high school, but this question had me confused.

"Mr. Lauden ran for state senate. He wrote that, 'you were an invaluable part of his campaign.'"

"I'll be honest with you," I admitted reluctantly. "I know the man, and I also know he is a politician. However, I had nothing to do with his campaign." This answer may have sealed my fate; I could have told a tale that would have impressed Donna Rice, but I didn't. At least I still had my integrity. In the morning, I flew back to New Jersey convinced I had just wasted my sunny March weekend and ninety-six bucks.

Two weeks later, I descended deep into the dungeon of the animal science building and stood in the doorway of Dr. Allen's man cave. I delivered the news as he squinted through the thick cigarette smoke trying to recall my name. I read directly from the letter from the Dean of Students of the University of Missouri College of Veterinary Medicine. "I am pleased to welcome you to the graduating class of 1988 at the College of Veterinary Medicine." I stood for a moment soaking in the approval through the white smoke. "I guess I didn't screw it up for someone else," I said sarcastically.

"I guess you didn't," he paused as he flicked ashes on his desk then brushed them off with his hand. "I guess you didn't. Good for you." The old fossil seemed sincerely pleased.

My acceptance arrived earlier that week. My mother enthusiastically opened the envelope and read those blessed words over the phone. She gave a typical mother response, "I always knew you could do it, luv. You're so smart. Thank God you're not like your father." I spent the next week ruminating on my victory. Because I had expended so much blood, sweat, and tears to see my goal to fruition, a unique realization came over me, one that I had not expected. I had slain the dragon. Now what? Would I be as obsessed with being in vet school as much I had been trying to get into vet school? I knew there were battles ahead, both academically and professionally. However, for now, I would enjoy the victory and hope the next beast would not burn me to ashes.

The next day I sent my acceptance letter certified mail to the Dean of Student Affairs of the Missouri Veterinary School-I was now a Missouri Tiger. Two weeks later, Ohio State reached a decision-I was on "the waiting list." This decision meant you sat on your hands through the summer waiting for another student to decline his or her acceptance, then you could take that space. In some cases, these final slots were not filled until days before the semester started. I had already made my decision. I respectfully declined my position and passed my seat to a more "qualified" student.

The first day of veterinary school started on August 29th, 1984. Ten days before, I crammed almost every possession I owned into my fourteen-year-old Chevy and drove 1,200 miles across the sunbaked plains of the Midwest to Columbia, Missouri. Who knows, with my luck, the unsuspecting town of Columbia would one day be the subject of the next storm chaser newsreel, with barns and trailers exploding under a black funnel cloud, to the delight of some sadistic meteorology club dweebs in short sleeve Arrow shirt.

CHAPTER 3

WELCOME TO THE JUNGLE

"I speak for all mediocrities in the world

I am their champion. I am their patron saint."

- The Movie: "Amadeus" (1984)

D r. Robert Bertram Kindle, the Dean of the College of Veterinary Medicine, stood in front of 76 neophyte VM1 students on August 29, 1984 (A first-year veterinary student was called a VM1). This day he proudly proclaimed was, "The first day of the next four years of your academic life and the next four years the most important four years of the rest of your professional life." He stood six foot- two had deep blue eyes which were framed by gold wire glasses and had thick white hair. Dr.

Kindle was, at first glance, very intimidating until you met his broad, cheerful smile and friendly soprano voice-he was a sincerely kind man. His resume of professional accolades was even more impressive than his height. He was a Cornell, Veterinary School graduate. This fact gave me solace if I was beaten out by a vet school candidate with half his potential their decision to pass me over may have been a just one. He spoke of how proud we should feel to be the thirty-eighth graduating class in a school which produces quality professionals who contribute to the advancement at all levels of the veterinary medicine. He spoke of a vocation whose scientific foundation had been built on the backs of one hundred years of talented veterinary professionals. We were now ordained to carry on their legacy. With the conclusion of his moving invocation, I for one, felt like standing up and screaming, booyah!

The second speaker was Dr. Kevin Niemister, Assistant Dean of Student Affairs, was a much less impressive figure; barely five-foot-six, thick curly red hair, and wire-rimmed glasses. He was a 1955 graduate of the University of Missouri. His job was primarily to act as a liaison between the administration and the student body. He explained the importance of being quality student professionals, promoting the academic reputation of the college, and supporting student activities like the student chapter of the American Veterinary Medical Association. He spoke passionately on being an active alumnus. Dr. Kindle was like the principle, whom you would see occasionally traveling the halls offering a vibrant "Hello there!" Then would quickly scurry away, probably to meet with the Governor about some important pending legislation affecting the college. Dr. Niemister was like the vice principal whose primary duty was to encourage loyalty to the school and guilt us to patronize some college club or some academic event. He was also the disciplinarian who could have been on a search and destroy mission. In my four-years our paths frequently crossed, on rare occasions, he was on a mission, and I was the target. If I saw him in the hall, I would quickly scurry away like a white lab mouse.

The next set of speeches introduced us to the instructors of our first-year subjects: microscopic anatomy (histology), physiology, biochemistry, and of course gross anatomy. If the first year had a strict orthodox religion, it was anatomy, and if that religion had an omnipotent god, it was Dr. Robert Mclean, head of the Anatomy Department. A balding man in his mid-fifties he had crammed in his head every anatomical term of every part of every domestic species existing on the globe. He was on the board of the International Committee on Veterinary Nomenclature; an international panel of veterinary anatomists whom every seven years revise the *Nomina Anatomica Veterinaria*. This document was a Papal decree for the clergy of veterinary anatomy to hold mass to lead thousands of veterinary students to the promised land of perfect anatomic terms. In our first year of vet school, these masses were 2 hours a day in lecture and 4 hours a day spent dissecting cadavers.

His sermon began: "Anatomy will be the bricks on which you build your veterinary school education- if you learn it right the first time that it will serve as a foundation which will support everything you learn in your next four years- learn it wrong, and your building will collapse. This year we will learn the normal anatomy first then next year you will learn the diseased or abnormal anatomy. Many of the terms have Latin roots; if you dissect them out, it identifies its function or its location. Such as the muscle aptly named, flexor digitorum superficialis which is a superficial muscle which flexes the digits of the forelimb. Another example would be the muscles of the cranial shoulder, the cleidomastoideus, cleidocervicalis, and cleidobrachialis each name identifies on what part of the skeleton it has its origin and insertion. It is simple once you know the correct nomenclature." Holy crap, I thought, I was listening to Julius Caesar- in Latin.

Finally, Dr. Christian Bastian, the director of internal medicine spoke of our third and fourth years in clinical rotations. The students at the University of Missouri were immersed in clinical duties in the third year, one year before most other veterinary schools. This schedule was an attractive benefit for those of us who by our third year would have already spent six years in a classroom. We would have eight clinical blocks of eight week's duration. Dr. Bastian was also the medical director of the small animal teaching hospital. He was a classic relax-fit Midwesterner who spoke with a slow cadence and quite deliberate speech. He tian spoke of pressure, stress and how to put the strain of veterinary school in perspective. Dr. Bastian gave some coping advice: "Imagine the absolute worst thing that could happen, what I call the worst-case scenario, and then anything else that does go wrong will not seem so bad. Like if one day the clinic burnt down, nothing worse could happen." No, I think failing out of vet school would be worse.

He continued, "Do you know which book has done more to damage the reputation of the veterinary profession than any other?" Dr. Bastian paused momentarily gazing over a silent audience. "Anyone? That would be, of course, *All Creatures Great and Small*, by the author James Harriot. I know that probably wasn't his intention when he wrote the book, but it has tainted the public's persona of our profession in a way we have been trying to reverse for over a decade. It is filled with anecdotes about his life as a veterinarian out in the farms of England, filled with piglets, calves, puppies, and kittens. He sees a couple of patients daily, covers emergencies twenty-four hours a day, seven days a week, and usually get paid in a couple capons, and maybe a dozen eggs-if his clients are generous, they will bless him with a slice of homemade pie and a cup of hot coffee. He drives out to the farms in a squeaky old sedan and performs his miracles out of a simple doctor's bag. His medical technology circa 1950 and seems to be independently wealthy because there is very little concern for making a living-he rarely asks the clients for money. I know, I know many of you read the books and probably were first exposed to the life of a veterinarian through James Harriot's novels when you were ten. Fortunately, that profession no longer exists. However, I am telling you to forget what you have read unless you want to spend the rest of your career getting paid in oven stuffer roasters."

I was shocked; I had spoken often of how these books were a model for my future vocation, and now I had been told they were nothing more than a naïve, fluffy, fairy tale. What were they going to say to me next, that Ronald Regan colored his hair? I did not truly, understand the point Dr. Bastian had made that first day of veterinary school until years later when the fairy tale turned into a harsh reality.

The first day of the orientation of the class of 1988 concluded around 5 P.M. Now I craved solitude as my head kept spinning from all the emotions of the day. The palpable fear of failure tempered my immense pride. I stood on a fifty- foot steel bridge in the wooded park at the northern edge of campus. The bridge rose fifteen-feet over a lazy stream flowing east through a shallow ravine. The shadows of the oaken trunks grew long into the small gorge as the sun dipped slightly below the veterinary school clinic which sat atop a hill to the west. In this bucolic setting, I stood, eyes closed against the glaring sun, hands folded on the steel rail and thanked God for giving me this day. Then I prayed that this mediocre student wouldn't jump off this bridge before I had a chance to graduate. Oh my God, I had four more years of school! Maybe I was crazy. Standing alone, I made a promise to repeat this ritual at the end of those four years. However, that seemed like a lifetime away; now I had to prepare for the first day of class which began at the unholy hour of 7:40 A.M. This class was taught by a living legend, Dr. Homer E. Dane.

I could not believe it; Lurch was teaching veterinary physiology! Dr. Homer Dane was a man in his late sixties. He had thin white hair atop a chiseled face, slight overbite, and extremely prominent chin. I could see my reflection in his coke bottle glasses as he stared me down from his six-foot-six-inch frame. Dr. Dane was lean and fit and moved across the classroom with the spirit of a man half his age. If some professors were old school, Homer Dane was Jurassic school. He graduated from the University of Iowa, Veterinary

Welcome to the Jungle

School some forty years before; in fact, this was his final year of teaching-we were his last class. The VM2's had told us that he was a likable man-but to be careful as he was passionate about physiology; that usually meant he was tough, and at 7:40 in the morning the last thing I needed was tough.

Dr. Dane relished surprising the class with early morning quizzes every week; he would slap a single page on my desk at 7:40 and would rip it off my desk at 7:50. If I was late I was burnt, the test was officially over when he reached his pencil-thin fingers down under my frantically scribbling Bic pen and tore the page from my grasp. I learned how to write very fast; I wasn't a morning person; I was habitually tardy. I believe he gave these quizzes, not to test our learning curve but to test our punctuality. The problem was that in the Northeast, the morning started at 9:00 A.M.-the definition of the morning in the Midwest was much different; it started at sunrise.

He taught with the precision of a computer program, long before power point, he lectured with only a whiteboard and his deep John Wayne voice. You either kept up with his lecture or faced Homer's wrath-he didn't take kindly to repeating himself. He may have taken his lectures seriously but his physiology labs he treated as sacred. Whether the experiment used a rat or a chicken, he would say, "These lives of these animals are being used to teach you something important. Don't waste my time and their sacrifice."

When he wasn't dead serious Dr. Dane had an endearing non-PC sense of humor- it was a combination of Hee Haw silliness and what might I call, "fun with physiology." He often spoke of his scruffy little white dog named Suki who was the hypothetical guinea pig for many of his physiological points. He would start: "My next-door neighbor has a cat he named Pussy. Suki hates cats, so the other day he saw my neighbor's cat and chased that cat up a tree. The fight or flight mechanism kicked in. Now what part of that cat's nervous system, sympathetic or parasympathetic got that cat up that tree before Suki could eat that pussy?" His lantern jaw would hang low with a broad smile as he waited for the bravest student to respond. We didn't know whether to laugh or pretend we didn't hear him. Did he say what I thought he said?

However, the patented Homer Dane joke, one he told all incoming freshman was during his anesthetic lectures, specifically his discussion of anesthetics and barbiturates. "Two lions were in a bar," he would jib, "and one just had a nice meal. He had eaten one of the local bar wenches, well he was feeling nauseous. So, he tells his friend, 'Listen I think I'm going to be sick.' The second lion looks at him and replies, 'Maybe that was the bar bitch you ate.' Get it? Barbiturate." I felt privileged to have been a member of the last class to benefit from his unique brand of instruction-a truly disappearing breed. The entire school viewed him as a passing legend-the following May after his final lecture the whole class gave him a standing ovation.

In veterinary school, there were essential courses, and then there were courses that were worthless; you just wanted to wipe off your shoe at the end of the day. Biochemistry was one of those courses. The fault lies with the instructor, Dr. Marcus Tomkins, his syllabus was twenty percent biochemistry and eighty percent bull shit. Dr. Tomkins was a short, rotund, gentleman with a poor imitation of a goatee which made Homer Dane's sense of humor tame by comparison. Somewhere between sexists jokes and racists remarks he would teach the Krebs cycle or maybe touch on gluconeogenesis. However, he had a serious side. His favorite off-topic subject was jurisprudence and the veterinary profession; and how we had to protect ourselves from "rich Jewish Philadelphia lawyers" who would take careless veterinarians behind the litigious woodshed for a whooping. This was not a mindful topic for a first-year veterinary student; we just wanted to dedicate ourselves to becoming a good veterinarian, not to be sued for malpractice. I guess he spoke from experience-practicing in the real world, or at least his version of it. Once when a student asked why he chose to teach over practice, he said, "If I had to clip one more painted nail of some senile old women's miniature poodle, I think I would have strangled both with the dog's leash." Ours was also his final class at Missouri; due to increasing pressure from the student body he was transferred to an administrative position at another college-not one student stood up and clapped at his departure. He would not be the last pointless professor to be booed off the academic stage.

The essential class of our first year was Anatomy. VM1's spent their life in anatomy, I lived and breathed dead animals soaked in formaldehyde. The professors dipped the cadavers in the formaldehyde mixture and pumped a latex liquid through the vessels of the dead specimens, where it hardened into a blue rubber like substance thereby filling the vascular system making dissection easier.

Now formaldehyde is a known carcinogenic. In 1984 I just knew it smelled terrible. The first semester I dissected dogs, cats, and pocket pets, the second semester I dissected farm animals. I spent four hours each day systematically peeling back the layers of each animal's body. I was either standing next to a hanging cow cadaver or hunched over the cold open carcass of a dog or meticulously dissecting out the eyeball in a horse's head. By the end of the spring semester, it indeed resembled a disturbing horror movie with hanging skinned corpses of goats and horses from some farm in Hades. Multiple professors taught two-hour lectures which enforced our daily dissection. Every other Friday I had a three-hour practical and a two-hour written exam. I immersed myself in anatomy, as a first-year vet student I learned from the gods of anatomy and I worshiped their formaldehyde preserved idols which hung from hooks in the ceiling of their smelly temple.

Dr. George Constankos was one of those gods. Dr. Mclean was exacting and business-like, monotonous and consistently inpatient where Dr. Constankos was a loveable balding, overstuffed teddy bear. He was a courageous man who escaped from the communist regime in Rumania years before. His knowledge of anatomy was extraordinary, but his most impressive talent was the ability to draw, freehand, any anatomical structure on the blackboard. He would draw symphonies in colored chalk. He had hundreds of illustrated publications and was internationally known for his academic artwork. His Sigmund Freud like accent and gentle voice made the study of anatomy romantic.

By spring, I was drowning in the Latin sea of anatomy. I would dream of nerves, arteries, and veins. I could name the muscles which made up the cuts of meat in the A & P. I even looked at my female classmates like they were walking anatomic models. I had quickly lost perspective. I wasn't alone; the depth and breadth of the workload was a monumental challenge, for some the bricks of Dr. Mclean's foundation were crushing them.

Most student attrition was in the first year. Some were either unprepared for the massive caseload or intellectually unequipped to handle the subject matter. We lost two students. Cody Perkins was the first. Cody was a gentleman who was in over his head from the very first day, and he knew it. He would sit in the lounge every morning and have what we called "the breakfast of champions." He would chug down a can of coke while nervously puffing on a cigarette. Cody looked like a man waiting for the verdict on his murder trial. He didn't have long to wait. The dean dispatched him with extreme prejudice in just six weeks.

The second casualty was a woman I affectionately call Penny Plucker. She sported old crusty jeans, white stained leather boots, and a utility belt packed with pliers and wire cutters. She worked at a local chicken farm-what she did there, I have no idea-it must have involved pliers, wire cutters, and chickens. Her face was weather worn; her personality was as crusty as her jeans. She was quick to criticize, and she was faster to castigate-I was one of her anatomy lab partners. That year I arrived back at school three days late for the start of the second semester. I must have broken some sacred commandment; my classmates were shocked; some even believed I had dropped out of school. Penny was especially perturbed. I assumed I could rely on my trusted lab partner to get me up to speed with the rest of the class. When I asked Penny where we were in the lab book, she squawked, "If you had been here on the first day of class, like the rest of us, you would know where we were. That's not my problem!" The following Monday our lab table had a vacant chair; we were short one student. The faculty expelled Penny for breaking the honor code; she allegedly cheated on the last anatomy exam. Karma is a bitch, and so was Penny Plucker.

In the class of 1988 ninety percent of the students were Missouri state residents, leaving the remaining slots for everyone else. This skewed picture, common among vet schools, was the direct result of the political pressure placed on admission boards to accept tax paying state residents. In the eighties, non-resident acceptance rates were less than twenty percent. Four of the seven slots were from New Jersey, one was from California, and two others were from Puerto Rico. One was a charismatic, full figured woman named Isabella, the other a jovial marshmallow named Victor. Victor Gonzalez had a loud foghorn laugh that reverberated through his three-hundred-pound body. He would bounce from one table to the next helping other students and telling silly jokes in a strong Spanish accent. Both comfortably meshed with our class as the language was not a barrier-he was consistently at the top of our academic.

I was like most egocentric easterners. I thought I was faster, stronger, and smarter than most country bumpkins. I equated a Midwest twang with ignorant rednecks and Midwestern farm boys with the cast of

Deliverance. I learned quickly that this was not the case. I struggled just to maintain my spot somewhere in the middle of the class. I sat inconspicuously hidden in the back of the lecture hall, more likely to crack a joke than ask a question.

In contrast, one of my Missouri classmates eventually graduated with a perfect 4.0, the first in the history of the school. He sat in the first seat, in the first row during every lecture. Because he was so close, I believe, he heard and saw things during the lecture, I didn't hear or see-and that is why he got a 4.0-while I championed mediocrity from the rear. I was typically sitting comfortably in the last row of the lecture hall, near the exit, ready for a quick escape just in case the boredom got unbearable. Many years later I noticed him at a national veterinary lecture and who do I see planted first seat, first row like an enthusiastic first grader? That's right, Mr. Four Point-O, listening ears on, pen ready to snag that top-secret Intel which would probably never reach the scrubs in the back. I was sitting in the back, as usual, I am glad there wasn't a test.

Most of us in class spent years in a desperate competition to get into veterinary school. Once I was accepted, I thought the contest was over. One of our instructors said during orientation, "Potential employers don't ask for your GPA or your class ranking, and if they do, you don't want to work for them." Long before convenient student portals, student test scores were posted on the walls outside of lecture halls, that's how you kept track of your grade. One thing I could never understand: Why would veterinary students act like rabid lemmings diving over a cliff, almost trampling each other to find their tiny printed grades on those brick walls? Who was competing with whom? I had a general idea of how I did after most exams; if I was getting a least a "C" I wasn't jumping off that cliff with the rest of the lemmings.

I was not a follower; I was not a joiner-I didn't need to be part of a group to define my worth. Combined that with my classic German obstinacy I was destined for a head-on collision with the academic hierarchy. I did not take kindly to being told what to do; in this case, it was joining the student chapter of the American Veterinary Association (SAVMA). Immersed in my studies, I had little interest in a political association which I felt would provide little personal benefit. Secondly, the seventy-dollar membership fee would buy a cartload of macaroni and cheese and hot dogs-I was still broke. In early October, the class president encouraged me to join. I refused. In late October, the senior President of the SAVMA attempted mild intimidation. I declined. In November, I had a sit down with Dr. Neimister. He gave an impassioned plea; he spoke of the last twenty-five years in which the SAVMA had one hundred percent student participation-it was a tradition-the class even got a shiny framed plaque. He spoke of the professional responsibility that starts while you're in school and he spoke of being part of a professional group which stands behind its members throughout their career; finally, he spoke of respect. In New Jersey when you have a sit down with a guy who talks about respect the next meeting is with two burly guys in black turtlenecks and crooked noses. I wasn't waiting for an offer I couldn't refuse. I may have been a stubborn loner, but I wasn't stupid. I joined the following week; I was in good standing for another year-and no, Dr. Neimister didn't kiss me on both cheeks when I left his office.

In my second year of vet school, I had a class called epidemiology, and my gonads were in hot water, again. I had epidemiology the spring semester of my second year. This course examined the origin and spread of disease; this was an important science in farm animal herd management. One of the class requirements was a visit to a Missouri slaughterhouse. This trip was used to introduce us to the role of the veterinarian in food animal regulatory medicine. These veterinarians are unsung heroes who spend their days as health and meat inspectors, who monitor slaughterhouse practices before and after slaughter long before the meat gets to your table. I had a good picture of slaughterhouse practices, and I didn't feel I needed it to be any clearer, so I refused to go. It wasn't because I was a vegetarian or an animal rights activist. I was weaned on Philadelphia's famous Pat's steak sandwiches. My time was just too valuable to waste a day watching cows get head bolted in a slaughterhouse; I didn't need that vision in my head while eating my next ribeye. Ironically, that bullheaded New Jersey attitude again brought Dr. Neimister out for another talk. I explained my objection in more of a moral, quasi-religious logic which placed him in an awkward position. We agreed on a compromise. I would write a paper on slaughterhouse regulatory medicine, and I could skip the class trip and pass the class. Dr. Neimister must have gone back to his office vowing never to admit another pain in the ass Easterner. Sorry Dr. Allen, I quite possibly might be screwing it up for someone else.

A vital class in the second semester of my second year was Pharmacology. This was a course full of complex concepts and more complicated words. I believe one of the basic requirements of teaching any class in an American medical school should be to speak proper English. Dr. Vincent St. Joseph's professor of pharmacology could not even pronounce "proper English" let alone fancy drug names. He was a native Jamaican, with the accent of the bartender mixing drinks on a beach in Montego Bay. He would routinely pronounce the words "hyper" and "hypo" as "hypa," as in "hypathyroidism" which is neither a word nor a disease. When asked for verbal clarity he arrogantly replied, "I said hypa, why can't you people understand?" For five years, the students filed formal complaints which made his tenure tenuous-Our class was the last straw. The administration had no other choice. Therefore, in the fall of 1985 the good people of Columbia, Missouri had two great victories; the Kansas City Royals won the World Series and Dr. Vincent St. Joseph was removed from the teaching faculty.

In the fall of 1986, I became a third-year vet student, but I will always remember 1986 for three tragic events; one was a national catastrophe, one was a class tragedy, one was a profound personal loss. In January, the school was preparing for a lecture by a prominent research veterinarian who was to fly on the space shuttle in the spring. This story was exciting; one of our own was going into space. A week before the lecture on the morning of January 28th the state veterinarian Dr. Robert Malkovich was to speak on Rabies prevention and control. He walked into the room at 11:00 A.M. and hurried to the podium, "I have some terrible news. The Space Shuttle Challenger exploded on takeoff twenty minutes ago, everyone on board was lost." He then left without another word. The scene was surreal as the class sat quietly in disbelief. The instructor quickly dismissed us for the day. I returned home, and like the rest of the nation, watched the fireball explode into the stratosphere- again and again. The loss of those scientists and an average school teacher shocked us back to reality. The fantasy we shared of astronaut veterinarians flying starships through space vaporized in an instant.

The second tragedy occurred during the winter break of 1986. Victor Gonzalez traveled to Puerto Rico to celebrate the holidays with his family. They had a family reunion on the sprawling luxurious upper floors of the Dupont Plaza hotel on New Year's Eve 1986. A fire was started in the late afternoon by three disgruntled employees. The fire soon spread upwards and onto the floor where Victor and his family were having their reunion. What still is the deadliest fire in Puerto Rican history killed 98 people and took the lives of Victor and his entire family. During his memorial service, we recognized Victor for his friendly demeanor, his vibrant personality and his willingness to always help other students. In his honor, a single seat was left empty at our commencement eighteen months later.

The final tragedy involved my mother. The next spring my mother called with disturbing news; Samantha, my dog was sick. My mother's divorce had left her homeless and destitute; for the last year, she had been living with a friend. Her only true comfort had been the Golden Retriever who had strayed onto our porch thirteen years before. I knew Samantha was failing. She was drinking and urinating excessively, had been vomiting for weeks, and she had lost over ten pounds. My mother was distraught, she was alone, and I could only provide distant moral support. She desired to save the dog, but her lack of funds and precarious living arrangements limited her options. Even in my second year of veterinary school, I knew my dog was dying, and there was nothing I could do to change the outcome-even if I were a real doctor. We both were in tears when we agreed together to put her down. The next week my mother and a friend took Samantha to the county shelter and had her euthanized as a charity case-she wasn't even allowed to be by Samantha's side at her death. A stranger held Samantha while a technician injected a lethal combination of barbiturates into her cephalic vein. In seconds, her heart stopped beating, and she slipped in death without a familiar face in sight.

In the years that followed my mother often spoke of Samantha's euthanasia. Always with guilt and deep regret. She blamed herself, not her circumstances. When I tried to ease her pain, she would say, "Bob, you have no idea how hard it was to leave her in the hands of a stranger. I'll never forget the look in her eyes the last time I saw her. It seemed like she knew; she knew I was leaving her to die." Even though the clouds of dementia which defined her waning years she would have periods of lucidity where she would lament the decision which would haunt her the rest of her life.

My emotions were trapped somewhere between the introverted child and the practical professional. Samantha was the perpetual three-month-old puppy which wandered onto my porch when I was nine years old-an answer to my prayers. She was my comfort when I was beaten up on the schoolyard, when my father left my mother, and when an insensitive veterinarian scolded me for not shutting the door on an angry cat.

A year after my graduation and three years after her death I walked into the county shelter and asked to see the euthanasia log for the spring of 1986. I found her name misspelled in pencil with five other animals on Thursday, April 24. I never knew her actual birth date, but now I knew the exact day she died. Along with my mother, Samantha was my inspiration to pursue a career in veterinary medicine. My mother introduced me to the love for animals; Samantha was the symbol for that love. I had kept a framed picture of Samantha taken when she was a puppy; I carried it through eight years of college and half-way across the country. Three decades later that picture still hangs over my desk in my office-an emotional tribute-a symbol of why I became a veterinarian.

Through the first two years of our veterinary curriculum, we took toxicology, parasitology, endocrinology and over ten other "ologys." By the time May 1986 rolled around we were "ologyed" out- it was time for something else. The faculty's answer was the dreaded Didactic block. These eight weeks were the veterinary school academic equivalent of "hell week." A solid eight weeks of intense medical and surgical lectures which combined everything we had learned the previous two years to prepare us for the clinical duties of the next two years. The best part of the didactic block was that we learned surgical techniques-we performed surgeries on live animals.

The clinicians taught the didactic block; in medical school, they would be called the attending physicians. Dr. Bastian was the medical director, and Dr. Jason Barack was the surgical director and technically the god of surgery. He was joined by a myriad of additional clinicians and residents in both small animal disciplines. Any confidence I had gained by this time was crushed by the horror stories of the didactic block. These were intense lectures taught by serious clinicians. Nursery school was over.

Dr. Bastian, who two years before shattered the James Harriot legacy, taught the methodology of case management. His medical flowcharts would serve to lead us on a logical path for diagnostics and treatment of our patients. He introduced the cornerstone of medical progress reports called the S.O.A.P. This was an acronym: Subjective, Objective, Assessment, and Plan. The S.O.A.P. quantified vital signs, objective appearance, their interpretation of the results and the plan for care. We wrote a S.O.A.P. for each pet, and every day we were bathed in Dr. Bastian's S.O.A.P.

Dr. Jason Barack was the chief of surgery and a world-renowned veterinary surgeon who did write the book on veterinary surgery in the 1980s. He was an internationally known speaker who placed a dynamic flare on small animal surgery-in theater terms he made love to the audience. Working alongside him in surgery was another story, that was another part of the legend. However, he gave colorful lectures which by today's standards are politically incorrect and sexually inappropriate-which also made him a world-renowned lecturer. He would plaster a pink, crusty, oozing wound on a twenty-foot screen at the front of the lecture hall. Pointing at it with his laser pointer he would joke, "Look at this thing, it's almost obscene. I'll teach you how to make it pretty again."

The first surgery of my career was on a futon, or more specifically a one-foot block of Styrofoam. In the first week, I learned how to manipulate needle holders and how to correctly hold a scalpel, making small straight incisions on the forgiving Styrofoam. I sutured these incisions closed and spent days learning how to tie square knots; the magical knot of the surgical world. I spent days learning how to dress for surgery in surgical gowns, gloves, and masks. I practiced sterile techniques to ensure sterility before and during the operation, getting my hands slapped if I contaminated the surgical field. The rudimentary focus on these basic skills formed a critical foundation for surgery. There is an inescapable logic; if a knot doesn't hold, a patient could bleed out; if a doctor brakes sterility, they contaminate the surgical site. I took it seriously because in two weeks I would work on a live animal.

In the mid-eighties, we could perform one surgery on a live anesthetized dog; then we would wake the dog, conduct a week of post-operative care, then euthanize the dog after completing the second surgery. Each dog had one survivable surgery. They had attained these dogs from private kennels who supplied these animals specifically for this purpose. They were neither shelter dogs nor stolen from unsuspecting pet owners. These live dogs were an indispensable tool because it gave us first-person experience on living, breathing, pulsing flesh. One of our early surgeries was the dog spay which is easily the most challenging routine surgery in veterinary medicine. We practiced on a live dog and experienced the complications on these sacrificial animals, not on someone's beloved pet years later. Secondly, by allowing the initial surgery animals to wake into a week of recovery, we learned the principles of postoperative care and pain management. Before each surgery, we would bury ourselves in the media room and review the surgical instruction VCR tapes until we knew the upcoming weekly procedure by heart-we had to be prepared-Dr. Barack would be watching.

In the years following my graduation, there was a progressive movement focused at veterinary schools across the country to reduce or eliminate the use of live animals in the veterinary curriculum. They even questioned the use of actual cadavers in teaching veterinary anatomy to veterinary students. The veterinary class which followed mine eliminated survivable surgeries in didactic block-they euthanized the dogs after each first surgery. The following decade saw veterinary students requesting computer simulators instead of real cadavers to study veterinary anatomy. There is a place for humane oversight in many forms of research and even teaching at many levels of scientific education. However, there is little place for this misguided logic which limits the use of actual live animals in teaching the practice of veterinary medicine. If I were contemplating hiring a new graduate who had never performed a surgical procedure on a living animal, it would be the equivalent of hiring a carpenter to build a house who has never worked with wood, except the house wouldn't bleed to death if the carpenter used the wrong gauge nails.

In the long eight weeks of didactics, we performed or assisted in six surgical procedures on live anesthetized animals. Three times these dogs recovered; we nursed, treated and administered to their needs for a week, monitored their recovering and maintained accurate medical records until their final surgery. It was an invaluable experience which prepared us for our future surgical block when we would be performing on actual pet animals. In those two months, in didactic block we learned more applied clinical medicine than we had learned in the preceding two years. The clinicians codified our previous knowledge into a coherent, focused view of what we would need to survive the upcoming medicine block. Medicine block, which began in six weeks, would be the most difficult block of the veterinary school. I considered this clinical rotation the true start of my veterinary career, and I was as eager as a yearling in an Atlantic City Racetrack starting gate. A-n-d t-h-e-y'-r-e off!

CHAPTER 4

DESCENT INTO THE ABYSS

"Mr. Hart, here is a dime. Take it, call your mother, and tell her

there is serious doubt about you becoming a lawyer."

- The Movie: "The Paper Chase" (1973)

Two years before I had stood on this same bridge in reverent umbrage of a deity who brought me to the mountain top. Now maybe I had gone too far. I was slipping off the other side into the dark precipice below, and I stood to ask, why? Why take all this time, expend all this energy to bring me so far away from home to endure this? I hated it! I was less than two weeks into my small medicine block, and I hated it. I despised the schedule, abhorred the subject matter, detested the workload, disliked the instructors, and even my classmates were starting to piss me off. How could things go down the toilet in just three weeks?

I was so confident the first day of medicine block. I was dressed in a white coat and tie with a brand new blue Littmann stethoscope around my neck, and a penlight in my coat pocket-I even had one of those little rubber hammers for testing reflexes. I was standing proudly in the prep room with my future colleagues. I was next to be called with one of the residents into my first real appointment. Following six years of school, I could easily delude myself into believing this was the first day of my career. I felt like a veterinarian and looked like a real doctor.

There I stood across the exam table from a female Yorkshire terrier puppy, laying weak and lifeless, eyes closed, it's breathing slow and shallow, barely responding during the clinician's prodding hands. It was dehydrated, pale and cold to the touch. Bloody diarrhea covered the dog's rear-an odor so pungent that an astute veterinarian could diagnose the disease by the smell alone. The clinician suspected immediately that this was Parvovirus, and this puppy was in critical condition.

Parvovirus is contagious viral enteritis, which in the eighties sickened and killed thousands of young puppies; before the development of a vaccine, the mortality rate could reach fifty percent. The small animal clinic had an isolation ward for confining contagious disease patients. The ward was a ten foot by ten-foot room wholly isolated from the rest of the hospital. Dressed in disposable gowns, masks, gloves, and shoe covers we entered through a small revolving door into this tiny brick and tile room. Like a low-tech version of the Andromeda Strain, the ward provided patient isolation while we administered fluids and supportive care we hoped would lead to recovery- most often it didn't, some died in only a few hours. It is still hard to forget the putrid odor of watery, bloody diarrhea in the confined poorly ventilated closet, and the vision of dehydrated young puppies covered in feces and yellow bile, barely lifting their head to whine as you could see their life quickly slipping away.

This case was the first of my small animal medicine block. The intern and I spent hours working feverously treating the puppy; we placed a small IV catheter in a barely visible cephalic vein and slowly pumped intravenous fluids, electrolytes, vitamins, and antibiotics into her tiny flaccid vessel. The only sign of life was a short faint high pitched whimper as the sharp stylet pierced her skin over the vein. We placed her on a heating pad and left her that late afternoon in that dank, lonely room. My first case in small medicine block died the next morning.

I had the weekend to reflect or maybe forget this disappointing first case. Tomorrow was Labor Day and another day outside of that environment would be cathartic. Sunday night, with my mind filled with visions of dying puppies and festering diarrhea I was unable to sleep, until 7:00 A.M. The phone rang ten minutes later. "Robert, where are you? You're late!" Barked a deep accusative voice.

"Late for what?" I was still half asleep, still fighting through the fog maybe the real question should have been: "Who the hell are you?"

"ICU!" Came the reply. His tone was rising another few decibels. "You're shift started at ten minutes ago."

"Wait." I shot back. "My shift doesn't start until 11:00 tonight. I've got the schedule right here." I fingered through a photocopied calendar titled "ICU DUTY" which outlined the days divided into three eight-hour shifts labeled "A" "B" "C." Today is Monday the third. "I'm shift 'C,' I start at eleven tonight."

"No this is a holiday, so we on a weekend schedule. Shift "C" starts at 7:00 A.M. Read your damn schedule!"

He was correct, in small Italicized letters was written: Holidays = weekend schedule. This meant the schedule was reversed. "I'll be there in 15 minutes," I replied in regretful defeat.

In addition to full-time clinical duties and case management students we were expected to cover ICU duties for the entire eight-week rotation. This usually amounted to one eight-hour shift a week throughout the small animal blocks. The weekend shifts were tolerable, the shifts during the week were tough, but the overnight shifts were killers; we attended clinics through the day, went into ICU at 11:00 P.M., monitored patients until 7 A.M., and then returned to a full day of clinics. Some days stretched on for thirty-six sleepless hours. The student was an acting nurse beholden to the medical directives of the attending clinicians. The orders included postoperative patient monitoring, medical treatments and, in many cases, babysitting the patients of some of the more anal-retentive residents. We would spend eight hours in a stark living room size ward with cages on one side and medical equipment and cabinetry on the other. It offered little amenities; an FM transistor radio and two sagging cushioned chairs. Our orders ranged from recording rectal temperatures every two hours to hourly tube feedings of aggressive cats. Although I was always with another student during overnight hours in ICU, we were the only humans in the entire vet school; this was a great responsibility. If I didn't perform a specific scheduled treatment or if I didn't identify a crashing surgical case I would have been crucified by some cocky clinician in the morning.

On my first ICU duty on Labor Day 1986 I was greeted by the agitated fourth-year student who phoned in my morning wake up call. He made a hasty exit leaving me, and another VM 3 student with an ICU full of patients-it was a busy weekend at the teaching hospital. The unit was full of challenging cases; we had an aggressive diabetic cat, a weak hypoglycemic puppy, two critical geriatric dogs in renal failure, one cat with a nasogastric feeding tube, eight other pending medical disasters and a special gift from the surgery department- a "Wobblers dog."

One of the most challenging cases in ICU was the post-operative care of the mature Doberman Pinschers with a condition known as Cervical Spondylomyelopathy, commonly referred to as "Wobblers Syndrome." This is a degenerative spinal disorder of the cervical spine causing weakness and paralysis; it was common in the Doberman Pinscher and other giant breeds of dogs. These dogs are weak in their back legs and sway as they walk, hence "Wobblers Syndrome." The surgical correction involved the decompression and fusion of the spine using bone grafts. This surgical procedure required a postoperative neck cast. In those days, it was a large plaster cast which started at the lower chin and continued down to the shoulders. The whole purpose was to extend and immobilize the neck during the weeks of recovery. Some of these dogs were in the ICU for up to a week. They were unable to walk and would lay on flat waterbeds until they were ready to go home, then they would use a cart or PVC frame to help them walk. During their ICU stay, we would hand feed the dogs, clean up their copious fecal matter, and periodically pass urinary catheters to relieve their bladders. We all dreaded these cases. Whether it was stress, pain or just frustration, these one-hundred-pound dogs would lay on their side and whine for hours. I can still hear to siren-like screams splitting the silence of the empty hospital.

Beyond the drone of the eighties pop on that cheap transistor radio it was the companionship of the other student which prevented psychotic breaks in the late- night monotony. I covered about thirty shifts in ICU in the final two years of vet school. During these long, tedious nights in that windowless little room; we learned the basics of patient care and postoperative management. However, more importantly, it was the responsibility, and teamwork which were the real lessons of ICU duty-it indeed wasn't the techniques of rectal thermometry. In the middle of these night shifts, I would sometimes resent these forced duties. I would remember my best friend who had graduated with an engineering degree two years before and had a real job in the real world. I was staying up all night for free. Then I would return to those depressing janitorial graveyard shifts when I scrubbed the floors in a middle school locker room; then cleaning the rear of a whining Doberman wasn't so bad. Late that day, with my first eight hours of ICU finished and only ten minutes of sleep I knew one thing; I was not prepared for the next day or the next eight weeks of small animal medicine block.

I hated to be on call. One night a week I would carry the little black beeper proudly on my side, like all the other students, ready to be summoned by the chief of surgery to assist in another life-saving procedure. However, the reality was impotent compared to the fantasy. The kind of emergency depended on the resident on duty. The better clinicians would only call students for major trauma cases. While those militant residents and interns would call you in for a broken nail-I considered these calls to be a complete waste of my private time. We could be summoned anytime in the middle of anything. I had constant anxiety. Students mainly observed, monitored and assisted the residents who treated these emergencies. The students did all the work for a little glory. Thus, did I answer the call or ignore the beeping of that little black box?

However, on Saturday night, a week after Labor Day, I answered the call, and I was staring at one of those militant residents over a dog who had been vomiting for three days. Dr. Mark Anderson was a tall, wavy black haired, twenty-eight-year-old resident who looked like John Travolta in clods, and he knew it. (The Vinnie Barbarino from *Welcome Back, Kotter*, Travolta, not the Vincent Vega from *Pulp Fiction*, Travolta). We spent three hours performing radiographs and bloodwork. We did not get a diagnosis, but we did reach a conclusion; he was never going to be my mentor, and I was never going to be his protégée. Maybe it was my lack of enthusiasm about this call specifically, or of the block in general, or because I just wasn't his type of student. Either way, Dr. Anderson offered some constructive advice before I left that evening. "Robert, if you are going to get through this block, you're going to have to put the time in, you're going to have to work harder. It's going to take more than just coming through the front door. If you don't do it here, you're never going to do it in practice. That's if you ever get to practice." In one short week, I lost my first case, was blindsided by an ICU duty, was derided by a fellow student, and was told I didn't have the attitude of a real veterinarian-I had reason to believe my career was on life support.

A week later, on a bright sunny day, I was passing through the veterinary diagnostic laboratory in a fog, with a visible dark cumulonimbus cloud following me down the hall, wishing I had stuck with meteorology, and I ran into the laboratory director whom I had known for about two years. Passing in the stairwell, he asked the loaded question. "How are things going?"

"Going? Not good. I'm a little bit overwhelmed. Maybe not what I had expected." I replied, fishing for a little sympathy.

"Well, you should have known what you were getting into." He shot back, without one ounce of pity to blow my cloud away.

Many students had similar feelings, criticized overworked, and unappreciated. Because it was my first clinical block, I just wasn't emotionally ready on day one to dedicate my whole soul to my first clinical rotation. There was a time or two during those first weeks where I would have considered, as a navy seal, ringing the bell in submission, if the college had a bell. However, it didn't have a bell or even an ocean; what it did have was endless Midwestern pastures full of cow pies. A metaphor for my future if I didn't pull my life together. If it wasn't for the long and windy road which brought me to this point, I might have given into the opinion of men like Dr. Anderson. However, I was never considered special before and I quickly learned I wasn't going to be special now. Most of the class fell somewhere in the middle of the student progeny and the desperately hopeless. Like the latter, we all hoped to improve; after all, we were all bought a ticket for the same ride. The former I regarded with contempt and avoidance.

One such prodigy was a fellow New Jersey resident, Franklin Kennedy, a bombastic narcissist-a classic cut throat and professional "brown noser." He would arrive in clinics at 5:30 every morning. When others were flexible and graciously switched schedules to accommodate a fellow student's special needs, Franklin would refuse. He was a favorite of residents like Dr. Anderson, but I think most clinicians past him off as just another cold fish. Franklin would make copies, shred papers, and perform the duties of a true loyal minion. Meanwhile, he was willing to throw his classmates to the lions for an "A" or a byline in the next journal article.

During our daily appointments, we would follow a resident recording the anamnesis, or preliminary history of the case. The student would present a diagnostic and treatment plan for any case upon admission. The residents would then evaluate that plan and have ultimate authority for the care and treatment of the patient. The student did all the legwork. These duties included administering medications, performing treatments, keeping records, following up on laboratory tests, and presenting the case during morning rounds. The clinician would monitor and subjectively evaluate every move the student made: the more complex the case, the more involved the project. If I had multiple cases, I had multiple projects each presented at group morning rounds at 7:30 AM.

Before rounds each morning, we would re-evaluate and S.O.A.P. the patient. We included the temperature, vital signs, lab results, and a complete well-researched case summary. Each case required about thirty minutes to examine, treat and notate the results. The students would present the results in rounds in front of the clinicians and fellow students to one's praise nor disgrace. After rounds, each entry would be signed by a clinician to prevent future additions or deletions. It was an essential part of our evaluation. Unlike Mr. Kennedy, I refused to arrive two hours early to prepare my report. Instead, I took the last page of the patient's medical record home the night before. Then I could write the SOAP for the next day, except for the morning vital signs. The following day, I would quickly examine the animal, record the vitals, and two minutes later I would return the completed case bin. I was in at 7:20 and ready for rounds at 7:30. This trick worked very well. My records were neat, concise, and complete; to the scorn of Dr. Anderson.

Will Rogers said, "The best doctor in the world is a veterinarian, he can't ask his patients what is the matter…he's got to just know." Every case, regardless of the problem, irrespective of the species begins with the owner. The human on the other end of the leash, harness or bridle provides the first clue to the condition of the animal. It is the job of the veterinarian to slice through the minutia and separate the sediment and emotions and from real clues which point to the pet's illness. In veterinary school, the goal of the instructor was to take the student, an amorphous blob of medical information and turn them into a valuable diagnostician and veterinary practitioner. This task is harder than it sounds. I have seen seasoned veterinarians take the most convoluted route to achieve a simple diagnosis. Dr. Bastian and the clinicians at Missouri performed a miraculous job transforming us into those neophyte practitioners. They gave us the tools we would use the rest of our careers.

Those tools were three essential lessons gleaned in clinical rotations: One, was the sixty-second physical exam. Dr. Bastian would say, whether we used a systemic approach (Heart, lung, skin, mouth), or head to the tail approach we should, be proficient in a sixty-second exam. To this day I have clients who miss my one-minute physical. "Doctor are you sure you checked the eyes?" I was also taught to look at the primary problem last. Take for an example a pet with bad ears; I look at the ears at the end of the exam; therefore, I do not miss another problem the client may have ignored. Second, we were taught to take a logical approach to every case. We would SOAP every problem and use medical flowcharts to lead to rule outs (r/o) or a possible diagnosis list. These signs could indicate these rule outs which we diagnose through these tests; if these tests are positive, it means this if these tests are negative it means that, then on to the next step. The foundation of internal medicine is logic. Third, we were taught to not look for "zebras in a field of horses." When you're are considering a diagnosis, consider first the most common diseases not the one in a thousand diagnosis, or the zebra in a field of horses. This rule is a common problem with new vets and clients alike, who spew out the exotic names of the rarest of maladies they find on a medical internet site when logic points to the more common disease.

Through the two months of medicine block, I learned to tolerate the rigorous schedule, the heavy workload, and the monotonous ICU duties. The eight weeks passed quickly, as I became somewhat more comfortable under the rule of tyrant residents-still more I was relieved to see it end. My next block was a legend, saturated with stories of mad doctors who saved lives with magical scalpels and hands blessed by God. We were these tall tales on the first day of orientation; for some of us, these stories were nightmares; for some of -us, these stories were wet dreams. However, had they been invented by fourth-year students to frighten the underclassman or was this the reality? I would find out in twelve short hours; my next rotation was small animal surgery.

What makes a good surgeon? The Hollywood version would be a brash, self- absorbed, egotists with a well-developed God complex. They treat their residents like unqualified morons as they focus passionate care on one and only one patient a week. If they are men; they are cocky, handsome, womanizers. If they are women; they are unadorned feminists with a chip on their shoulder. These stereotypes are just a fantasy invented to garnish Emmy Awards.

Real surgeons are gifted and well trained, sacrificing another four to six years to enjoy the privilege of being called a board-certified surgeon.

They are courageous; to cut into the body of a living being with full knowledge of the complications and risks associated with their actions-every procedure places their reputation on the line. A famous surgical proverb boasts; a chance to cut is a chance to cure. The good surgeons in veterinary schools were tough yet affable, critical but empathetic individuals who dedicated their lives to steer their students to one goal, becoming competent surgeons. Zeus ordained from Mount Olympus before time began for these gods of surgery to impart the mystical secrets of the scalpel blade on third-year students. Surgery is the indispensable marriage of anatomy, physiology and surgical skill. One crucial distinction unique to veterinary medicine is the veterinarian, upon graduation, is not only considered surgically competent to perform most soft tissue surgeries but is obligated to perform those surgeries their first day of practice without additional training. In those eight weeks, and only in those eight weeks, could we master the skills which would allow us to perform surgery on somebody's cherished pet competently? Surgery block was sobering work, it was challenging, and it was the most satisfying eight weeks of my academic career. Of course, my first day didn't start that way; on my first day, I was assisting Zeus, himself, Dr. Jason Barack.

Dr. Jason Barack walked into the surgical ward like a curly-locked Julius Caesar arriving from battle, minus the flurry of white doves and trumpeter's processional. When your name is highlighted in bold letters under the title, *Techniques in Veterinary Surgery*, you have every right to a parade before every surgery. Today he was performing a moderately challenging soft tissue procedure to correct an elongated soft

83

palate in an English Bulldog. This abnormally long soft palate is a congenital condition which prohibits normal airflow through the trachea. The surgery shortens the palate thereby facilitating airflow through the windpipe. Cutting the soft palate deep in the throat and suturing it closed can be a tricky and delicate procedure; it can have complications, such as fatal hemorrhage. He settled down on a stool, facing the gaping mouth. "Open it wider." He motioned to one of the assistants as he drove his hands deep into the throat. A hemostat clamp there, a quick cut here, and one running suture and he was finished. It seemed to me he had performed the whole surgery in under a minute. When I looked up again, he was floating out the door-release the doves.

He was an intimidating figure. I was happy to be on his peripheral vision, maintaining a safe distance. I knew if I didn't do anything stupid, I would stay off his radar. Franklin Kennedy was different. It was his goal to be as close to Dr. Barack as legally possible without being labeled a stalker. Franklin was a surgical minion of my block, following Dr. Barack like a hungry puppy performing all manner of embarrassing tricks. Sadly, after two months, Franklin Kennedy was discarded like so many others before him, like a wad of used tissues.

A lower deity, Dr. MacManus was a third-year surgical resident who defined the word intensity. He was specializing in orthopedic surgery and attacked some of the most challenging hard tissue surgeries. Unfortunately, sometimes they fought back. Orthopedic surgeries can be physically demanding, and surgically frustrating. The surgical suites were restricted to only essential personnel; because they were so concerned about sterility, they confined us to the surgical suite during the duration of the surgery. Traumatic pelvic fractures due to automobile accidents were inordinately common due to the absence of lease laws in Columbia. Most were large breed, big muscled dogs; these required bone plating and tension screws and a great deal of wrestling to place these devices. Things didn't always go as planned-plates broke, screws bent-Dr. MacManus would freak out. When I saw his eyes squint, his forehead grow flush, and I heard his muffled profanities I knew it was time to duck. He would fling a Gelpi retractor against the wall like a drunken dart player. We had to be alert; he was fast. I think it was all in the wrist. It was always exciting observing Dr. MacManus during one of his surgeries; it taught us to prepare for anything including unidentified flying orthopedics.

Every morning I would check the surgical whiteboard to choose the procedure and the surgeon; I was then committed as an assistant through the day. I not only assisted in routine soft tissue surgeries but could perform those surgeries under resident instruction. Before the end of the block, I was performing cat spays and neuters with minimal supervision. One of these routine cat castrations presented a problem. A testicle was missing; it was a unilateral cryptorchid. This is a rare condition in cats, one in ten thousand cats has a retained testicle-and I had the one. Unfortunately, I missed this minor problem on the pre-surgical exam. Now the cat was under anesthesia, and I had to find its hiding place somewhere in the abdomen. I opened the abdomen, and the testicle popped out like a prize in a cereal box.

I was lucky; it wasn't usually that easy. However, I wasn't one to turn down a gift.

Every afternoon at four we had surgical rounds with the students, residents and interns, every Friday we had grand rounds which included all the surgical clinicians including the gods of surgery. Here we would present our surgical case summaries and progress reports. I jumped at the chance to brag about my surgical conquest, and proudly tell my dramatic story of the cat with the missing ball.

"Dr. Cimer, clarify something for me." Dr. MacManus demanded. In rounds, he reveled in using the prefix doctor to pressure and intimidate his students. "You performed a successful cryptorchid surgery on a cat who was here for a routine castration. Did you check to see if both testicles were down before you put it under?"

"No, I didn't. I thought I checked them out earlier, but I guess I missed it."

"Let me give you some advice." His eyes narrowed, and his forehead turned a deep shade of ripe apple. "Every time you examine a cat for a castration, I want you to put your hands in your pockets and feel for your balls, then feel the cat's balls. If there is two of each you have a routine castration, if one hand comes up short one of you is a cryptorchid." I felt like hiding in my abdomen to avoid the burning gaze of Dr. Barack. I was lucky Dr. MacManus didn't have a retractor in his hand.

Surgical rounds may have resembled the Spanish Inquisition, but they were a crucial cognitive learning tool. Some days they were even fun. On one Monday in early December, a deer which was tragically hit by a car died on the way to the hospital. Five days later the deer returned as processed venison stew. In a tribute to Midwestern ingenuity, we ate the stew at the end of grand rounds out of stainless-steel dog food bowls-I can't recall if we used utensils.

If we were not on the surgery schedule, we routinely assisted the other students, even cleaning the rooms, if necessary. This was my duty on one afternoon at the end of a long, strained, surgical block. I passed Franklin Kennedy who was finishing a cat spay. "Hey Cimer, get over here." I could see his black beady eyes between his cap and his surgical mask.

"What do you need?"

"Get a mop over here, mop the floor where I spilled some blood." He barked as he pointed a hemostat at a small spattering of blood on the floor to his right.

I hesitated for only a moment, or maybe a bit longer, depending on your perspective.

"Do it now!" He barked.

"You must be frigging kidding me, no! I'm not cleaning up your mess; do it yourself when you're done." I stormed out before I was committed my next surgical procedure on Mr. Kennedy-the mop handle colonoscopy.

The next day in rounds, he filed a complaint with a South African surgical resident. "I politely asked Cimer to mop up a spill, and he wouldn't do it. I was in the middle of major surgery. I couldn't do it."

"That's not the way it happened; he ordered me to mop his floor."

"When I tell you to do something, you do it"!

"Screw you, you pompous ass! I'm nobody's bitch!"

"Oh, you're my bitch, when I say you're my bitch!"

Like a scene from The Jerry Springer Show, we both flung our chairs across the room and leaped at one another. Now, I had not been in a fist fight since the third grade, but I figured it was like golf, if I rotated my hips, kept my leading arm straight, and swung through the ball (his head), I would hear that unmistakable firm crack of a solid strike which makes the crowd say, "ooh-ah". So, I went for it. However, before I could get off my first right cross at his bulbous ego, we were split by Isabella, that gentle, big-boned Porto Rican third-year student, wedged between us like a first base coach between Billy Martin and a home plate umpire-she stopped the fight before it started. We retreated to our respective corners never to fight again. The surgical resident used great restraint and empathy calling it unsportsmanlike contact without assessing a penalty stroke.

I had survived the black forest of surgery rotation and the evil doctors who ruled over the kingdom; they were not so evil, and the rotation, not the horror story spun by the upperclassman. It was a necessary learning experience. Surgery is both a challenging and rewarding experience. Veterinary school can teach the basic skills and knowledge on which to build aptitude and excellence. One must reach a plateau to perform daily routine surgeries almost by reflex alone, as well as, the ability to improvise when challenged with the unexpected. Surgery is much different from medicine and other disciplines. There is great satisfaction with a successful surgical outcome; thus, the greater the risk, the greater the respect. Veterinarians either love surgery or hate it, they either fear or embrace it, but all of us respect it.

The final small animal rotation was medical services, covering radiology and anesthesiology. A technical block in radiology and had a minor introduction in 1987 to a promising technology, ultrasonography. Veterinarians routinely shoot and read radiographs every day, so a firm grasp on the diagnostic tool was essential. Veterinarians are also acting as their own anesthesiologists. The goal of the last four weeks of the rotation was to master the fine art of chemical restraint-to keep at pet under anesthesia somewhere between life and death-a rather lofty goal. A sign on the door of the office of the director of anesthesiology proclaimed: "Anesthesiology; hours of boredom followed by minutes of sheer panic." This was a time in history when veterinarians would monitor the heart rate and respirations manually. Today pets are monitored using pulse oximetry, ECG's, and a blood pressure monitor to maintain anesthesia. Veterinary technology has caught up and kept pace with human medicine. These factors have made for a very safe marriage between veterinary anesthesia and surgery.

What was not a very safe marriage: a golf bag size artificial vagina and a horny one-thousand-pound stallion. This odd pairing was the scene on the first day of my next block, theriogenology, or the block of all things, reproduction. After six months cooped up inside the white walls of the teaching hospital, I was in my first large animal block on a warm day in April observing this bazaar horse porno. The stallion was positioned behind a teaser mare in heat, while the farm assistant made ready to insert the baseball bat size penis into the water lined artificial vaginal. The other assistant would help the stallion mount a large dummy horse torso and when ready deposit his one hundred milliliter semen sample into his new, leather covered best friend. I often wondered, who had the most dangerous job? The guy who was holding the vagina or the guy who had to scrub the penis before the horse-mounted the dummy. It's hard to say, but they were both wearing helmets.

Missouri has a nationally respected theriogenology department and used techniques like this for scientific research in both reproduction and sterilization techniques in domesticated animals. The facility made advances in artificial insemination, embryo transfer, breeding soundness examinations, and chemical sterilization. The science, at that time, focused primarily on food animal and equine reproduction. Since then, these scientific advances have been used in pet animals; the science of reproduction in the dog and cat.

The collection of the semen samples was a fascinating distraction from our mundane studies. The collection has developed into fine art; in the horse using the artificial vagina, in the dog using manual masturbation, and in the bull using electroejaculation. In this technique, an electric probe is inserted into the rectum of a bull, stimulating the prostate gland. Fifteen volts and a few seconds later and the results are a sexually satisfied bull and scant seven milliliters of semen.

In 1932 R.M.C. Gunn, a professor of veterinary science at the University of Sidney noted in reports on human electric chair executions in the United States a strange side effect of electrocution, the ejaculation of semen in executed male subjects. He then transformed this information into a technology used in reproduction in the sheep industry. Then with the invention of the rectal probe in 1950 came the weird science of rectal electroejaculation.

One of these unwilling bovine subjects was a pure white three-year-old Brahman bull, named Prometheus. This twenty-four-hundred-pound humpback behemoth sported a fist size nose ring in between two black flaring nostrils. He had foot long floppy ears and thick brown horns which brought his height to over seven feet. He had his breeding exam and was diagnosed with balanoposthitis or an infection of the sheath of the penis. The technicians would wash the bull's penis twice daily and instill antibacterial ointment into the prepuce. After class, I would admire him from the outside of his stall, staring at my reflection in his black, orb eyes, which always remained eerily calm.

After two weeks of therapy, he was ready to go home. However, like the saying goes: where does a two-ton bull go? Where ever the hell he wants. Plan A was to wall off a pathway through the barn that leads into the truck; he then has no place else to go. The farmhands set the gates, opened his stall, and carefully steered him through the barn and onto the thirty-foot cement ramp leading down to the cattle truck. I stood safely behind a gate as he passed. His heavy footsteps shook the ground; his breath was thick and moist as he passed and moved down the ramp. One of the farm hands had taken a position a few feet behind his six-foot rump tapping him slightly with a long whip.

We all relaxed, the plan was working well, and the bull was a step away from the truck. I emerged from my hiding place behind the gate and started slowly down the ramp.

Then, in an instant, I saw the farmhand turn towards me, scream something in Spanish, throw his hands skyward, and dive headfirst over the metal rail. The bull barely missed his flying heals as he galloped straight back up the ramp-not twenty feet away.

Maybe Prometheus had his fill of penis soaks, or perhaps he had a flashback to his last date with an electrified rectal probe; either way, he was incensed, and he was charging my way. I honestly thought I saw my life flash before his black eyes. I spun and bolted back into the barn diving for the first metal gate I could find, scurrying to the top like a squirrel on fire. He passed a second later; his horn brushed my calf as he rounded the curve that leads back to his original stall. He planted his one-ton frame in the center of the pen and twisted his neck to look back.

He stood defiant, panting, torrid mist billowing from each faring nostril. He had enough, and so did I, it felt like I had just been dodging traffic on the Garden State Parkway. I dismounted the gate and trotted to my two-thousand-pound hatchback and drove home. I decided not to stick around for plan B.

Fortunately, most of our farm animal patients weren't crazy looney tunes characters, like Prometheus. The cows were mild-mannered and cooperative. Unfortunately, we spent an inordinate amount of time with our arms up their butt holes. Cows have two talents which keep them alive and off the dinner plate; making milk and making more little cows. One of the best scientific methods for identifying their estrus cycle is through rectal examination and digital palpation of their ovaries. The cows would line up in head gaits rear facing out like a chorus line waiting to be serviced. We would wear a shoulder-length plastic sleeve and insert our arm up to the armpit and manipulate the ovary through the wall of the colon. Each peristaltic movement would push feces towards our smiling faces, and we would rake the stool out onto our waiting rubber boots. We would then grab the ovary, like a firm nectarine and blindly feel the dimples and bumps to identify the stage of follicular formation, thereby the time for optimal breeding. I did get used to the sweet, digested vegetable smell of cow pies and even became quite adept at ovarian staging. Some of the shorter women in our group would stand on a stool and almost disappear into the poor cow's rectum; they would dodge the barrage of cow pies as they threatened to plop directly on their heads.

Horses were not as mellow; I was well out of my comfort zone standing behind their massive legs, their tail slapping me in my face as their vice-like anal sphincter clamped down on my arm to the point of numbness. I had lucid nightmares of my lifeless arm dangling from a clinched horse's rectum as my body was mercilessly kicked to death by an irritated ovulating mare. This memory along with raging bulls, dehorning and calf castrations on fully awake calves solidified my pledge, to never become a farm animal veterinarian-never.

One of the highlights of my fifth clinical block was the week spent in a Missouri hen house. Dr. Mortimer Capon, Director of Avian Medicine, looked like a chicken. Imagine Foghorn Leghorn as a sixty-year-old chain-smoking rooster-that was Dr. Capon. He was well over six feet tall, he had a long beak-like nose and full drooping cheeks and sported thin, spiked white hair that resembled a rooster's comb. Before class, Dr. Capon would sit in the front of the lecture hall, in a yellowed white dress shirt, and oversized black leather shoes, sucking on a long cigarette. Between puffs, he would frequently hunch down over his knees and have a coughing fit, a moist disturbing spasm which sounded like he was spewing up cancer-ridden lung tissue. In addition to chick sexing and hen necropsies, we learned to finer points of broiler house management. What better way to prove the point then a day trip to a broiler poultry farm; It was a sure way to bring this learning experience to life.

    I had heard rumors of these field-trips months before from classmate Larry Sommers a Beatles fan, and ironically a chain smoker-he called it "Dr. Capon's magical mystery tour." Then he added, "Make sure to bring oxygen." Dr. Capon drove five lucky students eighty miles south to the largest broiler farm in Missouri. He drove forty miles per hour with the windows closed in the ninety-five-degree heat of a mid-Missouri summer day. The airtight windows created a vacuum which trapped the cigarette smoke like a diving bell. Two hours and twenty menthols later we exited the vintage ford station wagon with a smoke cloud reminiscent of a Cheech and Chong movie. Larry's warning did not go unheeded; to prepare I brought a surgical mask and put it on with the first lite cigarette. Hunched down in the back seat I hoped to avoid breathing air saturated with floating carcinogens. Ten years before Michael Jackson's brilliant fashion statement I must have appeared odd to my classmates, hunkered down in the back seat with my face covered in a blue surgical mask. They never so much as batted an eye, in retrospect I think they wish they would have thought of it. "You can't have it," I thought. "The mask is mine, my precious."

The poultry barns were one hundred yards long and fifty feet wide. Large venting fans cooled them at each end which brought the temperature down about ten degrees below the mid-nineties outdoor heat. Long before the controversy leading to free-range chicken farming these broilers were housed in elevated wire cages the size of a toaster oven, barely enough room for the chickens to turn around. Long before organic farming, these chickens were fed prophylactic antibiotic powders. When I was a child, my Yugoslavian grandfather had hens. They nested in hay lined shelves with a ramp down to a large sand floor which led out to an outdoor courtyard. They ate, laid eggs, and socialized with other hens-this was not my grandfather's hen house. In the weeks from hatchlings to death, this disturbing scene of the broiler house defined their whole existence. I endured the mandatory two weeks of chicken jeopardy. "I'll take hatchlings for a thousand, Alex." I survived the ride through smoker's hell, had my introduction to the concentration camps of chicken farming. The two weeks codified my disdain for chickens and the broiler industry, but on a positive note, it did leave me with a deeper appreciation for the Surgeon General's warning on cigarette packs. Dr. Capon passed away a few years after my graduation. The cause of death was unknown-ironically; it probably had nothing to do with smoking.

The University of Missouri, Veterinary Diagnostic Laboratory is one of the busiest investigative and diagnostic labs in the nation. They process over eighty thousand cases every year. Because it is a teaching hospital, they serviced Missouri farmers at a significantly reduced cost-the educational value to its student was priceless. The farm animals were unloaded from the beds of pickups, horse trailers, and backhoes, some recently deceased and stiff others foul smelling and bloated-some had been dead for days. The carcasses were chained on ceiling mounted lifts and transported feet first on large stainless-steel tables. During this block, I learned the precise, systematic method of the necropsy on every species from the white lab mouse to the horse.

    I grew up watching the detective show, Quincy M.E., starring Jack Klugman. Each week the medical examiner would cut through murder victims looking for that shred of evidence which would lead him to the killer. During the opening credits, there was a humorous scene which dramatized four rookie police officers experiencing their first human autopsy which ended in everyone either vomiting or fainting flat on the floor. He was a coroner who solved murder mysteries, pushed social agendas, and even snagged the sexy ladies. I would like to see an episode of Quincy where Jake Klugman was waist deep in a thousand-pound cow; his rubber boots covered in slippery intestines, splashing in omasum fluid as he swings a bloody ax through the ribs of old "Bessie" the cow. Through sweat, flying bits of lung, and bloody goggles he would look not for an assassin's clue but parasites, toxins, poison plants, failing organs, and signs of nutritional deficiencies. Not as sexy but just as important.

    Farmers frequently brought live pigs to the lab for analysis. They were sick piglets who for the good of the herd were culled and necropsied to find the cause of the disease afflicting the farm. The dying pigs were restrained on their side and attached to jumper cables, one on the front leg, the second on the back. When The technician would throw the electric switch, it was like a gruesome scene from a seventies mob movie; in seconds, their body went rigid and lifeless. I thought this was cruel, but in the mid-eighties, the professional consensus was that this was a fast and acceptable form of humane euthanasia.

I had eight weeks of horse heads, bloated cow carcasses, electrocuted pigs, exsanguinated chickens, and dead puppies. Pathology block was an intense, unique and invaluable learning experience. One I neither would have skipped or repeated in my academic career. Following pathology block, I was genuinely looking forward to my last rotation, and touching a live animal again, even if that animal was a horse.

Almost everything I knew about horses I had gleaned from the racing form at the Garden State Race Track. I couldn't have put a bridle on a mare if the horse told me how to do it. I gained some respect for horses from my days in theriogenology. Who wouldn't be impressed by their tight rectums and their ample penises? However, it was their size and unpredictability which truly frightened me. All horse owners love their horses, but horses can be dangerous. This point became a brutal reality when ten years after graduation, a pleasant, well-respected classmate and experienced horse owner suffered a fatal injury at the age of thirty-six when his horse kicked him in the head.

A common problem in the horse is colic, a general term encompassing a couple of types of intestinal conditions. Some require emergency surgery; some require long term medical care. It is dangerous; it is sometimes fatal. The mainstay of medical care is IV fluid therapy to maintain hydration and prevent systemic shock. These horses would be in intensive care for days.

The student's duty was to stay with the horse, in a barn nightly during the horse's recovery. They would sit on folding chairs, in a cold barn, sometimes with another student, and occasionally alone. They would monitor vital signs and watch ten-liter bottles of lactated ringers slowly drip into the jugular veins of these half-ton patients. The equine barn was in the middle of the Missouri prairie, some fifteen miles south of the small animal teaching hospital, miles from the nearest store, not a deputy sheriff in sight. It made for a lonely night when you were sitting in a still barn on a deserted farm in the middle of a frigid pitch-black night.

During equine rotation, most students had weeks of over-night duties. There was never a shortage of colicky horses in the ICU barn-except during my block. The winter of 1988 was one of the coldest on record in central Missouri. There were whole weeks with subzero temperatures and daily ice storms. We spent most of our day in lecture, with very few live patients, and very little time in ICU. I made it through the equine block without one night in Intensive care. My classmates thought that was a shame; I thought it was a godsend.

Another godsend was Dr. Marcia Banks, equine medicine resident, and my instructor for two months. She was the fiancée of Dr. Mark Anderson, the Travolta wannabe who was a thorn in my butt during small animal medicine block. Dr. Banks was a beautiful, shapely, brunette who was quite striking in jeans and a suede vest, especially when bending over the back of a horse checking for laminitis. In those eight weeks, I learned two cogent lessons. I learned how to test a horse for laminitis, and I learned even absolute jerks could get a hot girl.

It was over. The last day of equine block ended before noon; eight years in college ended in a short final exam. I drove north and parked at the veterinary teaching hospital. On the way to the college park bridge, I passed a couple of VM1's heading to the cafeteria. They were talking about this morning's anatomy practical, "That wasn't a sesamoid bone," one said to the other, "that was the popliteal lymph node."

"Shit, you have got to be kidding. That means I missed three for sure."

"Did, you get the embryology question on the ventricles?"

"Not even close."

"I nailed it."

"Whatever."

"Don't worry; you'll probably make it up in histology."

"Ya, right."

With a sheepish grin and a nod of my head, I continued onto the bridge I had visited so many times before. I stood behind the icy rail, flicking small hanging crystalline sickles crashing to the frozen stream below. Squinting against the midday late winter sun, through the naked oak branches I could see clients dragging their dogs through the sliding glass doors. I took deep moist breaths exhaling eight years of strain, stress, pressure and personal doubt. Graduation was in early May, then the influence of the real world would shock me awake like a high-powered rectal probe. Before then I could celebrate the glorious victory of a mediocre student who once was warned by an advisor to "…not screw it up for someone else." I had passed veterinary school; I had passed my national board exams, and I would soon graduate with the pomp and circumstance of veterinary school graduation.

I don't know if I missed the circumstance, but I do know there was very little pomp. I was impressed by flowing black robe with gold piping, topped by an impressive gold and yellow hanging doctorate scarf. I was grateful for my mother and finance' who sat in the audience while I walked on stage as I shook the firm hand of Dr. Robert Kindle who beamed with a broad smile as he handed me the facsimile of my diploma (I would receive the real document in the mail one month later).

"Good job, congratulations. Dr. Cimer," he said with a handshake. Then we heard a brief prayer and listened to a speech by Dr. Kindle; he spoke of "respect and responsibility." Seventy-five students then recited the veterinary oath with one hand raised and magically we were transformed into seventy-five new veterinarians ready to save lives. It was somewhat anticlimactic and exceptionally frightening.

As I left the auditorium, my mother hugged me and said something I had heard a thousand times, "Oh, honey I always knew you could do it." However, on that hot day in May I started to ruminate on the haunting echo of another phrase my father used to say,

"If you're not careful Bob, you might get what you wish for.

CHAPTER 5

LAST PICKED FOR THE BIG DANCE

"If you don't know where you are going any road will take you there."

- Lewis Carroll, "Alice in Wonderland"

When I see a good old boy in a cowboy hat, I am always tempted to ask him where he tied his horse. Today I had my first professional interview, and that was the first question which popped into my mind when Dr. Randy Nelson answered the door to his office. He sported a jet-black Stetson, black vest over a white dress shirt and a pair of dark Levi jeans. He accented his ensemble with a pair of rattlesnake leather boots with gold tipped points. The only thing missing was a leather holster with two pearl-handled revolvers. He owned a mixed animal practice just outside of town. A mixed animal vet treated farm animals, as well as, pet animals. This practice wasn't my ideal choice for future employment, but he was the only practice in a ten-mile radius to offer a position. In a town of six veterinary hospitals and seventy-five hungry new veterinarians, I felt I was lucky even to get the interview-the sad part was Dr. Nelson felt the same way.

"So, you're not from these parts? I see you're from New York."

"New Jersey actually, just outside of Philadelphia," I replied.

"Uh ha. Did you see many farm animals just outside of Philadelphia?"

"Well, I rode by a swine farm twice when I was a kid."

"Uh ha," he responded, as he slowly rubbed his silver belt buckle which peaked out from beneath his bulging belly. The belt buckle pictured a tiger, the University of Missouri' mascot, inside a large black "M" over a white MIZZOU (the college nickname)- obviously, he was a proud fellow alumnus.

"Seriously, I got a good deal of experience with swine and sheep during my undergraduate training at Rutgers University. I also participated in a very extensive nutritional study in dairy cows where we tested feed additives for about a year." In my case participating meant graphing charts and collating data. I didn't have a lot of live animal contact. On occasion, I did pet a calf or two, usually right on the head between the eyes.

"Here, we usually do small animal office calls in the A.M. and schedule farm calls in the afternoon. Routine vaccinations, deworming, dehorning and castrations. Any problems with castrations and dehorning?"

"No, we did tons of castrations in farm animal block and quite a few dehornings." By tons of castrations, I meant three, by quite a few dehornings I meant none. I saw a dehorning once; it was bloody and cruel, and I honestly didn't understand the purpose.

"How about horses? Are you comfortable around horses?"

"Absolutely." I was tempted to say that I could tell a winner just from the way the jockey walked the horse around the paddock, but I thought better of it. After all, the joke about the pig farm fell flat.

Dr. Nelson then gave me a tour of his hospital. We stopped in treatment, and he led me to a lightbox alongside the x-ray machine. He lite the viewer to show an eleven by fourteen film of a horse's hoof. "This is a nine-year-old gelding with a limp. I saw it yesterday. What is it?"

Now I knew it was a horse's hoof, but I don't think that was the answer he was looking for, so I said the first and only thing which came into my head. "Laminitis?"

"No, it's navicular disease."

Damn, that Dr. Banks and her tight Calvin Kleins. For years, her designer jeans would be the only vision which would pop into my head whenever I thought of horses. I knew with that answer the interview was over. If Dr. Nelson had brandished two pearl-handled six-shooters, I would have been face down bleeding out in the muddy parking lot.

"I'll let you know." He said as he pushed me through to the front door. I don't think he even shook my hand on the way out.

My next interview was forty miles north at the Shelby County Animal Hospital. I drove on one of a thousand forgettable rural routes which led to the tiny town of Shelbyville, the county seat-population 492. I walked up to a one-story clapboard structure, little more than a trailer. I passed through the door and went back in time; I believe sometime during the Eisenhower administration. The waiting room was covered in vintage dark wood paneling and faded vinyl tile, both dustier than the road leading into town. Three wooden chairs and a receptionist table furnished the room. The walls had been tastefully decorated with framed paintings of hunting dogs; one had a black Labrador with a duck in its mouth, one had a Pointer who was standing next to a horse and a rider, another had two Pointers who were staring into the woods; perhaps watching the rider relieving himself on a pine tree. The only thing missing was a portrait of the Labrador, the Pointers and the horse playing poker. I soon learned, the receptionist doubled as the doctor's wife. She was delightful and told me Doc Johnson would be back in the office in thirty minutes. So, I waited with Mrs. Johnson, some classic artwork, and a phone which never rang.

As Midwest time moved slower than usual, my wait was closer to an hour. This pause gave me time to contemplate the reason I was seeking gainful employment in an unimpressive hospital with such Spartan conditions. The reason for staying in a state I had grown to dislike was simple. My fiancée was in her final year in veterinary school. Therefore, I was resigned to my commitment to remain with her to the bitter end; I wasn't going anywhere.

Doctor Johnson came in just before ten with three cups of coffee, one he gave to his wife at the receptionist desk; he offered the third cup to me. He was a tall, lean man in his late sixties with white sideburns and glasses. He was dressed in brown overalls, a plaid flannel shirt, and a St. Louis Cardinals baseball cap. He introduced himself, shook my hand and took me on a four-minute tour of the hospital. It was a tiny pet animal medical facility with some basic vintage Korean War era medical equipment. We sat in his office which smelled of moldy tile and Aqua Velva. He had a large framed picture of the Missouri mules on one wall and the other a portrait of Ronald Reagan.

"So, where you from?"

"New Jersey..." I touched on the high points of my small animal experience and skipped the jokes and embellished farm animal stories. However, I quickly realized old Doc Johnson had never read my resume; I even wondered if he remembered why I was sitting across his worn oak desk that June day.

There are three types of interviews: the best is the balanced input between the interviewer and the interviewee. The second is the when the candidate stumbles through a lengthy memoir while the employer reaches a judgment usually about thirty seconds after they start speaking, and the third is a lengthy soliloquy where the potential employer speaks of his accomplishments, his business savvy, and his five-year plan. Today I was a victim of interview number three. I heard the story of old Doctor Johnson and the Shelby Animal hospital, how he started twenty-five years before in a building smaller than this one-smaller is difficult to imagine. He told me he met his first wife at the state fair in Sedalia, Missouri thirty years before. I learned he had two children, a son in the Army in Georgia, and a daughter in a commune in

California. What I didn't learn was if he was genuinely looking for an associate or just needed a buddy.

"Ethel wants me to start thinking about retirement, but I don't know, I can still get up in the morning, and I still like what I'm doing. So, do I start introducing another doctor to my clients now, or do I wait? I don't-know." He would take long pauses and stare at the pictures on the wall, almost as if he was looking to the mules for advice. Then he would repeat, "I really don't-know." Then he would stare at Ronald Reagan for an unbearable amount of time. I was begging "old Dutch" to throw him an answer, or at maybe one of the mules-but it never came.

"OK." I interrupted. "I can see you're busy, and I have a couple more interviews down south. "So, I'll let you go."

"Oh, good, glad to meet you. Do you have any more questions?"

Later, as I slipped into my car, I remember thinking, "Yes, I do have one more question, what the hell was that?" However, as time would prove this type of interview was all too common among veterinarians. The "Sure I'm looking for a veterinarian, but not right now or maybe ever," interview. That day I learned a great deal about the life of old Doc Johnson, but I also learned veterinarians are an indecisive breed.

Now the radius of employment search was expanding faster than my student loan debt. The next interview was in the outskirts of St. Louis County, about 100 miles away. This was a new hospital with the audacious name of "Pet Animal World." The add was equally as impressive, "New 20,000 square foot companion, animal care facility, looking for a new graduate to be the primary leader for veterinary care in state-of-the-art facility, offering digital records, ultrasonography, surgical and medical care, as well as behavioral training, grooming, and boarding. Highly competitive salary and benefits to the right outstanding individual". I was speeding east for an interview the very next day.

"Wow, now that's what I'm talking about!" Driving down Interstate 70 I could see the neon sign more than a mile away-PAW in bold letters surrounded by a paw silhouette. I pulled into a newly paved parking lot on a sprawling two-acre property. Located at the very center was a shiny new white and gold two-story building. On the front of the building read the proclamation, "PET ANIMAL WORLD-THE GOLD STANDARD IN PET CARE." This hospital was no clapboard trailer.

Standing at the front door was a five-foot-eight black haired, well-groomed man, dressed in a black dress shirt and a dark blue tie-at first glance he resembled a young Joe Pesce. "Hi. I'm Dr. Vincent Santino. Glad to meet you." Years before I would have been nervous about meeting a man who looked like a connected Sicilian but after four years in white bread middle America, I welcomed the change.

"Let me show you around. We started this project about a year ago. We're about thirty days out from getting our CO. This puts our opening day, probably the first week in July. However, I would start any new hire veterinarian about two weeks before to get acclimated and finish setting up the medical facility."

We walked through the automatic louver doors and through a white cavernous reception area which resembled more a church than a waiting room with towering cathedral ceilings and ten-foot arched windows. We continued through to through the eight exam rooms, each with stainless steel exam tables, sinks, and computer terminals-a big deal in 1988. Dr. Santino led me to the heart of the hospital. Each area was a maze of ladders and contractors. The smell of fresh paint and tile adhesive filled the air. The rhythmic tapping of a carpenter's hammer could be heard from the floor above. The treatment area was bright and roomy and had more medical equipment than I had seen since vet school.

"Let's go upstairs," he said, as he started up a large staircase which led to a second-floor open auditorium. "This is our training area. We'll hold classes on training and behavioral modification. There is an elevator in the back, next to the grooming area. My whole goal here was to create the first all-inclusive pet center in the state of Missouri-everything under one roof."

I stood in awe. This hospital was easily the equal of most practices in the east. It certainly shammed most of those I had visited in Mid-Missouri. I had always dreamed of working in this type of hospital. It was a new, well-equipped hospital with a bright future. I truly wanted this job.

"Are you hungry?" Dr. Santino asked. "Let's get a bite to eat.

I hated to eat during interviews. It was like eating on a first date. I didn't want to come off as a pig, burp, or get lettuce stuck in my teeth. Besides interviews gave me heartburn burn and that wasn't conducive to proper digestion. However, this was a dream job, for a new graduate the position of a lifetime-so I agreed.

"Sure, let's go."

I was halfway through my Cobb salad, and I thought the interview was going very well. He had been impressed by my resume; we had exchanged pleasantries and compared biographies. Dr. Santino's was born in St. Louis and graduated from the University of Missouri two years before me. His family was originally from Long Island and later moved to Missouri and made their fortune in real-estate. His mother lent him 1.2 million dollars to build Pet Animal World, and he was "damn determined to make her investment work." I checked my teeth for lettuce frequently, swallowed my burps, and ate like a rabbit. It was going well until he posed a question which started the reflux of cucumbers up through my chest.

"If you don't mind me asking, how old a man are you?" In today's world, that question was a human resource nightmare-not in 1988. The reason he asked was apparent, I was by that time, bald. Thanks to genetics and a great deal of stress I had lost my hair by the time I was twenty-six, sometime during grand rounds in surgery block. He also asked if I was married and had children-again, not an ethical query. However, then the interview slid towards the inevitable abyss.

"I'm looking for a veterinarian with initiative who could run and grow this hospital. Quite honestly, I am looking for the top three graduates from your class. You must know them; do you think they would want to work here?"

Even to this day, I can't think of a witty response to Dr. Santino's question. I do remember thinking I could see Dr. Four Point-O working in this dream hospital while I festered in some pitiful hobble of a clinic fixated on hunting dogs chasing ducks. I certainly couldn't entertain the thought of Dr. Franklin

111

Kennedy, the elite brown nosier making his name in this veterinary Shangri-La. In the end, I said nothing, we finished our meal, exchanged false compliments, wished each other well, and left Applebee's in the quiet realization that we both wasted a perfect afternoon. On the long one-hour drive home, with tears from the late afternoon sun in my eyes, I recalled Dr. Bastian's advice on the first day of vet school: "If a potential employer asks for your grade point average or your class ranking, you don't want to work for them." Good advice, but I still did not handle rejection well.

My next interview was further into the heart of Saint Louis, over 125 miles from home. I was invited to spend the day with the head veterinarian Dr. Terry Wright. We met at one of three satellite clinics of an anchor hospital named Saint Louis Animal Care. Satellite clinics were intended to garner out-patient business from other sections of the city while utilizing the larger fully equipped founding hospital for surgical cases and overnight care. Dr. Wright was a small lean soft, spoken man, who looked more like Pee-wee Herman then Joe Pesce. He was affable and considerate. If hired, I would spend two days in this storefront clinic and four days a week at the primary hospital.

The anchor hospital was a fair size 10,000 square foot facility with a large surgical ward, eight exam rooms, and a boarding kennel. I was left to observe the daily flow for most of the day. Doctors would sit in a central pharmacy to wait to be called for an appointment. Clients would enter one door and the doctor another. The client would hold the pet, and the doctor would examine the animal, give the vaccines and again exit to the windowless sanctuary of the pharmacy-to wait until the next file was plopped in the door slot. This type of veterinary practice was common in the eighties, sarcastically referred to as "the assembly line practice"-this was the purgatory of veterinary medicine. Eight hours a day a veterinarian was sentenced to stand idle in a back-stage room ready to be called to action for the next fifteen-minute appointment. The doctor had little social contact with the hospital technicians or receptionists. The worst part, like Dr. Rankin in my hometown, was the small interaction a doctor had with the clients-doctors just popped in and out in ten minutes, like a peep show.

Two hours later I was summoned to finish my interview with the owner of Saint Louis Animal care, Dr. Theodore J. Mooney-not his real name but the resemblance was uncanny. Across an expansive dark laminated desk sat a large pear-shaped man with curly red hair and a handlebar mustache. Behind him was a large opaque picture window which lite his silhouette like a heavenly sunbeam. The late afternoon sun was so bright that I had to avert my gaze and focus on the side of his shiny desk. After lighting his African Rosewood pipe, he leaned forward so I could easily visualize his face beyond the glare. He began to speak with words that split the thickening haze of cherry and cream tobacco smoke.

"Dr. Wright told me you visited our Chesterfield clinic and got a feel for your responsibilities. I know this afternoon you spent some time here shadowing our clinicians. How does everything look?"

"Just great. I was very impressed." I was sincerely impressed, but not by the hospital; I was more impressed by this guy's office; wall to wall carpeting, hardwood shelves, a black leather couch, and gold-framed awards on every wall. It looked more like the office of a state senator then a Veterinarian.

"Did Dr. Wright fill you in on your schedule?"

"He gave me a general idea."

"As a new associate, you will work a staggered schedule which means you work Monday, Wednesday, and Friday from 8:00 AM to 4:00 PM. Tuesday and Thursday you work from 8:00 to 8:00 PM, and of course three Saturdays a month."

"I understand I would be doing surgery two days a week."

"Yes, your days in surgery would be Tuesday and Thursday after your morning appointments in Chesterfield. When the surgeries are finished, and the patent is in recovery you can leave. Sometimes surgery can extend through the early evening."

"Dr. Wright said something about Sunday and holiday duties?"

"Sure, the new associate covers the hospitalized cases for this main hospital, sometimes this requires the doctor to come in twice a day on the weekend. The senior doctors do not do treatments; that's the duty of first-year associates. Therefore, I require my doctors to live in town. This stipulation is spelled out in the contract. I know you now live in Columbia now, but I assume there is no problem with that move."

"No. I'm looking at a few places this weekend." This statement was false; I had no intention of moving to Saint Louis. This was the second bald-faced lie I had told today. The first was when I tried to convince Dr. Wright that my fiancée and I had decided against moving back to New Jersey and planned to remain in the Midwest. I had to convince myself-I needed the job.

"Good," he said as he relit his cold pipe. "I usually give a thirty-day window to find a new place."

"Could you tell me the benefits, like health insurance, vacation days and salary?"

"That is all covered in the contract. However, I can tell you we don't offer health insurance to first-year associates. But you do get one week of paid vacation, just to let you know that's five days' vacation, not seven days, many people make that mistake." He moved his leather chair back against the window obscuring his face once again. He fell silent; I think he was trying to ignore my question about salary.

I nervously shifted my weight as I began to squirm in my seat. Dr. Mooney had succeeded in making me feel guilty about asking about money. It took another minute before I gathered the courage to ask the question a second time. "And what is the starting salary?"

"Twenty-two."

Twenty-two thousand! A year! I was stunned. I had seventy thousand dollars in student loans, and I would be making twenty-two thousand a year, and that was before taxes. My dad, a union carpenter, was making more, an experienced janitor was making more, and I knew a rookie meteorologist was earning much more than twenty-two thousand a year. I would be working six to seven days a week; I would be the low dog on the food chain doing everyone's dirty work. I was screaming inside. You've got to be frigging kidding me you ginger headed, pipe toking, over-inflated toad.

"How's that sound? Still interested?"

"Oh absolutely, very much so," I said, swallowing my tongue and my pride. With one last ounce of courage, I asked, "Is there any room at all for negotiation?"

"Absolutely not! If you don't have any other questions, we will part company. Later I'll consult with Dr. Wright, and we'll let you know?"

"No. It all sounds very good to me. Thank you for your time".

Driving home that night I had such mixed feelings about the day. I liked Dr. Wright; he made the interview experience pleasurable while the cumquat shaped Dr. Mooney was less appealing. He was as impersonal as his practice. Maybe if I got the job, I could avoid him for four days a week for a year as I did with the eminent Dr. Barack in the surgical block. I needed a full-time position, so desperately I was willing to muddle through the boredom of the veterinary assembly line and torturous schedule, as well as, the four-hour drives each day. Sure, I wouldn't be medically challenged or socially stimulated, but I would be a real employed veterinarian. I was naïve about contracts. Long before I understood contract law and the tenacity of a good attorney, I convinced myself if it didn't work, I could walk away. Whom would it harm?

Then a lucid daydream popped into my mind. I was bent over, restrained in a metal stanchion. Dr. Mooney was powering up a large electric rectal probe- he was smiling as his spiked up the voltage. Nailed on the wall of the barn in front of me was the contract with my scribbled signature. "Your ass is mine, doctor, you're not going anywhere." The scene repeated with each mile I drove and not one scenario I could imagine ended with a happy ending. Maybe I would get lucky, and like the other interviews they would use my resume to line a cat cage, and I would never get the call.

I got the call five minutes after arriving home. Dr. Wright was as charged as a man who found a new best friend. His bubbling acceptance made my decision more agonizing. In the end, it wasn't the four hours of driving, it wasn't the abusive schedule, and it wasn't even the lordly Dr. Mooney which solidified my decision. I was worth more than twenty-two thousand a year. I was not greedy; that is not why I entered this profession. However, I was not going to compromise my integrity. I would leave that job for someone else.

Next, I entered the world of the relief veterinarian. A relief veterinarian is like a substitute teacher. The job was to fill in for a regular veterinarian who was on vacation. The advantages of this position were the higher pay scale, and minimal commitment and responsibility-you were there for a day or two, then you left never to walk into that practice ever again. The negative aspects were the fluid schedule and the lack of familiarity with almost any practice you entered. The pay was a significant amount in 1988-one hundred and twenty-five dollars for an eight-hour day.

My job the first day of veterinary practice was a relief veterinarian in a two-doctor companion animal practice in Kansas City, Missouri. The owner was Dr. Patrick Dorman, a meek, balding, middle age gentleman who from a short phone conversation agreed to hire me for relief. On Friday, I spent most of my energy trying to impress the staff; I didn't want them to suspect this was my first day of practice. Like most new graduates, I would stress over the simplest of issues: an itchy dog, oh no what could I give to stop it; a sneezing cat, oh no what could it be; questions on training a puppy, oh no what would I say? I had to hide all this anxiety while playing the part of the consummate professional. It was frightening, I had a library of information trapped in my head, but I had to learn to set it free for practical use.

The day had gone remarkably well. The cases were routine, there were few tense moments. I was expecting barbs and snickers, but I didn't detect a snarky comment or thinly veiled criticism all day. My last appointment was a simple suture removal. The female Pitbull was spayed two weeks previously, but it had two problems; she was extremely aggressive, and she enjoyed chewing out her stitches. She had already removed one set, and now I was looking at the new sutures placed one week before by the local emergency veterinarian. The technician held the muzzled, kicking, growling brute as I removed the second set of sutures from dog's abdomen — a simple ending to a good day.

The next day I arrived at eight o'clock in the morning for my final day of relief. Dr. Dorman approached me with an expression on his face like I had slept with his wife. He pulled me into his office and sat me down. "Do you remember the dog you removed the sutures on late yesterday afternoon?"

"Sure, the mad Pitbull."

"Well, the wound dehisced, the dog chewed through the sutures in the abdomen and eviscerated her intestines. When they found her last night, she was starting to eat her organs. The owner decided to euthanize her at the emergency clinic at three in the morning last night." He was truly agitated, truly disturbed and truly saddened by the incident. He continued as he started to wring his hands and wipe his sweaty brow. "I've decided to give them their

Last Picked for the Big Dance

money back for the spay, as well as, the cost of the euthanasia. That is just over $400.00. It's the right thing to do. They were good clients, and I feel we're responsible for their dog's death."

What he meant was that I was responsible for their dog's death. I was waiting for his order to go home, but his anger fell short. I was destined to suffer the remainder of the day with the weight of this disaster crushing my very being. Now I felt the scows and imagined the sarcastic remarks; my true nature had been exposed.

Four years before, the first day of vet school, when Dr. Bastian told us to think of the worst thing which could happen, and then anything less would not be so bad, should have explained that theory to Dr. Dorman. The next four hours I hid from his staff. By now the idea of faking my competence was a moot point. I stood, naked and exposed and counted down the minutes until I would never see these people again. At days end, Dr. Dorman dutifully handed me a check for $250.00 for two days of work. I want to say I gave it right back to him to pay for my part in this tragedy, but I didn't. I did have my integrity, but I also had my rent which was due the very next day.

In the years since I have often thought of this incident and this was a blatant example of the worst possible scenario; the dog who chewed through its intestines and had to be put down-I could not have imagined a worse outcome. However, this was not all my fault. This horrible scene was a combination of a dangerous dog, a negligence owner who didn't monitor the dog, and poor post-surgical instructions-my five-minute role just sealed this dog's fate. The timid Dr. Dorman convicted me far too quickly.

Would an experienced veterinarian have recognized the potential for disaster? I don't know, but if Dr. Dorman had taken a more diplomatic path, and was not so quick to cast blame, it would have a saved me years of guilt.

I never worked another day of relief in Kansas City. A short time later, I obtained a part-time position in a small animal hospital in Sedalia, Missouri. This position was the first experience where I started to grow professionally and gain the confidence to practice on my own-the owner was practical and always a supportive influence — his professionalism lite the fire which developed my potential as a veterinarian. Through twenty-five years of practice, working with a multitude of colleagues never has any surpassed the patience and dedication of this Midwestern practitioner. We would review cases after each day; he would offer praise when I deserved it. He would offer his corrective opinion when it wasn't. In one such case I had performed a routine dog spay; still for me a difficult surgery. He examined the uterus and discovered I had left a small bit of ovary in the dog-a mistake which could even allow the dog to still come into heat-the primary reason to spay the dog. He called me and just stated that I had messed up and to be more thorough. With a pig-pen full of disappointing encounters with other vets, he renewed my confidence in this profession. Dr. Clarence Foster, a nationally respected veterinarian, was both a mentor and a role model whom I have tried to emulate most of my life.

I obtained a second job to supplement this part-time position; that job put me wrist deep in a pig's cervix in the middle of a snowy Missouri night-that night one new piglet came into the world. Two weeks after the piglet apocalypse I was given an equally tricky task, and it dealt with a species I was even less familiar- the horse.

  Dr. Lister asked me to service a horse auction in Southern Missouri. My task was to obtain blood samples from horses before their sale. I was to perform a Coggins test, a laboratory test for Equine Infectious Anemia; a contagious viral disease transmitted by horse flies. The negative test is required for interstate travel and is an essential prerequisite in the sale of a breeding mare. This job all seemed too easy; I was to take a blood sample from a group of horses, fill out some paperwork, and bring the samples back to the state diagnostic laboratory. Taking blood from a horse was simple, even for a small animal doctor from New Jersey as the jugular vein in the horse is the size of a little water hose. I would be given a list from the office manager before the sale. Dr. Lister estimated there would probably be about twenty horses-half a day of work.

  It was a beautiful Saturday in December when I started my forty-five-minute drive to the Pettis County Horse Auction. I pulled into an expansive corral and barn complex just off Route 65. Horse trailers crowded the parking lot and extended to the horizon. I could see the tops of cowboy hats weaving between the trailers like leather shelled beetles. I entered the main entrance just after 8 AM and faced a scene I had only witnessed in true western movies. The smell of horseflesh and timothy hay filled the air; I could hear the quick tongue calls of the auctioneer rattling off one bid after another. There were leather boots, worn Levi jeans, suede vests and a remarkable number of chaps darting in every direction. The barn was cowboy chaos; it reminded me of a flea market on red bull. I snaked my way back to the manager's office and introduced myself to a pudgy man whose expression mirrored the confusion in the barn. He was signing and handing out forms like he had eight arms. I had to repeat my introduction three times before he acknowledged my presence, finally he handed me a piece of notebook paper with rows of numbers scribbled in pencil. These were the horse's tag numbers I was to test (4,7,12,16…) like lottery numbers-a total of forty-five.

"Forty-five horses! Where can I find all these horses? I yelled over the noise.

"Out there, some are in the barn, and some are in the lot outside."

"Is there someone who could help me?"

"Not today," he answered, as he twisted his body around in a dismissive gesture which screamed, "get lost."

I walked out into the bedlam and found my way to the barn. I could see aisles of stalls which stretched to the lot outside. I expected the horses to be in ordered stalls corresponding to the numbers on the paper; they weren't. They were in no apparent order, and there had to be hundreds of horses. After about fifteen minutes I found my first test subject. It was a gray mare with a brown mane. I tried to calm the horse and take my sample from the bulging jugular vein. It was quickly apparent that she was not holding still. Three times I tried without success. I needed help, so I decided to flag the first person who passed the gate; he ignored me and scurried down the aisle. Repeatedly, I was pushed aside like a beggar at a stop light. Just as my frustration reached critical mass, I got the attention of a teenage boy, six-foot tall and about eighty pounds, who offered to restrain the horse. I quickly filled the vacutainer tube and labeled my first sample. I turned to garner further assistance, but he had already gone. I was alone, again.

I now opened my folder with my Coggins Test Submission forms and was astonished at the amount of information required. In addition to the general information, it had a two-dimensional picture of a horse used to document coat color and markings. Instructions read, "White marking and whorls must be shown." What the hell was a whorl? I think we covered these forms in the equine block, but it must have been one of those bits of information I had filed under the heading, "Who gives a shit."

I finished my abstract interpretation of the gray mare and continued my search. Now I ventured into the endless expanse of the outside lot. It was 9:15 before I stumbled on my second victim. B-22, Bingo! Just before 9:45 I found another. However, after two hours I had two crucial epiphanies; I had zero artistic ability, and without help, I would be drawing whorls on paper horses through Christmas. The worst part was that I had to gather these blood samples before the horses were auctioned off. They were selling them faster than I could test them. So, I made an executive decision to drive home and get some help.

I picked up my fiancée, and we arrived back at the lot just before noon, I had squandered four hours and tested only three horses. The auctioneer continued to pop off bids, and I suspect some had to be horses on my list. Suddenly, as if the meteorology gods had finally discovered where I was hiding, the spring-like day turned into an early winter storm; it was forty degrees with freezing pellets of sleet. In spring jackets, we searched for our lucky numbers among an increasing number of empty stalls. By the end of the auction, my frozen fingers had bled a measly sixteen horses. I had missed twenty-nine tests. I reported the final total and handed the sixteen pink copies to the manager. He quickly asked for the rest. "I couldn't find them in time; there was no one to help me."

"That's not my problem," he answered.

"But, what am I supposed to do about the rest of the horses?"

"I don't know boy; I guess you're shit out of luck!"

"I'm shit out of luck!" Driving home in that cold night I imagined I was "shit out of a job." This blunder was just another incident to prove to that mild manner Dr. Lister that this cocky Easterner could be so irresponsible and dim-witted. The horse sale was not a good recovery from my previous misstep three months before. That day I was called out to a farm to deliver a calf. The procedure was a fine success. I handily manipulated, turned and delivered a healthy sixty-five-pound Holstein calf-The first and only one of my career. I was delighted that I alone performed this miracle with what I had learned in vet school. I always remembered my mentor, Dr. Park, repeating an Eastern dictum whenever he asked me to perform a task of which I felt unsure. I would always say "OK, I'll try" and he would reply, "You don't try, you do!" I did, and the calf was alive, but because of my internal manipulation, I thought it prudent to administer an injectable antibiotic to the heifer. The problem was the antibiotic I used carried a prolonged withdraw period. A withdraw period is the length of time needed before the milk from a cow was safe for human consumption. I guess that day I didn't check my farm animal library in my gold hatchback. In this case, the cow was out of commission for a full month-that is a lot of wasted milk. Dr. Lister was blunt in his criticism, saying it would be lucky if they didn't charge us for the lost milk. However, for me, that live calf made the call a complete success. Why cry over spilled milk? Sediment I didn't share with Dr. Lister.

Now three days after the auction he asked me how it went. I made some quirky remarks about frostbite and how finding the horses was like finding a needle in a haystack. Fortunately, he was in the middle of surgery and was somewhat distracted. I had thought I had put the subject to rest. A week later, I relived that terrible day with a quick, shocking statement.

"That guy from the horse auction refused to pay me for your work last Saturday."

"You're kidding, what was his excuse? I spent all day there."

"I don't know," he answered, shaking his head. "At first he didn't even remember you were there. However, then when I pushed him on it, he said he remembered you were there but said he didn't get the paperwork on time."

"I gave him all copies for all the samples I took that day," I interrupted. "The guy was a real asshole."

"Yes, I know, that auction bullshit gets old, really quick. However, you know, I've had problems with him before. That's why I personally don't do it anymore; it is a waste of my time. Don't worry about it. It doesn't surprise me. Let him get someone else next year."

I was relieved. I kept my job even after the horse auction debacle. Still, I did waste my entire day chasing lottery numbers in a frozen horse corral and eight hours practicing my skills as an equine sketch artist-all for a payday of $70.00. However, I did learn a crucial lesson-a degree in veterinary medicine does not demand respect. Indeed, not the respect of a real doctor. A lesson I would take back to New Jersey three months later.

CHAPTER 6

A RUDE AWAKENING

"Toto, I've a Feeling we're not in Kansas anymore."

- The Wizard of Oz (1939)

Driving past the Saint Louis Arch and over the Mississippi River for the last time I took comfort in the fact that is wasn't just the plains of Missouri I was leaving behind but the hills and valleys of my first year of practice. It wasn't all bad; I delivered a calf, a live piglet or two, independently honed my surgical and anesthetic skills- as I was on my own most of the year and I developed my laidback country folk bedside manner which I thought would be beneficial in the next phase of my career. I was frequently forced out of my comfort zone and learned to improvise and adapt to cases I could never have imagined five years before. I envisioned the past year as a practical internship with my victories and failures as letter grades soon to be forgotten. I would quickly learn; these Midwesterners were more forgiving than the critical Northeastern pet owners who would later haunt my dreams.

After working solo for most of the year in small one doctor clinics, I leaped at the chance to work in a large multiple doctor practice. Gone were the small paneled offices and the prefabricated metal clinics with attached large animal holding stalls. Behind me were the lonely farm calls in a pickup full of class notes and surgeries performed with one eye on the pet and the other on the breathing bag because there was no one to monitor anesthesia. I hoped I would never again put my arm up the opposite end of another cow. In these practices, there were always surgeons willing to back me up during surgery and colleagues to offer medical advice. They had technicians who scrubbed and prepped surgical patients and performed and monitored anesthesia. They employed assistants who restrained animals, technicians who answered the owner's questions, and hospital managers who handled billing and calmed agitated clients. Kennel workers cleaned cages and performed prescribed treatments, and an in-house groomer bathed and fluffed dogs and cats.

I was hired as the sixth doctor in a pet animal practice in an affluent Northern New Jersey urban community, fifteen minutes from Manhattan-a town filled with old money and new Jaguars. The owner was Dr. Richard Hershey, a short, balding, man with a developing middle age spread. He spoke softly and calmly, like he was always trying to put you at ease-he reminded me of how a hypnotist speaks just before he tells you to squawk like a chicken. The senior associate was Dr. James Stenson, an affable, well dressed thirty-five-year old bachelor, with a light blonde mullet-his specialty was treating cats owned by gorgeous young brunettes. The third doctor was a tall, dark surgeon, Dr. Tom Weissmuller. This squared jawed gentle giant spent his free time at Gold's Gym, proven by his pecs which strained his short sleeve dress shirts. Dr. Marilyn Jenkins was a thirty-year-old mother of two. She was soft, kind and a conscientious doctor. Not surprisingly she was well liked by the staff and adored by her clients. The youngest associate was Dr. Sarah Fox, a first-year Ivy League graduate. She was intelligent, inpatient, and didn't suffer fools lightly.

The Mountaintop Animal Hospital was established before World War II as one of the first privately owned small animal hospitals in New Jersey. It was still using the original three-story converted home from the late thirties. Years of additions and alterations had made a unique workspace of narrow hallways, sliding glass doors, and homemade wooden cages. There was an isolation ward made from an old carriage house located in the far rear of the property.

Winston, a sixty-five-year-old Jamaican man, maintained the kennels. He did all the dirty work, like walking dogs and cleaning cages; which I had done for almost ten years. He spoke very little English but had a unique mental connection with dogs-he was the Rastafarian dog whisperer. Winston would walk the dogs by opening the cage door and making a high-pitched call which sounded something like "poochie, poochie, poochie," followed by a loud whistle. Like magic, the dogs would run out of the cage through the kennels to the outdoor runs, never deviating from their appointed path. When they had finished, he would repeat the call and point to their respective cages, and they would inevitably run back to their cell without complaint-he never used a leash or needed a muzzle.

    Winston grew up in a small town, fifty miles north of Kingston known for its lush banana plantations, its muddy slums, and its ubiquitous feral dog population. He learned his gift in adolescence when his mother gave him the task of keeping stray dogs out of his family's barn. He worked in the banana fields from the age of twelve until his twenty-second birthday when he stowed away on an American cargo ship which eventually leads him to the port of New York. It was not clear if Winston was even a naturalized citizen-he certainly couldn't read or write. This fact made his kennel skills even more impressive. I will always remember his effervescent personality and the lite cigarette which hung from the side of his mouth. Most memorable was his rendition of "Day O," which he sang in his classic Jamaican accent as he meandered through the kennels directing dogs to their appointed path.

    Winston was one piece of the colorful mosaic of this new environment which was in sharp contrast to the monochromatic scene in white bread America. The bright lights of the big city also had enormous social and economic diversity. In the morning, I would see a gorgeous blonde professional in an Armani suit and Jimmy Choo shoes, carrying a miniature poodle sporting a Coach collar and one-hundred-dollar custom Poodle-cut. In the afternoon, I would see a tattooed biker in a leather jacket; fist cupped around a

A Rude Awakening

chain towing an aggressive hundred-pound Rottweiler. Both clients who were willing to pay any price for treating their pet. In Mid-Missouri, it was not uncommon for clients to decline even basic preventative health care. Here they didn't ask, and I didn't talk about money-it was not my job. I was responsible for treating their pets and highlighting my charges, as I received a percentage of every procedure I ordered. This was my first job with production-based compensation, and I liked it. I quickly realized this was the land of milk and honey. It was the post-Reagan era; it was the decade of *Saint Elmo's Fire*, and *Wall Street*. We were told if you worked hard you could be the next millionaire. It was 1989 in New Jersey, everyone was making big money, and I was getting my twenty-one percent.

A dark cloud in this promising picture was a gem we referred to a by the name of Cruella, the office manager, and the boss' wife. This arrangement was a common fringe benefit of veterinary practices during an era where running a business required more brawn than brain. In these hospitals wives commonly doubled as managers, it was a cost-effective management tool. Who better to enforce and protect the owner's interest than the person closest to his money? In some hospitals, it worked, in most, it didn't. In many hospitals, it created a tense atmosphere of distrust among the management and the hospital's best asset, the employees. Thus, she earned her second alias, the Gestapo.

Cruella would hide behind the front desk where she spent most of her energy courting good clients and exorcizing the bad. She extinguished fires with her scow alone-which was an advantageous trait in any business. Her reputation blossomed when she unleashed her charm on helpless employees. Her management style was as tight as her gray hair bun. She didn't tolerate sloth, tardiness, mistakes, miscues, insubordination, miscalculation, oversights or any fault which jeopardized profits or the hospital's reputation. She would perform a D & C (discipline and chastise) on those employees who had sinned. It didn't take very long for me to understand how much the employees disliked this woman. They resorted to great lengths to hide; slipping through the nearest kennel door when she walked down the hall, to avoid her gaze for fear of turning to stone. I was a doctor and not directly in her sights, but I too walked down another hallway when I felt the passing chill of her lifeless aura. This uncomfortable situation was my first experience in this kind of adversarial relationship between the employees and the boss. However, like everyone else, I didn't know how hard it was running a practice; I didn't trust management until years later when I became management.

 However, this was the ideal hospital where I could learn to be a competent veterinarian. Dr. Hershey was an excellent professional and a good role model. He was a conscientious, disciplined diagnostician using a logical approach to medicine. I was finally able to work cases up as we had learned in vet school; we could order radiographs, do bloodwork, urinalysis, hormonal assays, and endless bacterial cultures. However, I soon found the downside of doing workups is for every test you do you have to interpret the results. My quandary was not what to do when the results were abnormal; it was what to do when they were normal. In school, they emphasized

A Rude Awakening

the abnormal more than the normal-when everything checked out fine-I did not know what to tell the clients. Regular office hours ended at six o'clock, many nights I would be sitting catatonic long past eight in torturous indecision staring at a stack of unfinished files from the week. These clients had brought their cat in for excessive drinking, and the bloodwork was normal. This dog came in for panting, again all normal. The owners called for the results this morning. What was I going to tell them? I couldn't go home until I found an answer.

One Friday evening as the hour struck nine, Dr. Hershey was shutting the building down and noticed the glow of my office light. In an authentic touch of pity, he popped his head through the door and asked. "Is there anything I can do to help? It seems like you are always here so late."

"Well, it's just these workups are driving me crazy. Like with this eight-year-old cat, I was expecting something to be wrong, diabetes or renal failure. However, nothing. I don't know what the hell to tell the client. I did this whole expensive workup, and I found nothing."

"Listen to me," he said as he pulled up a chair. "There is an old saying in medicine, 'you can't find what you don't look for.' Meaning you as a doctor are obligated to recommend whatever diagnostics are needed to get the answer. The client gives you the presenting signs for the dog or cat, and you recommend testing, but you have no control over the results. If they are negative, then they are negative. Maybe one out of ten is positive; that's the one you're looking for."

"I feel like I have just wasted their money."

"You should not feel guilty about reporting normal results. Look at it this way; if you went to your family doctor because you had chest pains, he would give you a thorough examination, take X-rays, and run some bloodwork, and maybe an ECG. The next day when he calls which would you rather hear, 'I'm sorry it looks like you have blocked coronary arteries,' or would you rather hear, 'everything came back normal, I think it was just heartburn'?"

"Obviously, that everything was normal," I replied. "However, I sometimes don't know what to recommend next."

"You have to put that back on their shoulders. Let them decide if they want to pursue it any further. Referrals, more extensive testing, or do they want to take a wait and see attitude. You can always continue the workup later if the problem doesn't resolve. This is what I do; I always emphasize the good. Start off the conversation with, 'I have good news Mrs. Jones, Buffy's bloodwork was negative that means her kidneys are fine, and she doesn't have diabetes, thank God because that means you would have to give insulin injections for the rest of her life.' Hit on the positive note, then offer additional testing. More likely they will want to wait. This gives you time to investigate the next step. Doctors face this all the time in human medicine. Believe me; a sane person will not complain when their lab tests come back normal. Remember it is not a crime to say, 'I don't know.' Get used to saying it, because you are going to be saying it a lot."

Driving home that night I thought deeply on this crystalline logic. In veterinary school, we learned to work towards an answer, our brains were trained to find the etiology of a disease, and not to stop until you do. I was beginning to realize in the real world that living organisms do not always give up their secrets. Before I accepted this job, I had an interview at a practice which boldly stated in the classified ad in the Journal of the American Veterinary Medicinal Association: "Here every patient gets a workup, every workup gets a diagnosis, and every diagnosis gets a treatment." During my interview, I quickly understood the owner should have written; work up all patients, treat all patients, charge all patients. All he talked about was numbers; the number of x-rays, the number of CBCs, the number of bacterial cultures. It was, for this gentleman, all about the number of dollars.

In this practice, I was not pressured to produce; I was compelled to be a good doctor. This hospital was as far away from an assembly line practice as I could imagine; I had my own office where I would examine the animal. I would then write a SOAP with the plan of action, and the technician would take the pet with the written orders to treatment. They would then bring the lab work and any radiographs to my office for my analysis. My prescription would then be filled by the pharmacy technician who would explain the instructions to the owner and discharge the pet. I submitted the charges, and the receptionist at the front would check the clients out. I never provided an estimate, and I never heard a complaint-that was Mrs. Hershey's job.

In the late eighties, certified technicians (the equivalent of registered nurses) were a rarity, most learned by experience. Jim, the head technician at the Mountaintop Animal Hospital was exceptional. He was a fifty-year-old ex-military nurse who carried out the orders of six doctors to the letter. He would perform venipuncture, wound care, bandaging, and some minor surgical procedures. Today, most young vets would cringe at the thought of not personally performing these menial tasks-their egos, and their imagined legalities would not have allowed Jim's audacity. I liked the freedom; it allowed me you to practice real medicine and diagnostics-not taking blood and shaving hot spots.

In my early days, I also had a tinge of the doctors God complex. On one occasion, I examined a Pug who was limping on the left front leg. The dog had fallen down the stairs. Jim took a radiograph which I found to be normal; I noted in the file "tentative diagnosis a sprain."

Jim caught me as I started to leave treatment. "Tough break for the dog."

"What do you mean?"

"The fracture."

"What are you talking about?" I replied with a tinge of angst in my voice. "I didn't see anything."

"Sure, look at the radiograph again — distal humerus. I would be glad to go over it with you when I've got the time," he said, as he bent down to draw blood from a thirteen-year miniature poodle, forcing the end to our discussion.

I slipped the radiograph under my jacket and headed to the lightbox in my office. I was damn determined to prove this technician wrong. How dare he question my judgment. Who was the doctor here? When I lite the film, it took me only a second to see the break — a transverse supracondylar fracture just above the elbow. I don't know how I missed it; I returned to the client and gave him the news and then referred the dog to an orthopedic surgeon for internal fixation. Fortunately, the client never knew I had missed the diagnosis. Jim, on the other hand, did know. I shamefully returned to treatment and regretfully thanked him for his help. He then replied with words I have always remembered, "Listen we're on the same team if we can help the dog what difference is it who makes the diagnosis. I'm here to help you make the animal better. If it makes you look good, that's fine too."

It was in that instant that I learned to bury my ego and open my mind to others in this profession. Those with real-world experience can often trump two-dimensional textbook lessons. In the decades following that day, there have been innumerable cases where other doctors and technicians have offered valuable insight into a difficult case, saving both the animal and my ass. We are all on the same team.

However, it is the right of every young person to be foolishly idealistic. In my early career, I assumed that compassion and ethics were synonymous. I was in my second month at the Mountainside Animal Hospital. I liked my job and was proud to be working in a hospital with a real legacy and pristine reputation. Dr. Hershey had a similar reputation. He was the perfect personality to deal with those affluent clients who would spend anything on their pet but demand everything in return. They requested him because of his reputation and his ability to pacify their pedigree temperaments.

On Monday morning one of Dr. Hershey's special cases waited in treatment. Sasha was a typical two-year-old chocolate Labrador retriever, alert, friendly and frequently rambunctious. Today she was scheduled for euthanasia. Jim was on vacation, as I was the junior associate; I was responsible for some of his duties-regrettably this was a big one. The treatment area was astir, the young technicians and assistants were ogling over Sasha, questioning this bizarre decision. I assured them I did not have a choice; this was Dr. Hershey's orders. I didn't know why the pet owner had reached this crossroad, but it was out of my hands. The staff's dissension only grew stronger as they urged me to keep this dog alive.

"I would take her," said one young, blonde female assistant. Another female college student assured me she could find her a good home. Another judged it cruel "to kill such a great dog." Maybe it was my naivety, perhaps it was my mislaid compassion, or perhaps I just wanted to be the hero in the adoring eyes of those enthusiastic school girls. Either way, I acquiesced and hid the dog in the back of the hospital hoping to slip her out the back door covertly.

Thirty minutes later Dr. Hershey passed me in the hall and asked. "Any problem with that euthanasia?"

"Well, I didn't put her down," I quickly mumbled as I walked away. "We have decided we would find her a home."

"Wait, you did what?" He shot back as he started towards me. "Who's we?"

"Well, actually I made the decision. I thought I could…"

"Get in my office, now!" He chopped me off mid-sentence. He then spun and walked down the hall without even a glance to see if I was following.

A Rude Awakening

"Sit down!" He ordered as he slid the chair so hard it kissed the back of my knees. He then took his leather throne on the other side of his black steel desk. In two months, I had not seen Dr. Hershey speak a word of anger. I was beginning to think he was unable to raise his voice beyond a gentle whisper. However, when he was genuinely irritated, he would fondle the metal frames of his glasses-today Dr. Hershey was stroking the frames like he was polishing brass and his tone was not polite.

"I just thought…" I started; trying to plead my case.

"First, these people were good clients; they have been bringing their pets here for ten years. Do you think they came to this decision easily?"

"I don't---" He cut me off mid-sentence as I finally realized he wasn't asking for my input.

"They owned the dog for two years, they loved it, they took care of it, they did everything right. However, two weeks ago, it bit their three-year-old daughter in the face. She got sixteen stitches in her upper lip. Now, they refused to let this happen again. It was an agonizing decision. They were inconsolable when they left my office? Do you realize what would happen if next spring they were out for a walk and their dog, which they had agreed to put down a year before, was say, catching Frisbees in Central Park? Take a worst-case scenario; another family adopted the dog under your brilliant plan, and it bit another small child. Do you realize the liability we would have or the damage it could do to the reputation of this hospital?"

"I'm sorry I wasn't thinking, or I certainly wasn't thinking about the people, I was thinking about the rights of the animal."

"Whether you like it or not these pets are the property of the owners, they don't have rights. It is not our decision to question their motives, to question what is within their heart. Our job as veterinarians is to carry out their wishes as humanly as possible. Next time when I tell you to euthanize a pet, you better do it. Don't let it happen again."

Dr. Hershey fell short of using the "F" word. He would have been right to fire me, but he didn't. I was in a daze when I walked back to treatment. I ordered the staff to bring Sasha forward. I muffled the technician's protests with a fog of regret and frustration. I knelt in front of the dog as she lifted her right paw to shakes hands; I stared into her brown eyes, shot an overdose of barbiturates into her cephalic vein, saw her bodily go limp on the floor, and waited ten seconds for her healthy heart to stop beating.

Later that night I sat alone at my desk feeling like I had been slapped in the face and told to "wake up, welcome to the real world." Because for the first time I realized veterinary medicine was not about squeezing cute puppies and kittens and shaking the paws of obedient Labradors. Sure, it was about saving the lives of sick pets and alleviating their suffering, but it was also about relieving the pain and suffering of the owner. Their agony is more difficult to see, and for some to appreciate, but no less important than in their pet. When I was in vet school, my mother would mail me pictures she had hastily cut out of her *Women's Day Magazine*. They showed cute fluffy kittens and puppies, usually in the arms of a model in a white doctor's jacket; at the top, she would write, my name with a red heart. The problem with these ads; they were a fantasy like a fairy tale that permeates the public's view of this profession, a simple vision, hiding the hard truths, and the gut-wrenching decisions veterinarians face every day.

That night I sat alone in my townhouse garage and thought of my dog Samantha, how she was put to sleep in the company of strangers three years before; there I broke down and cried years of repressed tears into the hands that, earlier that day, were responsible for ending Sasha's life.

It was standard practice for Dr. Hershey to act as the heroic front man, impressing the clients with his medical expertise while delegating the hospital care to technician Jim or one of the other doctors. One such case fell on the lap of my colleague a, Dr. Arnold Weissmuller.

The day before Dr. Hershey examined Walter, an eight-year Old English Sheep-dog which had been anorexic and weak for five days. Diagnostic blood work suggested the dog had autoimmune hemolytic anemia; a life-threatening systemic disease which attacks and destroys the dog's red blood cells leading to a rapidly progressive anemia-with a mortality rate approaching 50%. Dr. Hershey admitted Walter Tuesday afternoon for supportive care and ordered Dr. Weissmuller to initiate immunosuppressive therapeutic doses of corticosteroids. The owners left with a promise from Dr. Hershey that we would do everything possible to save their dog. The dog was left alone in ICU for the evening; the doctor would reevaluate the dog the next morning. Dr. Tom Weissmuller arrived at eight o'clock to find Walter, stiff and cold, lifeless in a dark wooden cage.

Today's standard of care dictates that veterinarians inform the pet owner if they do not provide supervised after-hours care. In fact, in 2015 the New Jersey legislature passed "Betsy's Law," which requires veterinarians to post a notice if they do not have overnight supervision. The doctor must advise the owner of other alternatives, like a transfer to a referral hospital, which does provide overnight care. If they decide to leave their pet, then they assume the responsibility if the pet passes overnight. In 1989 this wasn't even a minor ethical concern, let alone, a legal matter. Sick pets were routinely left overnight, in intensive care on intravenous drips, without even a kennel worker to assist if the animal's condition worsened. Many veterinarians were small solo practitioners; employing staff to remain overnight just was not practical. I can recall cases where a critically ill pet was found in rigor mortis having died hours before the morning shift even arrived for work. Honestly, most of these cases were critical and would have passed even with adequate around the clock nursing care. Still, it did create a sensitive situation requiring a creative explanation.

Dr. Hershey found himself in that sensitive situation on a scolding Wednesday morning in July and Walter's owner was not open to creative explanations. The next morning, a severely agitated man carrying a large white sign over his head stood in front of the hospital. On the sign in bold black letters was written: "MY DOG DIED ALONE AT THE MOUNTAINTOP ANIMAL HOSPITAL AND NO ONE CARED!" This gentleman marched in front of that hospital non-stop for three days. A local radio station interviewed him; he even informed the local press of his grievance, and in twenty-four hours his horrific story was on the front page of the local

A Rude Awakening

newspaper-now that was creative. He even received food, water, and supplies from concerned citizens.

I had thought I had seen the worst of Dr. Hershey three months before with the Sasha incident but today was another plane of displeasure. The anger in his face that day was as if his son returned his Mercedes with an empty gas tank. Today his countenance was the rage he would have felt if his wife had run away with her female yoga instructor. He sat quiet, motionless, barely breathing, his hands folded on top of his empty metal desk, scowling through his polished framed glasses, peering straight ahead into the great abyss. No one dared to enter his office, we all scurried past his door like frightened mice avoiding a nasty cat. Even his wife, a woman prone to fits of indescribable rage, hid in her cubby behind the front desk. After three days on the picket line, the owner vanished, never to return. Some joked about finding his body in a shallow grave in the Pine Barrens of Southern New Jersey. Dr. Hershey probably made him an offer he couldn't refuse; probably a cash settlement large enough to ease his unrelenting sorrow-after all, with some pet owners, there is nothing like cold hard cash to relieve the pain of the loss of a pet. Money buys forgiveness, and in some cases a cute new puppy to replace the old one.

During my last year in Missouri, I had given considerable thought to the kind of hospital I wanted to work-especially when I considered the year in New Jersey as my first year of practice. Thomas Wolfe wrote, "You Can't Go Home Again." In my case, I wouldn't go home again. I could have chosen a quiet two doctor practice near my home town in Southern New Jersey. Dr. Park had talked about our partnership since my cramped hands conquered that vicious cat so many years before. He was a great man and had played a significant role in my success, but he was frugal. His clinic was a low-tech facility with minimal staff. I had worked in that type of hospital my last year in Missouri; therefore, I chose the practice with all the fringe benefits. However, the Mountaintop Animal Hospital had a cancer, discrete but incessant; it took months before any of us detected its presence.

I was making a good salary for a rookie veterinarian; I didn't get benefits or healthcare-but it was still good money. I was delighted with this new model of production-based compensation. I was young; I had no problem with hard work. The practice was unique for the day as it employed an in-house groomer who bathed and fluffed about ten pets daily. The practice had a policy that stated these pets had to be examined every six months and vaccinated yearly. This provided additional income for the practice and a nice bonus for me. I would skip to the back between my appointments and vaccinate as many pets as time would allow. In a six-doctor practice, it paid to be good friends with the groomer who reserved her patients for me. Some weeks I was making close to one thousand dollars, a substantial payday for a young veterinarian in 1989-but not for the average professional in Northern New Jersey, tristate area. The per capita income in my yuppie townhouse community was close to three times my meager paycheck. I was always struggling to keep my six-year-old Plymouth hatchback on the road and embarrassed to leave it out of my garage. Such was the downside of living in a town where your most prominent neighbor is Malcolm Forbes.

About six months into this daily struggle of ten-hour work days, and six-day work weeks, the other associates and I were becoming close friends, but the mood in the hospital was changing. We become allies because of increasing friction between the staff and Dr. Hershey, his wife, and his management minions. Dr. Fox was the first to illuminate a growing issue. Despite a jam-packed summer our weekly gross figures where stagnant. A few weeks later the other associates came to a similar conclusion-we were being short-changed. Their method of calculations was deceivingly simple — a register tape with only a weekly gross figure multiplied by a percentage and a final total. The computer program used in this hospital was a simple early version of veterinary management software. It was tough to pull up production data, and we had no way of accessing the records, we were all locked out of the accounting program.

The five of us, three men and two women, signed a scathing letter of intent to Dr. and Mrs. Hershey sighting gross financial discrepancies between our records and their invoices. We supported our claims with circumstantial proof and threatened immediate legal action. The doctors and I wondered if we would come in on Monday to locked offices and empty desks. We imagined Dr. Hershey seething, motionless behind his big black desk staring again into the abyss. We expected Mrs. Hershey, with her tight hair bun and her white diamond encrusted glasses, to storm from one office to the next slipping our newly signed pink slips under our door. We felt like we had just signed our declaration of independence. We knew if our ship sank, we would all drown together. "It was nice working with you." We joked as we left Friday afternoon. We waited all weekend in anxious trepidation for the other Hershey foot to fall. However, it did not happen.

"How was your weekend?" Greeted Dr. Hershey, as I scampered past his office.

"Uh good, really good. Nice, nice weather we're having?" I was barely able to find the words to mumble a reply.

"Looks like a busy week," he said. I've got Jim doing two low dose dexamethasone suppression tests today. What do you think, could I diagnose two Cushing dogs in one week?

"Sure, yes, definitely. Absolutely. Wow. Sure, let me know how it turns out."

"Will do," he responded. "You'll be the first to know." Then he stroked his glasses with one hand and patted my shoulder with the other.

I race-walked back to my office as I tried to suppress a colonic gas bubble that was spurting its way to freedom; seconds later I submitted my contribution to global warming. This was not good; I felt like I was in the *Twilight Zone*. I had to speak with the other doctors. We agreed on a clandestine meeting scheduled at high noon in the carriage house.

"Did Hershey say anything to you about the letter," I started.

"He didn't say anything to me, answered Dr. Tom Weissmuller

"Me either, he just stuck his head in my office and smiled. It was creepy," quipped Dr. Fox.

"You think that's bad, Mrs. Hershey asked me how my kids were doing. She has never asked me about my kids. I didn't think she knew I had kids," Dr. Jenkins added.

A Rude Awakening

"I know one thing," started Dr. Stenson. "If my wife is pissed at me when we go to bed and the in the morning she acts like nothing is wrong, then I know I'm screwed!"

"Do you think he got the letter," I asked.

"I put it into his mail slot on Friday night, it was gone by Saturday morning," Dr. Weissmuller replied. "I know he got it."

"Listen, guys," said Dr. Stenson, I don't think he's going to fire the five of us out of the blue, he can't cover the whole schedule himself.

"So, if the schedule stays the same, we're ok?" Dr. Fox asked.

"I wouldn't bet my job on that," said Dr. Weissmuller. "He's been screwing me since I got here. Remember he originally hired me on the promise of a ton of surgeries and a hell of a lot more money. Now, what am I seeing? Flea allergies and dying dogs with hemolytic anemia. I'll probably be the first one to go. He still blames me for the death of that Walter dog."

"Well, you touched him last," I said.

"Screw you! Your name wasn't in the newspaper. Besides, I think Winston was the last one to see that damn dog alive."

"You keep spreading that rumor, and you'll have Winston deported back to Jamaica," I joked.

"Listen," stated Dr. Fox, "I can't lose my job. I just started to pay back my student loans."

"Nobody is losing their job," rebuked Dr. Stinson. "We've got the leverage. Don't freak out yet. I think we just got to keep our cool and wait this out."

"Maybe so, but I've already started scanning the journal for jobs. I've got two kids, and I can't afford to be out of work either," affirmed Dr. Jenkins.

"Wait a minute," I asked, "you have kids?"

"Ha, Ha."

With that last word, our secret liaison quietly adjourned, and we slithered one by one back to our offices while the Hershey's were out to lunch.

Every morning for the next four days we expected some sign to show which direction the ball was falling. We listened for whispers around corners, phone conversations behind closed doors, and changes and omissions on the daily schedule. I even asked Jim if any significant changes were afoot. He would always answer the same way: "Didn't hear a word but I'll let you know if I hear something." Then he would give a sardonic grin and turn away. Dr. Hershey never seemed happier. We were beginning to doubt the whole thing ever happened.

Then on Friday morning, the seventh day since the letter, we received our usual paycheck, with a second yellow envelope; I was sure it was a letter of termination. The envelope contained a formal letter signed by Dr. and Mrs. Hershey which told a fantastic tale. They described a glitch in the computer system which started two months before, about the same time we experienced a change in our gross figures. This computer glitch neglected to count X-rays and bloodwork which reduced the total income figures for those eight weeks. They had fortunately discovered the problem before the deficiencies became too high. They gave their sincere apologies and greatly appreciated our patience in this matter. Lastly, they have corrected the problem and have calculated those lost wages. Included in every letter was a register tape with precise calculations and a second paycheck for almost two thousand dollars.

A Rude Awakening

We were in shock. The check was like a birthday present from my weird, reclusive aunt. Could it be sincere or was it sending a message? We held our next meeting later that day in the rear carriage house. This is indeed not what we had expected.

"You know this is hush money," started Dr. Weissmuller.

"Well, that may be, but considering we were all expecting to be out of work by this time, I think I'd be willing to swallow my pride," confessed Dr. Jenkins.

"That second envelope scared the shit out of me," I added. "I'm with Marilyn let's cut our losses and cash the checks."

"Yes," suggested Dr. Fox. "Let's cash them before they bounce. I'm sorry, but I don't trust little Dick and his wife, Cruella De Bitch."

"I don't think we have a choice," said Dr. Stenson. If we take it to the next level, it's going to get nasty. We would have to get a lawyer, subpoena the records to prove this whole thing was intentional; we would have to prove criminal intent. I've been here for almost ten years, and I will tell you that the Hersheys are never going to let that happen."

"Your right," I said. "That letter admitting to the 'mistake' takes the wind out of our sails. I don't think we can prove anything."

"I just don't know why they would take the chance to screw us over," added Dr. Jenkins.

"Oh, I think I know why," replied Dr. Stenson. "Last year he showed me the blueprints for a band new two-million-dollar hospital. Two stories, modern surgical suites, huge treatment area, four kennels, even a parking garage. The works. I think he needs the extra money to build it. However, that's just a theory."

"Those bastards," shouted Dr. Fox. "Theory my ass. I know how I can prove it. I'll take a clipper to Mrs. Hershey's man bun and shave it off if she doesn't confess."

"O.K.," responded Dr. Stenson. "Now as much as we would all like to see that happen. I think our only answer is, to see these checks for what they are, a peace offering, or if you feel better, hush money — Cash the checks. We'll keep our eyes open, and we'll see what happens next before we go any farther. However, we must be together on this. Agreed?"

"Agreed," we stated collectively.

The next few months went without incident. We didn't speak of it again, except in sarcastic innuendo. Dr. Hershey and his wife were ironically more amicable then before our letter of intent and before their payoff. However, for us, the trust was lost forever. Like in the movie "Mr. Roberts" where there was "disharmony aboard the ship," there was a great deal of underlying disharmony on this sinking ship. The tension was palpable. We were respectful, we did our jobs well, without complaint, but never would we ignore what went on behind our backs again-we kept personal records of everything which came across our desk. We all knew our time at the Mountaintop Animal Hospital would soon come to an end.

Dr. Fox resigned her position by the first of December. She abhorred the Hersheys; she would frequently confess that the sound of Dr. Hershey's voice sickened her. Dr. Jenkins left the following summer for a part-time position in a smaller practice which allotted her more significant time with her family. Dr. Weissmuller went later that year as he still wasn't reaching the compensation promised him two years before. Dr. Stinson stuck it out for another three years then left for a partnership in Northern New Jersey.

I submitted my resignation on May 1st, about six months after the infamous letter of regret. Once more I expected to be fired on the spot, but Dr. Hershey, the consummate professional, respectively allowed me to work the last thirty days in peace. Even though I was making decent money for a veterinarian, I was still a pauper in a land of princes, a Chrysler in the land of BMW's. However, my primary reason for leaving was the rapid disintegration of a position I had considered so promising and the loss of a real mentor.

My experience at the Mountaintop Animal Hospital illustrates how selfish and greedy management practices methodically can destroy the foundation of trust which is vitality important in a professional environment. Many of the para-professionals left for safer waters-some became veterinarians-most still tell stories of their servitude under the Hershey's tyrannical rule. I visited the hospital a few years ago, with my wife and children. Gone were the thirties era structure and carriage house which served well to hide our clandestine meetings. What stood in its place was an impressive white, two-story, stucco, palace with an Oriental rock garden and shiny automatic glass doors. I had no bitterness or regret. What did Jesus say in Matthew 23:27-28, about whitewashed tombs? "Beautiful on the outside but on the inside full of bones of the dead and everything unclean." Thankfully, it had been twenty years since my four colleagues, and I had washed our hands clean of the lies and deceit.

CHAPTER 7

YOU CAN'T CURE CRAZY

"A man is wise with the wisdom of his time only,

and ignorant with its ignorance."

- Henry David Thoreau

Again, I was in deep, I was almost up to my elbows, deep. Sweat dripped down my brow and into my eyes. My jaw tightened as my teeth clinched under my blue mask. My fingers were cramping, and my hands were drowning in sweaty latex gloves. Even my knees were starting to ache-next time I'll sit down-if I ever try this again. My gloves were greasy; everything kept slipping through my fingers like over-cooked linguini. My deep guttural breathes laid testament to my struggle. I strummed it rhythmically as hard as I dared and still, I couldn't get it out. It had been forty-five minutes since I opened her up and I still was only half done. This bitch was fat, and this spay was a bitch.

The text, *Fundamental Techniques in Veterinary Surgery* states, "Ovarian ligation in young dogs and cats may be simple." Lucy was a six-year-old Golden Retriever who was making this spay almost impossible. She not only had the body of a respectable brown bear, about twenty-five-pounds overweight, but she was also in estrus. In the veterinary world, this spay was the feared triad of evil; an old, fat dog, in heat.

The canine ovariohysterectomy or spay is the most difficult routine surgical procedure in veterinary medicine. Most veterinarians take years to reach a point of fearful respect for this procedure, and some never achieve this level-cringing at the thought of performing the next large dog spay. The public perception of this procedure is rather blasé; that it is routine. I believe this is the fault of our profession combined with the ignorance of an uninformed public. Twenty-five years ago, many hospitals were charging between one and two hundred dollars for a procedure taking close to an hour. Only until recently have the prices of these procedures increased-still a reasonable five to six hundred dollars. Still not enough for the skill needed and the risk involved with the spay surgery.

This surgery is an open abdominal operation to remove both ovaries and the uterus. The tricky part is the removal of the ovaries. They are held tight by the suspensory ligament, a sturdy band of soft tissue which prevents the ovaries from floating free in the abdomen by attaching them to the last two ribs. By strumming the ligament like a guitar string, it loosens the ovary just enough to get out of the two-inch incision opened in the abdomen. The problem is this ligament sits adjacent to the vessels which supply the ovary. In big dogs these vessels are large, and in obese dogs, these vessels are surrounded by so much fat tissue that all these distinct anatomical structures are indistinguishable from the greasy fat. This fat makes gloves and the instruments feel like they were soaked in bacon grease. In the case of a dog in heat, the vessels are twice the standard size, engorged and very friable. I tease, tug and pull this peanut size ovary as far out as possible without rupturing the pulsing ovarian artery, while my hands and my instruments slip and slide off every structure. If I am lucky, I will get a half inch to place two small ligatures around this amorphous mess- and remove the ovary. This painful struggle ends with a moment of truth; when the clamps are released, and the fatty stump slips back into the deep dark abdomen with a hope and a prayer that the ligations hold. If they slip the artery will start spurting blood, and the abdomen fills with blood like a rising, crimson hot spring. This surgeon's nightmare, called a dropped stump, is introduced in the surgical rotation in vet school and is feared even by seasoned veterinarians. It turns a routine surgery into a life-threatening emergency. This scenario plays in my mind during most large dog spays, especially fat dogs in heat.

When I finally tied my final ligature around the second ovarian pedicle, I was forced to embrace my moment of truth-psychologists call it facing your fear. After an hour in surgery I would call it facing my embarrassment; if I didn't finish soon, even the technicians would begin to question my ability. I carefully cut the pedicle, checked for bleeding and released it into the abdomen-no bubbling spring. Thank God. I could feel my blood pressure drop as my heart rate dipped below one hundred. Thirty minutes later I placed my final skin suture and removed my sweat-stained gown. Now I understood why even experienced surgeons admit that no spay is routine.

This was my first week at my new job. During my interview, I may have been guilty of creative embellishment regarding my surgical ability. When Dr. Murry Blevins, the founder of the Pinetree Veterinary Hospital, asked about my experience at the Mountaintop Animal hospital I assured him that extensive surgical experience had given me high confidence in surgery-neither was true. Dr. Weissmuller did almost all the surgeries at the Mountaintop Veterinary Hospital; he was the trusted surgeon while the rest of us handled most of the medical cases. It was nearly one year since my last dog spay; my confidence had left me months before.

My new position brought me into the surgical ward two days a week-a great chance to improve my surgical skills. In veterinary medicine, those surgical skills are honed under hot surgical lights-usually alone-having a surgical assistant, or even a nurse is a rare luxury. Human surgeons usually have one assistant and a nurse or two. I was always amused at fictional television surgeons who share the surgical theater with at least five other doctors and a sorority house full of nurses. So, when Dr. Franklin Willis, a senior associate, asked me how the spay went, I could only respond by sighing and saying, "She was really tight. I wish I had another set of hands."

"You know what they say about tight bitches?" He quipped as a grin ran across his face.

"I was so afraid I was going to drop the stump," I replied, ignoring the sarcasm.

"Let me tell you a little story. When I started here, some twenty-five years ago, I was spaying an old fat pit bull, like the big dog you spayed today. Halfway through the stump tore in my hands; in seconds, all I saw was a belly full of blood. I called for Murry for 'another set of hands.' Do you know what he said? 'You take care of it; you can't count on me to save you every time you get into trouble. I won't always be here.' Then he just walked away."

"What happened?"

"I took a deep breath and remembered two things I learned in vet school. The first was to apply direct pressure which stops the hemorrhage and gives you enough time to ligate the bleeder. The second was the old proverb, 'all bleeding stops; eventually.' Hopefully, the animal doesn't die before that happens. I got through the surgery, and the dog recovered just fine. If anything, it taught me not to panic when things go to hell."

Later that night I mulled over the day's surgery. The panic seemed so far away. I couldn't help but think of how dark my world would have been if the operation had indeed gone to hell. Lucy was someone's pet for six years; the owner had received the dog as a Father's Day present from his wife. Lucy was a protector and loving companion to their kids. I realized the character of a good surgeon wasn't just boldly cutting into an animal with the hope it goes well; it was about respecting the responsibility of the life in your hands, it was about being humble and confident, equally, it was about training and instinct capping the fear of failure. I practiced humility by offering a small prayer before and after each surgery; I trained by reviewing each operation, again and again, until it finally became second nature. I worked at this practice for six years and spent hours observing Dr. Willis perfecting his craft-a lesson no textbook or eight weeks in vet school could duplicate. He was deliberate without being reckless. He could spay a dog before I finished tying my surgical gown. A few months after Lucy's surgery I was wrist deep in another difficult dog spay and needed another set of hands; fortunately, Dr. Willis didn't just walk away as Dr. Blevins had done two decades before, he jumped in and helped me through the surgery. He rarely showed overt emotion; that day I was touched by his compassion. It wouldn't be the last time I had a difficult surgery. Unfortunately, I would not always have the aid of compassionate savior. Working without a net was common in this profession; for me, it happened a few weeks later.

It was 9 pm, the end of a twelve-hour day and the technician and I stood over another grossly overweight animal. (Why did it seem like all the pets in this town were fat?) Garfield was a twenty-pound, orange tabby who hadn't urinated in twenty-four hours. A mucus plug of blood clots and sand blocked his urethra. This condition once known as feline lower urinary tract disease is a costly disease of male cats. Phosphate crystals are formed in the urine which tears the bladder wall and can block the urethra like a clogged drain-this can prove fatal if the cat cannot urinate for more than twenty-four hours. My job was to sedate the cat and unblock the urethra with a plastic catheter. I had to place a tomcat catheter into an opening in the penis the size of a needle. Fat cats are always tough, sometimes just finding their penis is almost impossible.

Garfield, consistent with his cartoon namesake, must have been living on baked lasagna. However, what the children's story doesn't tell you was that his gluttony must have been compensation for penis envy, this Garfield had little reason to be proud. The technician held the cat's legs in an obscene splay-legged position as I repeatedly tried to find some evidence of his remaining tom-cat-hood. Time and time again the pee-wee remnant would poke through the preputial opening and slip through my gloves and back into the hole; I felt like I was losing a game of whack the tiny mole. Fifteen minutes later I trapped it and held tight while I attempted to slip the catheter into the small urethral opening. Sterile K-Y jelly made the plastic slippery and difficult to grasp. I bent the first and then the second catheter and still hadn't entered the hole. Finally, success, the third catheter progressed a half millimeter then stopped. I started to flush it with saline and nothing-the blockage was solid. I tried to push and flush only to have the catheter kink again. I looked at the clock; it was 9:30. I should have been on my way home already! My frustration rose exponentially; there was no other doctor in the hospital; there was no savior this time. I couldn't call the owner and tell her I couldn't unblock her cat; that would admit defeat. I wiped the sweat off my brow, sighed and took off my gloves and squeezed his bladder which felt like a hard coconut; maybe a little reverse pressure would help-nothing. I put on a fresh pair of gloves and opened a new catheter which I promptly dropped on the floor. Pacing back and forth

I tried one after another. Three attempts and thirty minutes later and I was finally advanced the catheter in a full millimeter, and I started to flush, hard.

We both bent down, our faces, inches away from the puny penis, "Flush you bast…" I pushed the plunger with a herculean effort, and the syringe and catheter exploded in a saline spray into both our faces, soaking our eyes in defeat. "Son of a bitch," I screamed, as I sprung up like a raging hulk, swinging my fist in the air hitting the surgical light which illuminated this disaster. The light swung around just missing my assistant head and slammed into the adjacent light like a billiard ball. Both lights exploded in a burst of sparks, stainless steel, and fragments of glass. The technician backed away in shock as the cloud of debris settled on the table. I bent over the cat again and ordered, "Get me another catheter!" I did not clear the debris which had landed on the sleeping cat; neither did I wipe the saline from my eyes-that would only be a sign of weakness. With squinting eyes and a dripping chin, I tried again. I mumbled a short prayer and tried one more time. I got some movement. Millimeter by millimeter, I held my breath, until the catheter smoothly slipped into the penis and out flowed the sweet nectar of success; the port wine colored urine common in a severely blocked cat. In the center of a pile of rubber gloves, used catheters (too many to count), tubes of K-Y jelly, glass, and electrical debris rested my patent after a successful surgical procedure. I would have made Dr. MacManus proud, maybe next week instead of breaking a light I could throw a hemostat or two. It was almost 10:30 pm and I was going home.

The next day I came in early to explain the surgical light incident. I told the harrowing tale of the blocked cat, I spoke of my struggle to thread the proverbial needle in a fat-stack and how I beat the odds and worked to 10:30 to save the cats life. Then I spoke of the intense electrical surge which came out of nowhere to blow up both surgical lights. We were lucky to be alive. Everyone was amazed. I was always good at telling stories.

Dr. Murray Blevins founded one of the first veterinary practices in the Pinelands of Central New Jersey. Decades before the area became a cheap retirement alternative for North Jersey seniors and the focus of mindless reality shows, it was dominated by poultry farms and poorly educated "Pineys" (A Piney is an affectionate term used to describe natives of the backwoods of the New Jersey Pine Barrens-essentially a redneck minus the confederate flag). Dr. Blevins, a mid-century Ivy League graduate, saw the potential in the sandy beaches and cedar water streams of Central Jersey. Equipped with a few thousand dollars and fifties vintage charisma he built the most extensive practice in the county. His surgical and medical expertise made a reputation still respected into his retirement, sixty years later. In the fifties, a veterinarian could spend little to start a hospital; property was cheap and technology minimal, legal risks were a non-issue. The downside was twenty-four-hour work days and treating everyone that called-sounds like a typical Missouri mixed animal practice.

His acolytes had three common traits; they were intensely loyal, wrinkled and grey, and unapologetically rude. They were the old codgers who saw the rugged, trustworthy, cigar smoking veteran and hunting buddy. They were the old widows who dreamed this handsome doctor was about to feel their swollen glands and check their temperature. Occasionally, I would mistakenly walk into an exam room with one of his clients to be met by a rabid, old woman in a house dress, with the voice of Fran Drescher, squawking, "Where's Dr. Murray, isn't Dr. Blevins here?" If she could have maneuvered around her walker, she would have kicked me in the ass as I hurried out the door. I would limp back to his desk like a dejected puppy and tell him another one of his disciples was waiting for the sacrament. Apparently, I wasn't their cup of tea, or prune juice, or even Viagra.

"Don't let it bother you; you'll have to get a little longer in the tooth before they accept you. Listen, most of these old women would believe anything I tell them. Like this old lady," he said, as he tapped the top of his white sideburn with the corner of the file. "A couple of years ago, she came in with this dog, a female Wheaton Terrier she had spayed at a local spay clinic a few months before. 'Dr. Murray you've got to help me. I need you to check out my Tori, I know he got to her, and you got to get it out.' So, I asked her. Get what out? 'Why the listening device of course. It was my son in law; he made that doctor put a microphone in my dog when he spayed her because he wants to find out where I keep my money. I told my daughter he was a gold digger, but she didn't listen to me.' So, I took an x-ray of the dog and of course found nothing."

"What did she say? I asked.

"Well, first she accused me of binging in cahoots with her son-in-law, which I denied. Then she asked if the device were plastic could I still see it on an x-ray. I told her I might not see the plastic, but I could see the

You Can't Cure Crazy

batteries, even real spies haven't figured out how to hide batteries from my X-rays. Big surprise, I didn't see any batteries."

"Did she believe you?"

"Well, she still comes here. Doesn't she?"

He slipped into the exam room and emerged ten minutes later with a wide grin on his face. He reached into the top shelf of a cabinet in the pharmacy and pulled out an unlabeled medication bottle. "Want one?" He asked as he counted out the tablets."

"Want one what, what are they?"

"Sugar pills, I prescribe these for my wacko clients with stories like this one. Today she says that her dog is having nightmares, she can tell because the dog whines in her sleep and then twitches its left leg for five minutes, always at the stroke of midnight."

"Wow, that is crazy."

"No, that's not the crazy part. The crazy part is she thinks it's the new cable box that sending the dog signals which are giving her precious puppy nightmares."

"Then why doesn't she just call the cable company?" I asked.

"She did, they just told her to turn off the cable box. I guess they thought she was crazy too. Now, its Dr. Murray to the rescue, again. These pills will stop those nasty nightmares," he finished as he walked back into the room with a quick wink and his thumb in the air.

Dr. Blevins was sincere when he said his clients would believe anything, he told them-they would trust him with more than their pets. He told one story of a plus size women who adopted a cat with ringworm; which is a contagious fungal infection. She was seriously concerned; she thought she had contracted the disease from her cat. "Dr. Murray, could you just check my rash," she asked as she lifted her shirt, pulled her middle age thirty-eight double "D" s out of her bra, and pointed to a red spot under her left breast. "Tell me is this ringworm?" Always the consummate professional he responded with the calm assurance and told her it was just a mild case of impetigo and just put some salve on it.

He had a remarkable way of respectfully addressing their concerns no matter how outlandish their claims. Making them comfortable instilled trust. One example was the woman who was convinced the dog she had brought in for surgery in the morning was not the same dog she took home in the evening. He assured her it was her precious Marla, but she could take the dog home for a week, and if she weren't happy with the dog, he would be glad to take her back-she never returned the dog; either the dog was indeed Marla, or she fell in love with a brand-new dog.

Dr. Blevins was not the only vet with eccentric clients; we all had our share of clients who were one parkway exit from the twilight zone. One such woman was a sixty-five-year-old widow and proud owner of an eight-year-old female Labrador. This dog was her pet, her friend and quite possibly her dead mother. I respectfully submit for your perusal the story of Mrs. Erma Winkleman and her dog, Molly.

On an otherwise unremarkable Friday afternoon, I stood alone in a room with a white-haired old woman and her middle age, black Labrador Retriever. The file read: "Bad ears."

"Hi, is this Molly? Are we going to check her ears today?" I asked as I patted Molly on the head.

"Yes, this is Molly. My mother says her ears are itchy."

"Has your mother been cleaning the ears?"

"No silly, she can't do that," she answered dismissively. Followed with a high-pitched cackle which grew into a deep laugh which lasted about a minute. Then she continued, "She can't clean her ears, she can't get her paws in there. What Molly? She thinks you're so funny?"

I stood for a moment trying to understand; maybe I was confused. I started to examine the ears with an otoscope when I asked again, "Have you or your mother been cleaning the ears?"

"This is my mother? I told you that, "she replied, as she placed her palms over the top of her head, twisting the curls of her ill-fitting, gray and white wig between her fingers. This time her laugh was almost mocking as she said, "Say hi to my mom."

I was years away from the tact of Dr. Blevins; I approached uncomfortable situations by the method I had mastered called shear avoidance. I walked out of the room without saying another word. I didn't know if she were playing mind games or was genuinely certifiable. I gave the technician, an unsuspecting young college girl, the task of explaining the treatment for her animal, or mother, or whomever. Mrs. Winkelman made a final statement on her way out the door. "Tell the doctor my mother really loves him."

The following Tuesday afternoon she was back again. I opened the file with trepidation, my first thought; the ears had not improved. Instead, the file read: "Check puppies." I walked in the room expecting to new puppies sitting on the exam table. I wondered, could this be her grandchildren?

When I entered the room, it was just her and Molly-no puppies. "So, Mrs. Winkelman, I understand you have a new puppy." I began, fully expecting the front desk had made a mistake.

"She had six puppies over the weekend," she answered.

"Who had six puppies over the weekend?" I continued, knowing I had just started down a perilous path.

"My Molly had six puppies."

O.K., honestly not the answer I had expected. Molly was an eight-year-old who had been spayed years before. "Mrs. Winkelman, Molly is spayed; she can't have puppies anymore."

"She did have puppies, six of them, and I have come to take them home, now."

"Mrs. Winkelman, we don't have any---"

"Now!" She interrupted, as the color of her face turned from a pasty white to a flaming crimson. Her thick glasses accentuated her bulging, injected eyes. "I know they're back there; get me my puppies, or else."

"I'll be right back," I said as I skirted out the door so fast, I almost dove into the hallway. It was time to implement my avoidance protocol. I stood in the pharmacy, frozen, able to utter only one word: "Puppies?"

This time it appeared to work. I could hear the other door in the exam room open and the sound of her footsteps as she stomped to the front desk. Maybe she will leave. However, that would be too easy. The next thing I heard was a loud, "You bitches give me my puppies. I want my puppies!" I could hear the chain leash strike the counter shattering the Milk-Bone jar as it tumbled to the floor.

I knew she was getting out of control, so I had the receptionist summon the police. When I walked to the front, I found Molly wondering free and Mrs. Winkelman pacing the waiting room, like an angry tiger, kicking the chairs, mumbling profanities, fist held high in the air. She seemed to have a real issue with the water-cooler, slapping and calling it names. I believe she used the C-word (cooler!). I apologized for the misunderstanding but encouraged her to sit quietly, until we could sort this mess out. She then seemed to resign herself to defeat, she became calm, reattached Molly's leash and slowly sat down on the waiting room bench. Now I was sure this woman truly needed professional help, soon they would be here to take her away. I started to walk down the hall and turned-she was gone, she had quickly skirted out the front door. I knew it would be best to keep her in the hospital until the police arrived; I raced after her as she was starting her late model Chevy. I quickly put my head through her open window as I spurted out, "Mrs. Winkelman, wait, the puppies are here. Come back in, and we will get them for you. Won't you turn the car off and come back into the hospital. The puppies. Remember?"

She bent low and glared over the top of her black-framed glasses, one hand squeezing the steering wheel the other pointed at me. "Doctor," she said as a strange grin spread across her face. "We both know there are no puppies." Then she backed out of the parking lot and drove in the direction of the parkway probably headed for her special exit, the one that leads to the *Twilight Zone.*

In the weeks that followed we all had a good laugh at Erma Winkelman's expense. We didn't expect to see her or her dog Molly again. We sent her a client termination letter and a copy of her records instructing her to seek other veterinary medical care. The following month my wife and I had a five-day seminar in Washington D.C. When I returned, Susan, the head receptionist asked me an unusual question, "Did you know you were missing?"

"Missing. Missing what?"

"No, not missing what, missing from here," Susan answered, as she looked at the other receptionists who in turn started to giggle. "Someone filed a missing person report with the state police."

"On me?"

"Yes, you."

"Who filed the report?"

"Your wife."

"My wife? That doesn't make any sense; my wife was with me all week."

"Not that wife, you sly dog. Your other wife."

"What other wife?"

"The one with the coke bottle glasses and the dead opossum wig."

"You're kidding?"

"That's right, Dr. Winkelman. Erma filed a report which stated you had been missing for a week. A state trooper was here on Wednesday, asking about her beloved husband, Bob. She told the police you had been married for eight blissful years. Why didn't you tell us?" By this time everyone in the reception area was laughing loudly.

"You know, you guys think this is funny, but I could end up chained to a stove pipe in her basement, a real live sex slave for a geriatric Jeffrey Dahmer. Then we'll see if you're still laughing."

"You're right; she could go Kathy Bates on your ass."

"I sure hope someone cleared things up."

"Well, I think the state trooper new her story was crazy, especially when they found out you were only thirty," Susan affirmed. "What is she like ninety?"

Later that day I spoke with the police sergeant who told me she recanted her story and withdrew the report. Still, it didn't make me feel any safer. When I left for home that evening, I asked Susan a favor, "I'll give you ten bucks if you will you start my car for me." She declined my offer. I guess I had to fend for myself with this eccentric client.

Three days later, Susan grabbed my arm in the hall, "Come with me. I want you to hear something." She led me to the front desk closet and pointed to the answering machine. "Listen to this."

There was a scratchy female voice which was difficult to hear over the background sound of a television, "Murry, Murry it's me Erma. I'm at the Parkway Motel. It's Ten o'clock, and I've been waiting here for two hours. Where are you? I'm waiting. I'm waiting. I'm waiting for you."

I could not believe what I had just heard. This woman whom I had seen in two bizarre visits, who shared with me her schizophrenic delusions, who professed her dog/mom's love for me, who told the police we had an eight-year fantasy marriage; this woman was having an imaginary affair with another doctor-there was Dr. Murry's vintage charisma again, stealing my woman. With all the wackos who came to that hospital, he had to steal mine. Hell, hath no fury like a doctor's scorn.

Later that day I spoke with Dr. Blevins about the message, "So I understand you had a rendezvous with a hot lady at a cheap motel. To be honest, I'm a little pissed. I thought she was my woman."

"Sorry," replied Dr. Blevins. "As I said, you have to be a little bit longer in the tooth to impress my clients. Besides, I had to dump her; all she did was talk about you the whole time."

This was an all too familiar tale; a precarious lover's triangle between an old vet, a young vet, a confused old woman, and quite possibly an eight-year-old Labrador Retriever named Molly; all with an eight o'clock rendezvous at a cheap motel in the *Twilight Zone*.

In a business where cortisol levels spiked from one crisis to the next Dr. Murray Blevins calmed the waters of client discontent. He was the Henry Kissinger of veterinary medicine. On a cold day in February in the early seventies, an illiterate assistant made a fatal error which cost the life of a healthy pet. He was ordered to bring a decrepit old beagle from the kennel for euthanasia; instead, he brought the technician a healthy young beagle who was in the hospital for routine grooming- the dog was dead before they discovered the error. This could have been a fatal moment for the reputation of his hospital, but he worked his magic; expressed his sincere regret, offered condolences, and before the end of the week had bought the client a new purebred Beagle. Absent were the protest marches and damaging news reports which tormented the owner of Mountaintop Animal Hospital. The difference was Dr. Blevins' integrity and pose. Dr. Hershey focused on his clients to promote profits in the guise of good medicine while Dr. Blevins focused on his patients, respected his clients and knew that profits would not be far behind. I would experience regretful disasters when I finally owned my practice; then I would be the man who stood naked and exposed in front of an angry and judgmental client. During those moments, I would always remember him as the calm statesmen who accepted responsibility and met those problems with compassion and professionalism.

Dr. Murry's practice philosophy was circa 1950. His methods included: bartering, billing for services, discounting medications, freebies and diagnosing over the phone. His ways created a loyal following but generally was considered bad business. When I entered vet school, this antiquated system, like the James Harriot novels, was a danger to the profession. Years earlier this simplistic view of the family practice in human medicine, like the *Marcus Welby* fantasy, was becoming obsolete. This change, to Dr. Blevin's disappointment, was transforming his hospital. Ten years before his son had joined the practice and was now implementing modern business logic to streamline the practice, which would lead to fiscal culpability for all of us, even Dr. Murray Blevins.

When Dr. Murray was scolded for giving away services, I should have refrained from doing the same- but intelligence is not always the foundation of common sense. In this hospital, the doctors were given the responsibility of providing estimates and talking dollars and cents-a somewhat uncomfortable position for most veterinarians. We also had access to computers. Which allowed us to input charges or in some cases delete or discount services-management discouraged the latter. In one such case, I hospitalized three six-week-old kittens with a severe upper respiratory infection. They had crusty swollen eyes and conjunctivitis, most likely a viral infection called Rhinotracheitis. I treated the two-pound kittens in the basement isolation ward administering fluids, antibiotics, and nutritional supplements. They slowly improved and were discharged after three days. The client's bill was well over eleven hundred dollars, about three hundred and fifty dollars a kitten. I thought the charges were excessive, so I reduced the total to about three hundred dollars. I discreetly deleted one charge after another, items I thought were overpriced for the amount used on two-pound kittens. Who would know?

The next day my phone rang. "Bob, this is Ken Blevins, I need to speak with you about something. Got a minute?"

"Sure, what's up?" I hoped for a pleasant conversation, but Ken Blevins didn't call me at home to discuss the American League pennant race.

"I want to talk to you about the Mendum case, the three kittens you treated this week."

"Oh, they went home last night. They did pretty well."

"Yes, I know, but that's not why I want to talk to you. Did you take charges off their bill?"

"Yes, I just thought, eleven hundred dollars was ridiculous for three kittens, I just figured it didn't cost that much to treat two-pound kittens, probably pennies a day."

"But, that's not your call. Why do you think you have the right to delete charges in this hospital? It's more than how many syringes you use or how much Penicillin you give. It's about your time, the kennel staff's time, and everything else that keeps that isolation ward operating. You have no idea how much money it takes to run this hospital."

"Mr. Mendum started talking about putting them down from the time I gave him the first estimate."

"Again, that's not your decision. That's his call," he paused. "What would have you have done if the kittens died, not charged him at all?"

"No of course not, I see your point, but I don't know if he would have agreed to treatment if he knew how expensive---

"All right, enough already," he interjected abruptly. "We could go around and around all day and get back to the same place. Let me reiterate you do not discount service unless I authorize them first. So, unless you want to work for free, I wouldn't do it again!" The rest of my conversation consisted of regretful apologies and an embarrassing amount of groveling.

He was right. It may seem to be logic based on greed, but more precisely it is good business. If every one of the six doctors in this practice randomly altered charges based on fairness the hospital could not survive. Human hospitals don't ask the doctors and nurses if the price of aspirin is exorbitant-the charges are the charges. This concept is the toughest hurdle for veterinarians. Most have great compassion for their patients; most became veterinarians because they love animals. It is easy to talk about saving a pet's life; it is hard to talk about the money needed to do it. It often becomes a negotiation for the life of the animal, but it usually is the veterinarian who feels guilty when the owner cannot afford or refuses to spend the money to save their pet. I have worked with veterinarians who experience guilt for charging their clients any amount, and those who reduce the estimate to encourage the client to authorize a service. This situation doesn't happen with physicians; no one negotiates a deal with the surgeon when you tear your knee skiing, it needs to be fixed, regardless of the cost. Veterinarians are frequently treated like they work behind the desk at a muffler repair shop. "I'm sorry, that's expensive, can't you put a patch on it until payday?"

I was sheltered from the money matters at the Mountaintop Animal Hospital, but that was not the norm. Because most hospitals demand their veterinarians deal directly with fiscal issues. The Pinetree Veterinary Hospital experienced a constant wave of issues from doctor's estimates which were far too generous and clients who were unaware of the mounting debt they had incurred until they had picked up their pet. The sticker shock at check-out created a tense scene which usually ended with the reduction of the bill or the signing of a promissory note which could be as worthless as a promise in the wind. In the days before the existence of pet insurance, many bills went unpaid. In the seventies, veterinarians would keep the pet until the bill was paid-now this solution would be considered illegal and unethical. This pressure to get the bill correct and get the client to pay was sometimes more significant than making the animal well. My position at this hospital first introduced me to this insidious stress which grew when I owned my practice. They never warned me in vet school that I would be expected to be a client's accountant, their moral compass, as well as their veterinarian.

I always took responsibility for my mistakes. Of course, the notable exception was the surgical light fiasco, as I said, we were damn lucky to be alive. I, on occasion, would have to accept blame for my faux pas. I did not suffer fools well and in this profession, we suffer through a ton of fools. Germans consider impatience a virtue and in my early years I had a reputation for rude impatience. One busy Sunday morning, I ran head-on with a naïve, indecisive young man, who spent most of his intellect, debating forwords and backwoods, on a relatively simple choice: should his dog take the antibiotics I had prescribed or continue to battle the skin infection ravaging his body? After thirty minutes of indecision I could take no more, "It is your choice, give your dog the pills or don't either way, stop wasting my time!" I scolded as I slammed the door behind me.

A day later I got the call from Ken. "Did you tell a client last Sunday to stop wasting your Time?

"Sure."

"May I ask why you would say that?"

"Because he was wasting my time," I answered.

"Oh." Then he thought and paused for a few seconds, "You know you can't say that maybe you can be more tactful next time." Even he couldn't argue with German logic.

However, sometimes I could not win, regardless of how accommodating I tried to be. Minutes before closing one frustrating Tuesday night a woman called demanding an immediate appointment for her dog who had been scratching for a week. I thought it could wait and I offered the first appointment in the morning. Because she didn't get her way, she put her husband on the phone. This gentleman then informed me: "I am an important man in town, you are screwing with the wrong guy, and I certainly can and will make your life hell!" I did not know his identity, neither did take his threat seriously, but to keep the peace I finally agreed to an immediate appointment. He quickly responded, "Forget it, too late pal, you sealed your fate. You wait for it!" The next week I recognized his name in the local newspaper; he was most assuredly an important man, an attorney, a wealthy businessman, and a politician. The paper covered his life in a brief biography, a beautiful, positive story, filled with accolades and compliments-a rather fine obituary. He had died of a massive stroke, two days after we had spoken. I respectfully declined to attend his funeral.

The following July, common sense took a summer vacation. A twenty-five-year-old woman brought her one-year-old neutered cat in for inappropriate urination; the cat was urinating on her clothes and occasionally in her shoes. I knew it was either a urinary tract infection or a behavioral problem, so I needed a urine sample to which she responded, "I don't understand why you need a urine sample I know what it is." I was fool enough to ask the foolish question of what "it" was.

"It's the third testicle."

"I assure you that is highly unlikely, or impossible. Cats only have two testicles." I boldly proclaimed, then I thought twice about putting my hand in my pocket to check. Remember, I have been burned before, during surgery block in vet school.

She then picked up her cat in her arms and waved her fist in my face. "How dare you doctor, don't tell me! I know my brother has three balls. Are you calling me a lair?"

"Really, your brother has three balls. If I were him, I would take the next pitch and draw the walk." I quipped, unable to resist the temptation.

She stormed out of the room and slammed her money on the counter, "Your boss is such an asshole, this is the last time you'll see me in here."

Later when the receptionist asked me why the client was so angry, I could only answer, "I guess she wasn't a baseball fan."

When I was young and still struggling, it was difficult to endure the low level of respect I would receive every day; sarcasm was starting to replace avoidance. I wasn't getting paid enough to tolerate the abuse. Human physicians do not have to endure our level of disrespect-I thought I was still on their level even if my patients were animals. However, like a colleague was so fond of saying it was the client's "perception of the need." What they thought was an emergency was rarely an emergency. If your dog is scratching for a week, where were you five days ago? Obviously, busy. Oh, I forgot it was March Madness.

Then of course "the perception of the need" was different than "the perception of the cost." One example of that dichotomy was an elderly couple who brought their sick cat to the hospital, most likely suffering from geriatric organ disease. I recommended a workup which they refused due to the cost, thus making a definitive diagnosis impossible. Their response, "Well, why can't you do the blood work for free, after all, don't you vets love animals? Aren't you supposed to help pets?" Or, the owners who equate the cost of treatment to the pet's weight; we shouldn't charge as much for a four-pound Chihuahua than a Great Dane because it takes up less space. Or the pet owners who believe we shouldn't charge the same amount for an elderly pet because they're just not going to be around much longer. Or one excuse I will always remember: "Don't get me wrong Doc I would spend anything to save my dog, but there's a point…besides, I honestly think he is suffering. We're taking the kids to Disney next week, and I would hate for something to happen while we're away."

Eight years of school could teach me how to treat sick pets but to treat pet owners required decades of patient endurance. Through twenty-five years of practice and a thousand frustrating pet owners I have softened, I have become more empathetic, I have even become numbed to the illogic of the common leash holder. Understanding and sometimes ignoring their part is one of the secrets of happiness for those who consider veterinary medicine a vocation, not just a profession. Many never achieve that goal; pride and stubborn resistance will always conflict with the high maintenance pet owner. These veterinarians will never be truly happy.

My years in large practices exposed me to the gambit of characters and bedside manners from the comforting philosophy of Dr. Blevins, to the brash, no-nonsense approach of Dr. Willis, to the unyielding, pretentious personalities of many of the new doctors. Some methods worked well, while some failed miserably. I grew up in the seventies, and my favorite show was *M*A*S*H*. My favorite character was Hawkeye Pierce; he was a brilliant surgeon who saw the only way to survive the stress of daily life was to sweeten the pain with sarcasm and dry humor. He would never feign professionalism for the sake of appearance. After graduation, the prestige of the title "doctor" ended after one long first day when I drove home with the realization that my Plymouth Horizon, traveling on the lonely Missouri road was not the only thing speeding, blindly into the pitch-black night. I never adopted the doctor's ego. I hated when someone told me I had to be more professional; I had to act like a doctor, I guess I still held a grudge with Dr. Anderson who scolded me for my lack of dedication in the third year of veterinary school. Of course, I tried to be professional when dealing with clients, but when it came to my work environment, I enjoyed the interaction I had with the non-veterinary staff. On Monday morning, Dr. Ken Blevins gave me a verbal reprimand for what he called, 'fraternizing with the lay people.' Rough translation: 'I treated the receptionists like human beings.' God help us all. I could only think, "If I wanted to hang out with boring dweebs in short sleeve Arrow dress shirts, I would have become a Meteorologist-but I don't think he would have understood.

In 1995 my marriage was falling apart faster than an old Ford pickup on a Missouri dirt road. Therefore, I found solace in the relationships with these 'lay people.' I believe the feeling was mutual; they didn't see me as one possessing the doctor complex. In my first year at the hospital, I placed a small note on the inside of the pharmacy door which would be seen by the first technician in the morning and the last technician at night. It was a two-item checklist:

AM duty: Tell Dr. Cimer how great he will be today.

PM duty: Tell Dr. Cimer how great he was today.

That kind of light humor formed a real bond with loyal employees; a friendship I would always defend. So, I was leery of new employees. I had a fear they would ruin the dynamics I had worked so hard to develop. Therefore, I was always observant during interviews; most of the candidates were young and most were women. I didn't conduct the interviews I just peered from around the corner that wasn't as creepy as it sounds. One summer day, Jennifer the office manager was finishing an interview with a twenty-year-old high haired, blond in a silk pink, pants suit which accentuated her slim, tan legs and shapely butt-all right maybe it was a little creepy.

After she left, I asked, "So Jennifer, how did the interview go?"

"OK, but she's young and doesn't have any experience."

"I think you should hire her."

"Why do you think I should hire her?" She asked with a grin.

"Because she has nice legs," I replied.

"Dr. Cimer, I cannot hire a girl because she has nice legs."

"Why not?"

"Because that breaks a least three human resource laws." Then she put the file in the cabinet and added, "I'm not going to explain to Dr. Blevins why we hired an unqualified applicant based entirely on her looks."

"Again, why not? Consider it affirmative action for hot women. After all, Bill Clinton can hand-pick his interns for the Oval Office, but we can't hire hot girls because of their looks. I personally think charisma-based hiring is a fantastic method of staffing a hospital."

"You're sick. You see what trouble that got him. God forbid you own a practice someday, and you use that kind of logic, you're sure to get sued." Jennifer added.

Jennifer hired another young applicant with flatter hair, shorter legs, and apparently better qualifications. She was a good receptionist-if the definition of a good receptionist is one who spends her shift arguing with her boyfriend instead of answering the phone. Let me clarify; she did answer the phone when she wanted to argue with her boyfriend.

Two months later Jennifer handed me a personnel file. "This should make you happy."

"Why, what is this?"

"I just hired Elizabeth, the girl you liked a few months ago."

"What the blonde? Is she taking the place of that new girl? If I hear her scream, 'Yo Joey, don't frigging talk to me like that,' one more time I'm going to reach through the phone and personally smack him upside his head."

"No, sorry, she's not leaving," Jennifer replied. "Margo is moving to North Carolina; she's leaving in two weeks. This girl will be taking her place."

"Really, that's good news, now we'll see which hiring method work best."

"We'll see," she replied.

In my career I had always been happy to see Dogs, cats, rabbits, and rodents, basically anything with fur. I didn't, under any circumstances see reptiles or birds. I can still blame my aversion to feathers on post-traumatic stress disease suffered on Dr. Capon's ill-fated trip to the Missouri broiler house. My employees knew this from a catchphrase that reminded them to avoid scheduling a bird or snake when I was the only doctor on duty-most employees except the new ones.

"Who gave me this message?" I screeched as I stood in the center of the reception area. "Who gave me this message about a cockatiel?" I repeated waving the message stub in my right hand.

"That would be me, I gave you that message, as you can read my name is at the bottom of the paper," said the young blonde girl on her first day of work. "They just wanted to know what to feed their cockatiel."

I looked her straight in the eyes and scolded, "If it doesn't have hair, I don't care! Everyone knows that." I flipped the message on the counter and left the room without waiting for a response. "I certainly told her, she'll never give me another bird message," I thought, as I hurried back to my desk to hide.

I realized later I was unfair to the new receptionist on her first day. I was sometimes hard on new employees. However, was I just being a jerk or was I, as a third grader, metaphorically dipping the pigtails of a girl I liked in the ink well? I don't know. However, I do know she made quite a criticism after I left, "If he didn't care about things without hair then he must not care about himself." Later she would tell her mother after her first day of work, "That one doctor was a real asshole." Some would have quit after that first day; fortunately, she stayed in that position for more than five years. I would be reminded of that encounter frequently and for many years after that day; because Elizabeth not only became a great receptionist but four years after our first meeting, she became an outstanding wife and years later the mother of my three children. Twenty-five years after that interview she still has nice legs; proof that charisma-based hiring indeed does work well.

I left the Pinetree Veterinary Hospital after six years with greater respect for the founder of that practice, a tepid recommendation from his son, and a smoking hot wife. Indeed, better benefits than I could have expected from most government jobs.

CHAPTER 8

WARLOCK'S APPRENTICE

"Two things are infinite: the universe and human stupidity; and I'm not sure about the universe."

- Albert Einstein

Veterinarians are a strange breed-we share a common trait. We love animals, more precisely we prefer animals over people. I will go as far as to say, some of us hate people. When I was young, I envisioned my future career as a Hallmark commercial teeming with purring kittens, bouncing puppies, and prancing ponies. My dream lived in a perfect snow globe of youthful idealism insulated from the harsh realities of life: demanding clients, depressing cases, anorexic wages, business failures, and the occasional lawsuit. My four-year veterinary school curriculum focused almost exclusively on technical training and did little to prepare me for life outside the globe. Even when a professor would explain these harsh realities, I thought they were just bitter and couldn't hack it in the real world. I imagined I was different; these problems aren't going to taint my dream. Why should I care? I love animals-all I want to do is save lives. Since I graduated, veterinary schools have added mandatory courses on professional ethics and jurisprudence. These courses focus on the veterinarian. However, do they ignore the logic and the ethics of the pet owner?

Many veterinarians become disillusioned and resentful when faced with the realization that they don't just treat the pet; they also treat the client. Some purists would say they would never compromise good medical care based on the needs of the pet owner-but we are asked to do just that every day we stand on the opposite side of that stainless-steel exam table and offer our professional opinion. These factors combined with modest wages and anemic retirement plans have produced veterinarians who have grown old with resentment, who regret the profession which they have chosen.

In October of 1996, I was starting my second marriage and beginning a new job. A year before Dr. Ken Blevins told me that I had reached my proverbial glass ceiling. My salary had skyrocketed from $33,000 to $42,500 in six long years. If I was a member of the United Auto Workers, working in some repetitive factory job and I had to endure such pitiful raises, I would have been on the picket line before the whistle blew. However, associate veterinarians have little clout for negotiating a better deal. These large practice owners can hire a new graduate to work more for less compensation. Even if they're not as competent as a more experienced veterinarian, so what, in the end, the bottom line is king. In my final year at the Pinetree Veterinary Hospital, I was offered a three percent cost of living increase and negotiated for an additional $500.00 a year. Dr. Blevins agonized over the request for two days before he would agree to increase my salary $9.60 a week; it wasn't worth my breath. When I first graduated, my brother a successful CPA, warned that I was delusional to believe I could pay off my student loan debt on such a pitiful wage. Six years later I was starting to see he was correct.

I was still working at the Pinetree Veterinary Hospital when I received an offer from a multi-hospital group in southern New Jersey. The pay was only slightly higher, but there was a promise of advancement. They had given me a tour of three of their largest hospitals and they had promised me the Chief of Staff position in the fourth hospital, a smaller satellite clinic; I accepted the offer sight unseen. One week later we agreed to meet at this forth clinic to sign the contract. I was excited; I received an offer for a position as the director of this new modern clinic; new equipment, clean floors, and shiny cages. However, that morning I walked into a tiny, disorganized space which, to my best guess, started its life as a Wendy's restaurant. In high-school, I worked for two years in fast food, so I could easily imagine the bubbling fry station, the sizzling grill cooking those juicy square hamburgers, and the frosty machine. What I couldn't imagine was the veterinary clinic I was supposed to direct. The technician on duty showed me my future office which was an old broom closet which had the door removed. The surgical ward and treatment area were small with no frills and little equipment. I was alarmed by the physical state of the clinic; the others were newly painted, well-appointed with clean floors and new countertops. Here the cracked tile floors and pealing counters reminded me of my interview eight years before in that small dark practice in Northern Missouri.

Dr. Schmidt, the senior partner, arrived ten minutes later and led me into the unfinished basement to finalize the contract. As I walked down the wooden stairs, I started to understand why I had not seen this fourth clinic until now-I was taking home a Yugo when I had test driven a Mercedes-the old bait and switch. I scanned the three-page contract, with each page I could feel my anxiety building exponentially. This deal didn't feel right. I imagined working every day in this office, and the thought sickened me. The partners worked in their new hospitals, and I was going to manage a dilapidated practice out of an old broom closet-like my first job offer in Saint Louis, Missouri. I just thought I deserved better. Except for this time, it wasn't the money; it was the environment, I had come too far professionally to compromise my standards. Unfortunately, I wasn't here for an interview; I was here to sign the contract we had agreed upon-I had no idea how this scene was going to play out.

"So, what do you think, did you familiarize yourself with the office?" Dr. Schmidt asked as he sat down on the folding chair across the white banquet table.

"Your technician showed me around. I appreciate her help."

Warlock's Apprentice

"Do you have any questions on the contract?"

"No, no, not really." I pushed the contract to the center of the table. "This is a one-year contract, and it is effective when?"

"Yes, sign it now, and you'll be on board immediately. You can start September first." He replied, as he hastily scribbled his name on the last page and slid the contract and his silver Montblanc pen back across the table.

I picked up the pen and slowly rolled it in my fingers as I again leafed through the three-page contract. At this point the words were starting to blur as I was beginning to lose focus, I thought if I stared intensely on the white of the page maybe I would be transported somewhere else, anywhere else.

"Anything wrong?"

"Well, there is a problem," I paused. "I can't sign the contract. I have to decline your offer respectfully."

"You what?" Dr. Schmidt asked, as his entire countenance transformed into the face that resembled the Grinch when he heard that infernal singing coming from Who-Ville. I can remember my father having the same scow when I would ask him for money. "What do you mean, we had an agreement. I've already scheduled you for the next three months. You need to fulfill that agreement. I'm already working six days a week, in three other hospitals, I can't fill in here anymore."

"Sorry, I can't."

"What is this? Is it about the money? What is the reason? I need a reason. Give me a reason!" His stood up, his finger pointed in my direction, as his entire face turned the color of a ripe Macintosh apple. "If you truly are a professional, you'll fulfill your commitment and work your schedule for three months until I can find someone else."

"It's not about the money I just can't work here. It just doesn't feel right. I'm not signing on for a year when it doesn't feel right. If this were a marriage, I would have already left the church." (I already made that mistake once). I was starting to have a small amount of sympathy for this man until he taunted me with the word "professional." I couldn't believe he expected me to work for three months; I think he thought I was quitting when I hadn't even been hired. Still, I could not admit the real reason I withdrew my acceptance-the place was a dump. I saw no purpose in hurting his feelings. I laid the unsigned contract on the table and rolled his pen off the other side. 'Nice pen, asshole,' I thought. "I'm sorry, I've got to go," I whispered as I slid the chair back and stood erect, turning for the door.

I kept looking back, as I expected to see one of those folding chairs thrown at my head as I scooted up the stairs. I left that fast food restaurant never to return-please, cancel my order.

One day later I received a call from a veterinarian who was seeking a candidate to fill an associate position at his two-doctor practice. I was genuinely excited as this could be a promising offer, except there were two problems. This peculiar gentleman had a reputation as a tough, disagreeable veterinarian-it was said he had the bedside manner of Dr. Kevorkian. More importantly, his hospital was located only three miles from the Pinetree Veterinary Hospital. This was well within the perimeter of my five-mile restrictive convenient I had signed the previous year. A restrictive convenient is a legal restriction which prevents a veterinarian from working within a certain radius from the hospital for a specified period following the termination of their employment. This clause prevents their ex-employees from stealing their clients. I knew Dr. Blevins would do everything in his power to enforce that clause in my contract.

Dr. William Klein was a man short of stature but tall in personality. Five foot- six, with curly black hair and thick-framed glasses. His reputation gave me pause before we even met. Mythical Legends, good or bad, tend to be somewhat disappointing in person. I had heard so much of this man as he had been practicing in the area for over twenty years. He also had been employed fifteen years before by the Pineland Veterinary Hospital; of that experience, Dr. Murray Blevins said of him, "Good old Bill, a good vet, but he should have chosen another profession, one that didn't have to deal with people."

When I arrived for my interview I was impressed by the facility; it was simple, clean and well designed. It was comfortable; I could easily see myself working there. When I walked into the building, Dr. Klein was on the phone with a client. The clinic was small so that I could hear the conversation through the open door of his office; he was in a heated discussion with someone about a sensitive matter.

"Mrs. Stanley listen to me, you brought your cat in here to be spayed, but I can't spay it, because it's a male cat… No, no I've checked it, I've been doing this for almost twenty-five years, believe me, I can tell the sex of a cat…I don't know, my technician brought the cat in, I guess she just assumed you knew the sex of your cat…I'm not trying to accuse anyone, but if you've had this cat for a year someone should have checked to see if it had testicles…Well, that's why it didn't come into heat because it's a male…No, it's not pregnant, it's just fat…What? It has what? Nipples. Male cats have nipples. All animals have nipples…Yes, I'm sure…Mrs. Stanley, Mrs. Stanley. Please let me speak. You have a husband, right? Ok, then the next time he comes out of the shower check if he has nipples, I guarantee he has two of them…Fine, fine…Yes, yes I can castrate him…Yes, I sure will but quite honestly I don't think he cares…Absolutely, I have my receptionist change it…See you this afternoon."

Dr. Klein quickly trotted out of his office and passed me by without notice, swinging a file in his hand, he tossed it on the receptionist desk. "Jenny, make sure we change this cats name in the file. Now that I have convinced Mrs. Stanley her cat has balls, she is going to let us castrate him. She is going to change his name from Fluffy to Franky like the cat gives a shit. She's been calling it Fluffy for a damn year. Jenny, is this woman blonde? I'll bet she's blonde."

Then, as if coming out of a trance he saw me, shook my hand, and said, "Do you have nipples? I have nipples. Everybody has nipples. I wish half my clients had a brain; I'd be happy if they even had half a brain. Bill Klein. When can you start? Or maybe you don't want to start. Who knows? Let's talk."

We went into his office; a small room where each doctor had a metal desk which sat side by side-it was intimate setting-which could prove touchy if he and I did not get along. He spoke little of the job, the talk of his struggle to run the practice despite an uncooperative and uneducated public dominated the conversation. When his attention did turn back to me, he asked several inappropriate personal questions; such as, if I was married, my wife's age, how many kids I had, and why I wanted to live in this middle class, backwoods town? When I handed him my resume' he pointed to the Pinetree Animal Hospital and ignored my experience and focused on his stint fifteen years before.

He was an accomplished surgeon and practitioner who earned a slot as a partner. He declined the offer because he knew Dr. Blevin's son was guaranteed the job as the future director of the hospital-he refused to be subject to the rule of a favored son. One year later he broke ground on his practice right under the unsuspecting nose of Dr. Murray Blevins. Three months before opening his office Dr. Murray was notified of the betrayal by a friendly building inspector and promptly fired Bill Klein, one week before Christmas. So, when we spoke of my restrictive covenant, he just looked me in the eye and said, "Well at least he can't fire you. If you're not worried, I'm not worried."

I started two weeks after my wedding. I would be under Dr. Klein's scrutiny for over six years. Those years would prove his reputation was not entirely without merit; as he routinely meddled into my personal life, was occasionally rude and judgmental, was a class A personality, an incurable control freak, and quick to call me out on my failures. However, he was a principled, honest man, and an exceptional veterinarian. He was a complicated man, who for better or worse had a significant influence on the rest of my career.

I had worked with Dr. Klein for an uneventful month before receiving a legal cease and desist order from a prominent town attorney representing Dr. Ken Blevins. It ordered immediate cessation of my present employment or I would be liable for all damages incurred by the Pinetree Veterinary Hospital. I did my best to keep my job a secret, but one of Ken Blevins' client let the proverbial cat out of the bag. Ken Blevins must have looked like Popeye just after he eats his spinach; eyes were popping out of their sockets, ears spewing pure steam, black smoke rising from an old corn cob pipe. I knew I violated my signed contract, but I was genuinely amazed that one doctor would threaten a multi-million-dollar hospital in a tiny clinic on the other side of town. All I truly wanted was to work, undisturbed in my community. Dr. Klein and I were in full agreement as we had no intention of luring loyal clients from his hospital. This decision was a credit to his integrity, given his frosty relationship with Dr. Blevins, he could have started an unbridled war against his old nemesis.

 I had a moment of weakness when I had suggested offering an olive branch and personally settling the matter with a quick phone call. However, I then remembered my last phone conversation with Ken Blevins just before I left the Pinetree Veterinary Hospital eight weeks before. By then I had lost all enthusiasm for my job; I was living in frustration and treading water until my last day. I was being pushed out after giving him six loyal years. Because I was the only male doctor in the hospital, I knew he was eliminating the last vestige of competitive testosterone. Dr. Blevins had taken control of his father's practice a few years before; any man who challenged him was a threat, and I was always a constant challenge. One late evening I had lost my patience with one of the technicians. This girl was a full-time spy and part-time snitch.

"Bob, its Ken Blevins."

"What's up, Ken." I was waiting for his opinion of the Yankee's playoff hopes, but it never came.

"Listen, I've heard from some of my people that there have been a couple of issues, tense moments between you and a couple of my employees. You were short, maybe even rude. Did you tell June she was a waste of space?"

"No, I said she was just taking up space," I quickly corrected. "I guess I'm under a little strain, with losing my old job, getting married, you know trying to find a new job, and wondering how I'm going to pay my bills. Lots of changes after six years. Sorry, I'll had a moment of weakness. I'll try and keep it under control from now on."

"Well, you know what, you have a little over a month left. I'm not happy with what I'm hearing. You have had a couple of weak moments lately. I don't believe it's going to change. I think maybe its best we part ways, now."

I didn't know if I was hearing him correctly, but I think he was firing me. I didn't care as much about being fired after six years of loyalty as I did about the loss of six weeks of pay on the eve of my wedding. So, I had to interrupt, "Well you know Ken, if it's all the same with you I'd rather stay until the end of next month. No, I won't be going anywhere right now. Thank you, but no thank you." I passed on my option to be fired-it worked. The Jedi mind trick worked, he let me stay. I was living a charmed life; a month before I had refused to be hired to work the drive-through in that fast food/veterinary hospital and on this night, I refused to be fired.

However, now it was communication through our lawyers who wrote thousands of dollars of fancy letters back and forth for three months of legalese that would gag a pregnant sow. The attorneys were only doing their job, more to blame was the new school business acumen of Ken Blevins. It was about principle without logic or what a Missouri farmer would call "horse sense." He could have reached out, and I would have promised to stay away from his clients, and I would have kept my promise. It was the new wave of cold, impersonal veterinary medicine that was changing the Pinetree Veterinary Hospital and this profession forever. It wasn't about medicine or bedside manner; it was about techniques for success learned at business seminars: contracts, P/L statements, HR laws, OSHA regulations, maximizing profit, minimizing expenditures and squeezing every dollar out of every patient coming through the door. Dr. William Klein and I found it very hard to subscribe to the new veterinary management style. Greed was not why we became veterinarians.

The attorneys agreed on a final out-of-court settlement that was binding for three years. Basically, like the unknown comic, I had become the unknown veterinarian. I could not do any advertising; I could not place my name in the phonebook, ads, and signage. I couldn't even sign my name to any official hospital documents like rabies and health certificates. We could not see any of the Pinetree clients even if they decided to switch on their own. If someone called explicitly seeking me out, we had to pretend I didn't work there. Lastly, the staff, at the Pinetree Hospital were prohibited, under penalty of termination from divulging my current place of employment. Of course, we had a client or two who told Ken Blevins to shove his agreement up the business end of his P/L statement, they were taking their dog to whomever they wanted, and he wasn't going to stop them. Like Moses, my name has been stricken, forever, from the walls of the Pinetree Veterinary Hospital, especially the note that told the techs to "tell me how great I was that day." This agreement ended three years later without any clear violation. Thankfully, that multimillion-dollar practice didn't suffer any damages that lowered their bottom line or Dr. Ken Blevins' retirement nest egg. However, paybacks were a bitch and my time was coming.

With the lawsuit settled I could concentrate on practicing veterinary medicine. Working in a two-doctor practice was much different than in a large practice. With each passing month, I adopted more of the Klein philosophy; it was us against them-them being the clients. The foundation of his philosophy was his belief that clients were idiots until proven otherwise. He thought his primary job was to treat their pets, despite them. If you wouldn't listen why did you come and ask for his help in the first place? He would never reprimand me for telling a client to stop wasting my time he would have called to compliment me. More than once he led clients out the back by the right arm with an order, "Don't ever walk through my doors again!" He loathed their perception of the need. Most of all they needed a brain. The irony was, compared to him, I had started to soften, grow patience, and face uncomfortable situations with empathy instead of avoiding them. Dr. Klein began calling me the gentile Doctor; because I was soft-spoken, kind, and didn't make clients cry, as was the scene on a warm May afternoon.

"I don't understand. This started two weeks ago." Dr. Klein's voice became progressively louder with each pointed insult; I could easily hear the conversation through the door of the other exam room. "Two weeks ago, your dog started vomiting, now today, Friday, at 5:30 in the afternoon you show up at my door and expect me to make everything better." I could hear a barely audible response, followed by a whimper. "I don't know if I can," he responded, as I heard the door slam behind him.

I calmly excused myself from my appointment and headed outside to assess the situation. Dr. Klein was sitting in his office head in his hands; a bundle of frustration, he was refusing to finish the appointment. I could hear the client crying through the closed door. The technician urged me to intervene; thus, I was unanimously elected as the damage control officer. I walked into the room to a young woman sobbing over a twelve-year-old brown Labrador, who was motionless on the exam table. It was apparent that the dog was extremely sick; the abdomen was bulging, and his breathing was short and shallow. I briefly apologized but tried to focus only on her dog and the decision she had before her. I explained that we could perform diagnostic testing to identify the cause of her dog's illness and then formulate a plan for treatment. However, given the dog's critical condition making a diagnosis would only be academic. In my opinion, nothing was going to change the fact that her dog was dying.

"The other doctor said if I had gotten to him sooner, he might have been able to help him. I didn't know he was that sick; he seemed to get worse overnight." She continued to sob as she picked up his limp head off the steel table.

I don't know if it would have made a difference if she had come in earlier, but I wasn't going to make her feel any worse. "Listen, dogs don't always show you they are sick. Labradors are happy until the day they die. If you did get him into us earlier, I don't think it would have made a difference. I believe this a terminal disease, there may be nothing you can do.

"Do you think he is suffering? What would you do if it were your dog?"

"I think he is suffering. In fact, I think he is dying. I would put him down." As I looked in her eyes, her tears started to flow as her facial expression mirroring the grim reality.

She shook her head in agreement, buried her face in the thick fur of her dog's neck, and wept over him as I injected the euthanasia solution into his back leg; she sighed as her dog took its last breath. A few minutes later she said, "Thank you, doctor," and left without another word.

Dr. Klein cared deeply about his patients and especially about that twelve-year-old Labrador. He would become frustrated when an owner would present a dog who was long past the point of no return. Whether he could have saved him if he had seen the dog earlier was irrelevant; the fact that he felt the owner neglected the signs for two weeks and then had unrealistic expectations of saving the dog; that was the crime. It was like tying the hands of an artist and asking him to paint a portrait.

In veterinary medicine, the owner's plays a vital part in the health of their animal. Basic health care, timely routine vaccinations, and preventative medicine is the primary responsibility of the pet owner. We can send reminders and recommend treatment; we cannot go to their homes and start vaccinating their stray cats without their consent. Dr. Klein took this responsibility seriously. When it came to surgery, he saw it as a religious obligation. When he performed surgery, he expected the owner to carry out post-surgical instructions to the letter when they did not; they had to stand tall before the man.

Years before Dr. Klein saw Casanova, a six-month-old German Shepherd who jumped off a two-story deck and fractured his radius. It was a clean, simple break called a greenstick fracture. Dr. Klein placed a plaster cast on the front leg and sent the dog home with strict instructions to keep the dog in a cage with only short leash walks for a period of six weeks. Three days later the dog returned with a shattered cast and now a full spiral fracture. In disbelief, and pure frustration he asked the owner what had happened. The owner admitted she let the dog outside to play with the kids and the dog must have come down on the cast while trying to catch a Frisbee. When asked why she let the dog outside she stated, "Because he wanted to go out and play with the kids. What was I going to do, say No? He loves playing Frisbee."

Now Dr. Klein had to spend two hours placing an intramedullary pin to repair the cracked radius. That evening he sent the dog home again with a stronger definition of cage rest and a warning: "If you can't keep the dog confined and the dog injures the leg again, you can go straight to an orthopedic referral service." He was finished playing games. Two weeks later Dr. Klein received a call from an orthopedic surgeon in Northern New Jersey. Casanova was chasing after her boys, ran onto the highway and was struck by a car. He shattered the leg and broke the pin- this time the leg was unrepairable; the surgeon had to amputate the leg. A healthy six-month-old German Shepherd would now live out its life on three legs because of the incredible display of stupidity, not once but twice. Dr. Klein knew he would never truly trust another client to follow simple instructions again- idiots until proven otherwise.

Owner compliance refers to an owner's ability to follow and carry out the veterinary instructions-a major stumbling block in this profession. The mistakes made in Casanova's case are obvious; some are subtle. Three months before I had seen a dog for a urinary tract infection; three months later the client was back to see Dr. Klein with a major grievance.

"What seems to be the problem?"

"Cooper's urinary infection never really went away. We were here last month, and the other doctor gave us some antibiotics, but they didn't seem to work."

"Well, reading the file I see you were here three months ago, not last month. Where have you been?"

"Are you sure? I thought it was last month?"

"Yes, that was on June 15th it is now the end of September. By the way, did you use all the antibiotics?"

"Sure, in fact, I have some left right here. I started them again yesterday to see if they would help." She proudly stated as she raised the half-filled bottle in the air.

"First, you were given a two-week supply which you were supposed to finish. Every pill, the bottle should be empty."

"Well, I don't really like giving my dog medication. I know antibiotics weaken the immune system, so I stopped after five days. I didn't think it was working."

"However, if the dog wasn't getting better why didn't you bring Cooper back in June as the doctor said?"

"I don't remember the doctor telling us that."

"He absolutely did tell you that, in fact, it's written in the file, right here! He also recommended X-rays, which you declined." Dr. Klein's voice rose three decibels as he held the file in front of the client's face and circled my sentence, 'recheck the dog in two weeks if not better." Most people would understand their mistake and agree to finish the antibiotics, but she declined to use the antibiotics and try Cranbury juice instead.

If there was one thing Dr. Klein hated more than a client not following his instructions was a client who accused us of not doing our job. He hated defending himself, and he certainly didn't want to waste his time defending me. Remember "CYA" (Cover Your Ass). It was an important proverb of veterinary medicine only second to another proverb: "always putting it in writing." It was difficult speaking on behalf of another doctor when it wasn't written in the file. Dr. Klein liked the evidence in print so that he could prove his point with an exclamation point.

Many pet owners do not realize that medicine does not come with guarantees. We may not always get a diagnosis; some patients relapse; some diseases are incurable-the pet may not get better. A blocked cat can be heartache to the owner, a headache for the veterinarian, and occasionally a broken surgical light. Because even after the initial recovery the same cat can block a day later or a year later, especially if the owner doesn't follow strict instructions. Dr. Klein was adamant about letting the client know the potential for failure so that we wouldn't be blamed for the impending disaster. "You tell the owner," he would say, finger pointed in my face, "that she is going to spend over six hundred dollars and the damn cat could block again. I don't want her coming back on Saturday morning bitching that we didn't cure her cat. If he does block again, then she must start thinking about a perineal urethrostomy, that's another twelve hundred dollars." (A perineal urethrostomy is a corrective surgery which removes the penis, thus preventing future blockages). He wasn't cruel; he realistic, a rare trait in some pet owners.

    I did explain these factors to clients each time I encountered one of these blocked cats. In the years before prescription urinary diet foods, a fair percentage of cats did re-block. Here I learned to live by the credo, "CYA." Many clients would choose to treat their cats, some would not, fearing their cat could block again. One of the most gut-wrenching cases was a young woman I had seen whose four-year-old cat was at this crossroad; she didn't have the money to treat him. Dr. Klein even offered to unblock the cat at a reduced cost, but the owner declined, she was afraid he would block again, and she didn't want to put him through the stress of another surgery. So, with weeping eyes and trembling hands, she signed her name to the authorization form to put her cat down. As she left, she vowed never to own another cat.

Decades before the presidential election of 2016, Dr. Bill Klein was the Donald Trump of veterinary medicine. He spoke without a filter about bold truths; statements which would offend clients. Truths mere mortals dare not say out loud. He had little patience for bad dogs. Aggressive dogs were a threat to his employees; a dog bite could put a technician in the hospital and out of work for days. Keeping a client was not as important as the safety of his employees. He loathed those clients who would joke, "Veterinarians should expect to be bitten; that's all part of the job." He would reply, "That's idiotic. That is like saying a cop should start his day expecting to be shot before the end of his shift." (I spent a day in the hospital, a week out of work, and I sport a three inch scar on my hand as a thank you gift from an aggressive Chow Chow.-because he was a bad dog).

Little nippy Chihuahuas, uncontrollable Shepherds, and rotten little Terriers were always a challenge. However, long before the Pit Bull became a feared and mostly a misunderstood dog the breed which topped the bad dog list was the Rottweiler. In the late nineties, the Rottweiler breed was one of the top ten family dogs-these dogs held a special place in Bill Klein's nightmares. Hopeful new puppy owners would prance joylessly into our office with an eight-week-old "Rotte" puppy and expect the doctor to perform the sacrament of the blessing on their precious new arrival. Instead, they would hear Dr. Klein's gentile opinion, "This is a dog which should never have been breed, I wouldn't give you a plug nickel for the whole lot of them."

His opinion may have offended the owners, but it did give voice to many in our profession who saw the Rottweiler as a primitive, and potentially aggressive breed. This breed was unpredictable. When even mildly offended, as with needles, ear cleanings, and nail trims they would lash out unprovoked; at home, they were gently family dogs-in our office they could be intimidating hellhounds. When a Rottweiler gets mad, it becomes dangerous for everybody in the room. The popularity of Rottweilers has decreased dramatically over the past twenty years, but the stories of "the nasty vet who insulted my sweet, innocent 'Rotte' puppy" have lasted to this day.

Barbara Woodhouse who wrote the book, *No Bad Dogs: The Woodhouse Way* should have been in the room when a hundred and fifty-pound, intact Rottweiler named Damien took offense at a simple pedicure. This dog who had the thigh muscles of a miniature bull and a head the size of a bowling ball. He broke loose and threw three assistants to the ground and attacked a female technician so severely she would have permanent scars on her face and hands. This outcome is not what any of us had in mind when we decided to dedicate our lives to helping animals. Dogs are instinctual animals who lack logic; they don't reason through a situation-they are fearful, they retaliate when hurt, and they bite. Some bad dogs are like bad people; some are beyond rehabilitation.

What is worse than nasty dogs are pet owners who use money as an excuse, under the guise of a pet's suffering, to make decisions about the care of their animals. People know when they are shading the truth to decide the fate of their pet. "You know me Doc, I would spend anything on my dog, but five hundred dollars is a lot of money, especially when he may not get better." Meanwhile, there are driving a fifty-thousand-dollar pickup or preparing for their weekend in Myrtle Beach. If they think their pet isn't worth saving, they should say, it's not worth saving. Why did they get the pet if they are not willing to pay for their care? Dr. Klein could see through their smoke screen and would administer a harsh tongue-lashing which would either compel them to approve treatment or result in expulsion out the back door.

Fortunately, these owners are in the minority, more common are those who sacrifice much for their pet. One exemplary family faced the difficult choice of corrective orthopedic surgery on their dog or a family trip to Disney World. This family chose their pet, authorized the operation, and delayed their vacation for another year; now that is a sacrifice.

What Dr. Klein lacked in tack and sensitivity he made up in honesty and integrity. He lived to perform his job correctly for a fair price. "I have a conscience," he would say, "I like to be able to sleep at night, knowing I did the right thing without charging like a whore." He didn't agree with the philosophy of new graduates. Instead of new veterinarians relying on instinct they were becoming dependent on expensive diagnostics and costly treatments. In the nineties, large specialty referral practices were growing and slowly transforming the general veterinary practitioner. Once veterinarians would perform most surgeries, most diagnostics, and most treatments in their hospital-there were not many alternatives. Now severe surgical and medical cases were being referred to twenty-four-hour facilities-good care for the pet at a higher cost than the small-town clinic. Ultrasounds, digital x-rays,

MRI's and multiple specialists are costly. In 2016 these facilities are everywhere; their quality and intensity of care are positively propelling veterinary medicine into the future. Some are on equal to the best human medical centers. In the nineties, they were a new luxury in veterinary medicine. Dr. Bill Klein didn't resent these facilities because of the lost revenue as much as his lost opportunity to diagnose, treat, and cure his patients; he thought those who chose them used them as a crutch.

I would carry his voice and the call for quality medical care through the rest of my career, but I would also take his philosophy of reasonable medical costs into the next phase of my career; to start a practice of my own. Although I could sleep soundly with my personal fair price doctrine, I was kept awake through many a midnight hour taunted by ghosts of accountant's past, "Yes, your prices are fair, you're not a whore, but how the hell are you going to pay your damn bills."

I started a family in October of 2000 with the birth of my son. Twelve years into my career I was still earning only about sixty thousand dollars a year. Not nearly enough to support a family. I supplemented my income by working weekends at a local emergency clinic. In an eight hundred square foot, poorly equipped strip mall facility I worked nights with a single technician seeing a myriad of medical and surgical cases. Managing cases alone galvanized my medicine and the confidence to consider starting my practice. Dr. Klein and I talked about a potential buy into his hospital, but time and apathy seem to wisp that possibility into the wind. After six years with Dr. Klein I started to tire of working under another veterinarian without any hope for a partnership; I also tired of his critical opinions and rash judgments. I guess having a desk inches away from your boss for over half a decade could strain any relationship. In six years, I spent more time with Dr. Klein than I did with my wife.

In the mid-nineties and the decade which followed, the robust economy created most of my generation to become entrepreneurs. The goal of most of my peers was to start their own practice. "Are you crazy? Why would you work for someone else for the rest of your life? You're putting the money in somebody else's pocket. Just borrow a few hundred thousand and start your practice." New small storefront practices were opening everywhere. Banks were eager to lend to a profession with extremely low default rates-veterinarians are a reliable breed.

It took almost two years of planning before I could follow my colleagues into the brave new world of practice ownership. I committed to my decision two weeks before September 11, 2001. When the twin towers fell early that fateful Tuesday morning I started to wonder if this was a bad omen. If I was jumping head first into a foolish endeavor on the eve of what some predicated was the next world war. (This was years before the banking crisis and recession of 2008 destroyed the economy for the following ten years-bad omens, maybe).

Again, I had a couple of significant problems. I was challenging another restrictive covenant of three miles outlined in my original contract set six years before. I was also betraying the trust of a man with whom I may not always agree but did respect highly. It was as if history was repeating itself when twenty-five years before he left the Pinetree to start his practice. I could only imagine how quickly I would be yanked out the back door by my right arm and told never to return.

We often spoke in vague terms of starting in my practice. He would respond we his typical words of wisdom, "You don't want to do that and put up with all the bullshit I have to deal with every day. Bills, inventory, advertising, and employees who take advantage of every chance they get. There are two parts of my job, the practice of veterinary medicine and the business of veterinary medicine. That's not what you want. I don't know if you have it in you to run your own practice." That was it; I made my final decision that very moment. Like so many of the residents, advisors, and doctors before him, they criticized me for not being the ideal veterinary professional. Dr. Klein had thrown down the gauntlet. I felt like Marty Mcfly when they called him a chicken, so I foolishly slammed on the gas pedal and raced toward my density. Sorry, destiny.

I answered in one final statement of defiance, "You have no idea what I can do when I set my mind to it." I believe he still thought these were empty threats, and he characteristically ignored them like I was just another foolish client.

The tricky part about starting my business was not investigating demographics and market shares and developing a thirty-page business plan, it was not securing a two-hundred-thousand-dollar bank loan, it was not locating and renovating a business office, or even finding the right professionals to staff my budding practice, it was telling Dr. Klein what I was about to do.

I waited until I had received my business mortgage approval, knowing very well I wouldn't open my doors for another six months. I did this for two reasons; I wanted to give Dr. Klein time to find another associate, and I didn't want him to discover my secret from a local building inspector. I practiced my speech for weeks, imaging each scenario and every response so to prepare for what I was sure was my immediate termination. I notified the staff on a Friday morning in January for the big reveal. It was to go off at high noon. "I don't care what kind of shouts, screams, or unearthly sounds you may hear. No one is to interrupt us."

When I closed the door and leaned on my desk, which sat so uncomfortably close to his, I felt like I just closed the lid of a coffin. I was shocked by the grim realization that in one sentence I would permanently change my professional and personal relationship with a man who, whether imagined or a reality, mentored me for over six years. It was the most difficult conversation of my professional life.

When the office door opened thirty minutes later all the pressure of the last few months of dread escaped like steam out of an autoclave. What the staff and I had assumed would be a major blow out, a barrage of obscenities, and my rapid expulsion from the hospital didn't happen. Instead, I left Dr. Klein's office with a handshake and a nod; I picked up my jacket and went back to work.

My unexpected announcement shook Dr. Klein. However, I explained my reasons; my desire to make more money, build something of my own, a business I could perhaps leave my children. I assured him I would not solicit his clients; neither would I compete with his practice. My goal was to attract the clients from the surrounding hospitals actively; the primary target would be our mutual enemy; the Pineland Veterinary Hospital. The end of our discussion concluded in an agreement which would have even impressed Henry Kissinger; with sincere intentions of logical men, a pack for our mutual benefit. He needed a veterinarian to work until he found a suitable replacement and I needed to work until I could open my doors for business. We both agreed I would work for the next few months until Dr. Klein hired a new associate, or when I was close to opening my hospital.

We worked almost four civil months together without one rash comment or critical remark. Dr. Klein had every reason for resentment, but his professionalism and respect remained intact, even though some around thought he was crazy for letting me stay-some also encouraged him to file a lawsuit. In mid-April, I left his hospital for the last time with a handshake and a wish. In the year which followed Dr. Klein hired a gentleman who eventually bought the practice. A short time later Dr. Klein left his hospital, forever. We both kept the agreement to my last day. Even after I went, I didn't solicit a single client while he still owned the business. It was ironic that a big-time practice owner sued me because his cold business logic ordered him to slash and burn all possible enemies. While a small practice owner who was arguably more vulnerable respected my desire to make my mark. He even visited my office a couple of years later armed with his typical sarcasm and a critical remark or two.

I had no intention of stealing clients, but I had planned to take one of his young technicians. Karen was a twenty-four-year-old talented technician who had impressed me in her two years at Dr. Klein's hospital. She had become increasingly unhappy with her employment and had asked me for a position in my new hospital. When I left in April, I told her she could join us as the primary technician as soon as we were ready to open.

A few weeks before opening day Karen sent me a personal letter in which she officially declined my offer for employment. She felt it prudent to remain with Dr. Klein; she was concerned about the risk of switching jobs at what she called a sensitive time in her life. I was disappointed, but I had to seek a replacement quickly. I opened my doors in mid-summer of 2003 a month after Dr. Klein's practice was under new ownership. In September Karen called me applying for the technician's position I had offered three months before. Unfortunately, I had already filled it. I tried to lessen her disappointment by assuring her I would keep her in mind for any future openings. She took the news in polite consolation, so I added, "Hang in here, I might be able to get you in soon. You're a very talented tech. Please, don't take another job until I get back to you."

Two days later I received a call from Dr. Klein's head technician, Robin, who in exasperation asked, "Did you hear? Did you hear about Karen?"

"No, I didn't. What happened?"

"She's dead. Her father found her dead in her bedroom yesterday morning. They think it was an overdose."

"Oh my God," I responded. "I talked to Karen the night before. She was looking for a Job, but I didn't have an opening. I didn't know she had a problem."

"Between you and me she had gotten involved with some bad people a few months ago. Then last week she was fired from here for alleged criminal actions. I guess that's why she called you for a job."

Three days later I attended her funeral. Dr. Klein and his wife were in attendance. We realized this was infinitely more important than any professional conflict. I was in still in shock as I stood in front of the open coffin of this beautiful, young girl. Her voice again echoed in my head from a few days before; she was so calm and polite, she never pleaded or begged- if she had I probably would have offered her a job-I tend to be a sap in such matters. We would never understand what happened the night of her death. Was it suicide, or an accidental overdose? My question is: What would have happened if she had taken my original offer three months before, or I had offered her a job during our last phone conversation? It may not have changed her life, but it did illustrate that the decisions you make when you are a business owner can profoundly impact a person's life — a lesson which would lay the foundation for future decisions as a boss and a business owner.

CHAPTER 9

THE STINKY KID ON THE BLOCK

"If you build it he will come."

- The Movie: "Field of Dreams" (1989)

"Two weeks, Bobby, we'll be done in two weeks. Don't worry we'll be out of your hair in two weeks. Oh, I'm sorry Bobby I forgot you don't have any hair," quipped the stocky Italian as he drove as another six-penny nail into a two-foot piece of crown molding.

I don't know what bothered me more: That he called me Bobby; my mother always called me Bobby, or that he focused on my incurable affliction; male pattern baldness, or that he repeated the mantra he had been chanting for almost three months; "Two weeks... We'll be done in two weeks."

When I first started my practice, I rented a tiny twelve hundred square foot office space in a small professional complex; my office was the smallest of three spaces on the ground floor of a '50s era brick building. A fourth space; a slightly larger office was on the second floor overlooking the front of the building. My office offered the bonus of a partially finished basement but had a significant disadvantage of being in the rear of the building; almost completely hidden from public view. The changes I needed in this office were minimal. I had expected this simple renovation project to last about six weeks-that was a week before Presidents Day. Now it was Memorial Day, and I had only a fool's hope of opening before summer. I should have known my best-laid plan was destined for failure when the day after I had received my new set of keys to the building New Jersey was hit by one of the most significant snowstorms in ten years; the Presidents Day blizzard of 2003. I had to plow through twenty inches of snow to walk through the front door to stare at a fully carpeted dermatologist's office vintage *The Dick Van Dyke Show*. Apparently, the yellow plaid carpet was all the rage in 1965. Although my business plan had included renovation costs, I had always hoped to avoid a major renovation project and perhaps do most of the upgrades myself. However, as I stood in the in that cold, convoluted space, I realized I

216

needed a contractor to transform this office into a modern, fully functioning veterinary hospital.

I should have been more selective and not chosen my contractor off the placemat from the local diner-especially the one with the slogan: "Forget-a-bout-it! Call JERSEY BOYS CONSTRUCTION when you want your building problems to 'just go away.'" When I called the number, I did just what the deep voice with the classic North Jersey accent had asked me to do, "How you doin'? Got a building problem? Don't worry 'bout it. We'll take care of it. I'm goin' to ax you to leave a message at the beep. I'll get back to you."

Two weeks later I met Vincent Capella, the owner and brain trust behind Jersey Boys Construction's advertising campaign. He was six-feet tall and four feet wide. He sported a jet-black pompadour reminiscent of a lead singer in a '50s quartet. He wore a faded Metallica t-shirt, torn, distressed jeans, and high-top white sneakers. He was in an outfit the eighties were screaming not to give back.

"Call me Vin," he said, as he squeezed my hand so hard, I could feel the blood rush back up my shoulder. "Can I call you Bobby?" He asked as we walked through the front door. I will always regret not screaming out an emphatic no, as he would then and forever call me, Bobby.

After a quick tour, I showed him my rough blueprints and a printed version of the renovations needed to create a logistically appealing hospital. Most would be minor changes and additions; a short wall in treatment, a countertop in reception, a new tile floor, and a decent paint job to cover forty-year-old paneling. The basement would serve as my office and an employee lounge. Vin gave me a quick estimate and an even speedier time table: "Two weeks, I can get this done in about two weeks. Maybe three or four tops."

I had to ask him if that was a genuinely realistic time table. After all, if this was true, I could be open by April fool's day-sounds promising. "I can guarantee it, Bobby. My hand to God, two weeks. My-hand-to-God!" Who was I to doubt such a religious man?

What I didn't understand was when he promised he would finish in two weeks that didn't mean fourteen consecutive days; Vin said that he would spread that fourteen days over three months. My first mistake was to write a hefty check for a fifty percent deposit to secure his services. Which he promptly deposited and returned three weeks later with two helpers starting to dismantle some old cabinetry and dispose of the remaining carpets. When I asked where they had been since our last meeting, Vin spoke of finishing a commitment on another Job in the next county. "Don't worry, we're all yours now, Bobbio." Oh, I forgot, he often called me "Bobbio."

He didn't keep his promise. After one week, his pledge was about as reliable as the next weather forecast. I would drive by the office each day hoping to see Vin's blue Ford F150 with the big white JBC letters on the door. Sometimes he would say, "We'll see you tomorrow Bobbio." Other times he would finish a full day of work, and he would pull me aside and repeat the same two phrases: "I won't be here tomorrow, I gotta take the guys off this job and do some work up in Staten Island." Then in a vailed attempt to comfort my fears, he would add, "Don't worry Bobby, we got about two more weeks here, then we're done." After Vin and his men would leave for the day, I would stand in the partially completed waiting room in growing disbelief that anyone but me would ever be waiting in that room. I should have paid good old Vin on a scale based on progress, not promises. An error I would not make again.

My second mistake was assuming this general contractor would organize the various professionals to do the job; like the plumber to install the oxygen supply, or the electrician to hook up the X-ray circuit, or a tile man to install the tile. I had to find and organize these contractors on my own. One spring day I took delivery on an eighteen-wheel tractor trailer full of cabinetry and using a small hand truck I pulled twenty cabinets into the office and out of the pouring rain. I was starting to realize I could have done this job myself in half the time, a third of the cost, and a hell of a lot fewer Bobbios.

Finally, two weeks after Memorial Day Vin made an announcement, "One more week, Bobby." I couldn't believe it fourteen weeks into a two-week job, and we were close-so close. When he said, he was going to call the building inspector to see if we could get a CO by the end of the next week, I was so happy I wanted to kiss that big lug on the cheek; my hand to God.

The inspector came at 9:00 am the following Monday. Vin must have been at a Job in Statin Island because I stood there alone answering questions like I was on a nighttime game show, "Are You Smarter Than a Contractor." I didn't know all the answers and I wasn't good at bluffing. The inspector seemed perturbed that "Mr. Crappolla," as he called him, wasn't present for the inspection. "He should have been here," he said, as he started to make red slash marks on his sheet like he was grading a test. "What's this going to be used for, storage?" He asked as we walked down to the basement. "You can't have people down here; there is only one egress. It wouldn't be safe if there were a fire."

'Absolutely not, just storage." I quickly replied. "Yes, I know, no people just drugs, bandages, and supplies. Not even dogs or cats." I was smarter than a contractor-I would have told him anything if it would have got me my CO. I even thought about leaving a present on the basement stairs on our way up, "Oh, look at that, Mr. Inspector, did you drop this crisp, new $100 bill? It's amazing what you can find in these old buildings." After all, I am from New Jersey. What was I to do; threaten his family? That would have been Vin's job. However, it didn't matter; he refused to sign off on the office until he could speak to the contractor, personally.

Five minutes later I left a rather terse message on Vin's answering machine, after the beep, of course. One week later the inspector finally got his answers, and I finally got my CO. I was scheduled to open July 7th, almost five months after plowing through knee-high snow drifts on a cold February night. Two weeks, Bobbio, two weeks!

I was truly gratified and confident that on that final day of renovations Vin and his Ford F150 would have sped away with my final check in his one hand and his worn hammer in the other, never to return. However, as he loaded his truck with his last toolbox, he spoke of his sister's dog. "Bobby, my sister Lisa has a Jack Russell Terrier, named Carl. He needs his shots, so I'm going to have her bring him here. Remember that new door we put up in the bathroom and the paint job on the walls downstairs. That wasn't in the original estimate. Here's what I want you to do, take care of Carl, gratis, as a personal favor to me, and we will call it even."

What was I going to say? The guy carried a graphite hammer in his work belt? So, I agreed. For the next two years, I saw his sister's dog five times, always at no charge. Extortion? Maybe. I think that was the safe thing to do for the dog and me. I knew that when some guys asked you to do a favor, they only ask you once; and believe me you can't refuse; so, I sucked it up-leave the hammer, take the cannoli.

I thought my troubles were behind me. I finally could start seeing appointments, perform surgeries, and treat patients in my brand-new clinic. However, I needed patients; only a handful of clients knew I was open. I had distributed flyers, placed ads in the local newspaper, and supplied grand opening brochures to all the local groomers, but the phone was almost as quiet as that rural clinic in Northern Missouri fifteen years before. In 2003, Facebook was just Mark Zuckerberg's wet dream; the annual printed phone book was the only opportunity to advertise a business at a reasonable cost. Word-of-mouth is the most forceful advocate in veterinary medicine, but that takes time. I shared space in a small professional complex with an insurance agency, a dentist, and a psychiatrist. This building didn't even have a sign to advertise the businesses in the complex, so most of the people in the neighborhood didn't even know we were there. A sign seemed the logical solution.

I spoke with the landlord, Dr. Bernie Caplin, who agreed to allow a sign under two conditions; that all the tenants agreed on its design and that I paid for it. The easy part was paying for the sign; my biggest hurdle was to convince three total strangers they could not live without my sign. Thus, I handled everything from the design to the installation; all they had to do was provide their company name and their signature on the dotted line. I brought them a plan which I had hoped would appeal to each tenant and assumed they would approve without reservation; after all, it would not cost them a cent. I quickly learned that the sign wasn't the problem; I was the problem. The other tenants didn't care for my hospital or me, or to be more precise, they despised me and resented the fact that I had opened a veterinary clinic in their quiet, professional complex.

First, I walked to the next office to speak with the manager of the insurance agency. I sat down in front of a middle-aged, blonde haired woman with lavender designer glasses. She made some notations on a file as I started to speak, "I'm Doctor Cimer, I own the Veterinary Hospital next do---."

"I know who you are, and for the life of me I can't understand why Bernie let you rent in our complex."

"I'm sorry is there a problem?"

"You bet there's a problem. This is a professional office complex, not a dog kennel. Did you even get zoning approval for that place?"

"I assure you I did. In fact, the zoning officer brings his dog to me."

"Oh, is that how it works?"

"Is that how what works? I don't understand did I do something to offend you?"

"Not just me. All of us. No one in this building is happy you're here." By now she had closed the file and was glaring straight through me. "Why do you think I rented in this small complex?" I begin to answer, as she quickly addressed her own question. "I'll tell you why: two reasons; it's close to my home, and it's quiet. Now I must put up with hearing barking dogs on the other side of the wall, and my employees have to worry about walking in crap and getting bitten in the parking lot."

"Ma'am."

"Don't call me ma'am! My name is Ms. Eldridge. Janis Eldridge. I've been here for almost five years. Now, what am I supposed to do, rent space across town, drive another fifteen minutes because of you? We were here first."

"Ms. Eldridge I've been here less than a month. I haven't had a dog even stay overnight yet. First, there is a brick wall between us you so probably can't hear anything going on next door. Secondly, my parking lot and entrance are on the other side of the building. You probably have never even seen my clients."

"I can see them out my back window when they walk their dogs. Now we can't even open our windows on a nice day because of the smell from those dogs. Believe me, if you think I'm pissed wait till you talk with Malcolm in the front office. He's already tired of the crap all over the yard on that side of the building."

I was starting to feel like the stinky kid in gym class that no one wanted on their team. I was shocked; I suddenly struggled to remember why I had come into this retched office in the first place. "Listen it is my employee's responsibility to police the area very closely, and I will assure you they will continue to make sure the other tenants aren't in any way inconvenienced. You have my word. Let me tell you the real reason I am here. As you know this complex has never had a sign at front advertising its tenants. Dr. Caplin has agreed to put a sign in the front of the building with each tenant's name and ---"

"I don't need a sign," she interrupted. "I work with a lot of established businesses, and I don't need to advertise to get new clients. I'm not paying for something I don't need."

"No, see this sign won't cost you a cent. That's the beauty of it. I've paid for the entire cost out of my own pocket; all you need to do is let me place your company name on the sign. Believe me; my business depends on this town knowing my presence in this complex."

"Why don't you just put a sign up then? Why are you wasting my time?"

"Because Dr. Caplin will not allow me to put me to put one up without all the tenants agreeing on a sign."

"Oh really, well I tell you what, I'll agree if one, it doesn't cost me anything and two, the other tenants agree. However, I better not get one bill for this asinine idea."

"OK," I said reluctantly. I'll come back when all the other tenants sign the consent form." I stood up and reached my hand over the desk to solicit a handshake. Ms. Eldridge pulled her chair back and turned to the side to face her computer screen; she offered no handshake.

"Oh, I just want to let you know," she said as I was leaving her office. "I have already started looking for another office to rent. I started the day you moved in, so this may be a total waste of your time."

I left her office feeling like I had just been beaten unconscious an awarded a draw. After all, if I couldn't get the other two tenants to agree I still wouldn't get my sign. As I headed for the next office, I wondered if the psychiatrist would be as brutal. Would he live up to the hype? Only if he agreed, would she sign on, this would take subtle diplomacy to get me my victory. If not, the stinky kid would get thrown off the playground.

I walked into the office of psychiatrist, Dr. Malcolm Jessup for the first time since I rented my office space six months before. He was a lean, six-foot-tall man with thinning brown hair-imagine if Ebenezer Scrooge was a psychiatrist. His continence at our first meeting was the face of strained annoyance. His boney forefinger motioned me through the reception area into his office in the rear of the building.

I took a seat on the far side of his desk as he settled down in a large leather chair against the wall. His office was small and unadorned with only a single-family picture on the paneled wall behind his head; it was one of those staged pictures in front of Cinderella's Castle in Walt Disney World. He was wearing the same face in that family picture as he did today. I have heard of Grumpy Cat now I met grumpy Doc. "Hello, I'm Dr. Cimer. I own the---."

"I know who you are," he interrupted. "I Know what you are."

I was starting to get a complex. I couldn't even finish a sentence around these people. After a prolonged uncomfortable silence, I realized the therapist wasn't big on small talk; so, I started, "The landlord has agreed to put up a sign at the front to advertise our businesses and has instructed me to get the other tenants to sign on to the design."

"Waited a minute," he said, pointing his finger first out the window then at me. "He asked you to get the tenants to sign. Why did he ask you to do this?"

"Because this is my idea, I'm the one who designed the sign."

"Why, did you design the sign."

"Because the complex needs a sign, and no one else here came up with the idea. I don't know if you need a sign, but I do, so per the landlord's stipulations I have to including everyone in the decision."

"Obviously, the decision has been made. You took it upon yourself to make these big plans without informing us first."

"Well, I'm informing you now. You still have time to make any changes before it goes to the sign maker. Besides, I'm doing the footwork to get it built, I'm paying for it, and now all I'm trying to get the people in this complex to agree to my blueprint." I pulled the design out of a folder on my lap and placed it on his desk.

Dr. Jessup pulled the blueprint closer and sat motionless for a full minute before responding. "Why is your name at the top of the sign when I have the front office? I don't like it. I'm not signing anything." Then he flipped the paper across the desk and back into my lap.

"My name is at the top because I'm the one putting out the thousand dollars for the sign, besides I thought no one cared, or there would be a sign up already. Believe me, if I could do it without you, I would." I was losing my patience; I was getting tired of repeating the same thing to people who just were unable or unwilling to understand this simple concept.

"You know I don't know what bothers me more," he said, as he slowly raised out of his seat. "The fact that I have to be careful now. I must be careful that I don't step in dog shit when I walk out into the side yard, dog shit from your patients. Or," he continued, as his laser-like glare pushed me back in my chair. "Or, the fact that in the months you have rented your piss ant space in the back of this 'professional' complex this is the first time you've come into my office and introduced yourself. Why now? Because you want my help to do something which offers absolutely no benefit to my business. We're done here."

I then stood and graciously started to exit his Spartan office. As I began to walk down the hall, the eminent Dr. Jessup fired a parting shot. "Doctor, let's be clear; I won't be held hostage over a sign."

On my walk back to my office I was stunned by the reaction of the first two tenants to something I thought would be so easy. The lack of respect was disturbing. I had a five-year lease next to two people who wanted me to disappear; I was the dog crap they wanted to scrape off their shoe-the day was not going well. I had struck out twice, and I still had to see the last tenant. The psychobabble phrase, 'I won't be held hostage over a sign' kept dancing in my head. What the hell does that even mean? No wonder people leap off a bridge after they see their psychiatrist.

My mind drifted as I started to walk up the stairs to the second-floor dental office of Dr. Tom West. I imagined my next challenge would find me tied in a dental chair as the pudgy Dr. West drilled a hole through my front tooth asking me that profound question from Marathon Man. "Is it safe?"

When I walked through the door of his modest office, it was Dr. West who was sitting in his dental chair reading the Asbury Park Press. He cast a glance above the sports section, as he motioned me to the back of his office. "It looks like the Yankees have a good shot this year," he said. "Jeter had another great game."

"I didn't see the game, but your right Jeter is hot right now. I have to agree, they could go all the way," I said confidently, although I hadn't been following the Yankees since spring. (My prediction was correct, in 2003 the NY Yankees made it into the World Series only to be defeated by the Florida Marlins in six games.)

"Have you been to a game this year?" He asked as he flipped the paper on a stainless-steel instrument stand.

"No, not this year I've been pretty busy getting my office set up."

"I hear that. Let me know if you want to go to a game. My brother-in-law has season tickets. Maybe we can get there before the end of the season. Tom West, nice to meet you," he said as he reached his hand over the stand.

"Bob, glad to meet you," I answered. I was afraid to say, doctor, it didn't go over well with the other tenants. In the twenty-five minutes, we sat together we had a friendly conversation which circled back to baseball a couple of times, including some light-hearted barbs on my home team, the Philadelphia Phillies. I spoke of the speed bumps I had encountered getting my office renovated and my quest to build my sign. He was receptive, encouraging, and even offered to pay his share of the project. I assured him the only thing I needed was his simple signature. He shook my hand as I left his office and I realized at least one friend existed in this world. In one day, I had completed one consent form out of three-not a bad average- for baseball. After all, Derek Jeter had a .324 batting average in the 2003 season, and he was a future Hall of Famer, I was just a lowly veterinarian still struggling to build my sign.

It took another two months and the landlord's intercession before I finally saw my name at the top of that four-foot by four-foot, blue and white sign. The landlord placed it directly in front of Malcolm Jessup's office; the psychiatrist who told me he wasn't going to let the sign "hold him hostage." Now it would remind him every time he peered out his office window that he truly was second best in his little "professional" complex.

The unfriendly insurance lady did leave by the following summer without so much as a nod when she saw me in passing. The dentist moved after about two years without ever taking me to a Yankee's game, but it was kind of him to ask. The psychiatrist stayed for over five years after the royal rumble sign battle of 2003. I would occasionally get a forced grin if he saw me, but we never spoke again. The sign I had fought so hard to build did not last as long. Neighborhood vandals destroyed it on mischief night of 2006-I found shattered letters of my name, mixed with Dr. Jessup's scattered throughout the parking lot-I never attempted to have it rebuilt.

Five years passed quickly. The practice grew substantially, and so did our need for more space- we were falling over each other and running out of cage space. I started to think about two things which made my blood run cold, two things which would haunt my dreams for many years to come: borrowing more money for expansion and hiring a contractor to renovate another building.

This time I did it the smart way; I took out a loan for five times the amount I borrowed the first time, except at a much higher interest rate. No, that wasn't the smart way. What was smart? I hired a real contractor who did a beautiful job without ever uttering a single, "Bobbio."

Two things attracted me to Angelo DiMaggio: his name; an ethnic gem that, like Bruce Springsteen, screamed, "Jersee," and his slogan; "the oldest and the best." We met while he was doing some work for my previous landlord. He had impressed me with his craftsmanship, and he had astounded me with his energy. His work did seem like the best and if his age was accurate, he might have been the oldest contractor still above ground- he was eighty-six years old. Angelo stood five-foot-six, had a full head of white hair but had only seven fingers-three on his left hand and four on his right. Three fingers were severed in a workplace accident in 1944-a year before Truman dropped the bomb. He looked like Burgess Meredith, spoke like Popeye, and swore like Joe Pesce. However, his most impressive ability was the way he controlled a job

The Stinky Kid on the Block

site-he was like George Patton with a pearl-handled nail gun.

Angelo had two indispensable officers with whom he shared endless responsibilities while on the work site. His brother-in-law, Joe, the second in command, kept the men in line. Joe always reminded me of Dean Martin, but instead of a romantic crooner with a golden microphone, he was a talented, soft-spoken carpenter with a golden hammer. His last assistant was a man named Ron; a talented young man who was skilled at everything from framing to painting. He was Angelo's boy Friday; he also took the brunt of his cantankerous personality and brash insults. Fortunately for Ron, he couldn't hear a word; he was completely deaf- hence Angelo's politically incorrect nickname for Ron, 'The Mute.' Angelo's method of direction was to scream profanities in his gruff, New Jersey voice; if he weren't satisfied, he would even grab the hammer out of the worker's hand and show him how to do it correctly, "This is how you do it, you useless son of a bitch!"

Watching his interaction with Ron was a special treat. Angelo couldn't speak to Ron, so to get his attention he would fling the nearest projectile at his head; that may have been a rule, a level, or a paint brush. He would raise his three-fingered left hand in the air and shake it in a primitive form of sign language that I could only imagine was used by the earliest Neanderthals. Ron would wave his hands in a similar motion then expel a grunt that sounded like Chewbacca on helium in bold affirmation. In most cases, he would do a perfect job, but when he didn't his handicap became a rare godsend; he deafness made him impervious to Angelo's condemnations.

I had the opportunity to rent a forty-five hundred square foot square, single story building which had was administrative offices for over fifty years. Angelo's job was to convert this unusable office space into a logistically appealing veterinary practice. Unlike the first office which had limited potential, this space could be designed from scratch to be what I had always wanted in a hospital.

Human doctors have it easy. They can rent a much smaller space; all they need are a couple of exam rooms, a reception area, and a waiting room. They don't have to worry about barking dogs, urinating cats, and cages to put them in. Most don't have an x-ray machine, grooming tubs, lift tables, surgical suites, treatment areas, or isolation wards. The family doctor's offices I visit still sport decades old tile and wallpaper, and few patient comforts. Many don't consider logistics like; traffic flow, ventilation systems, patient stress levels, noise reduction, or patient waste containment.

The veterinary hospitals of the fifties were unaffected by the standards of modern veterinary facilities. Today the standards of care set by the American Veterinary Medical Association and American Animal Hospital Association equal those addressed in human medical centers. These improvements are good for veterinary medicine but can be cost prohibitive to the small veterinary practitioner. In the fifties, a veterinarian, like Dr. Blevins, could open an office out of his home for a five-thousand-dollar investment. An investment which grew through their career into a multimillion-dollar cash cow. In contrast, the cost of equipment and renovations for my new building would rise to a figure one hundred times the original investment; old Dr. Murray laid on that stainless-steel surgical table fifty years before.

    I was shocked by the strict standards set by local building code enforcement and OSHA regulations which I had avoided mainly in my first renovation project. Plumbing, electrical, X-Ray certification, medical waste disposal, oxygen delivery systems, and waste gas removal are all closely monitored during construction. Again, these regulations would protect the employees who would spend a third of their life in my hospital but would exponentially increase the costs of each phase of construction.

    It was a rainy afternoon in late April when I stood, alone for the first time in the quiet of a dark, empty building trying to imagine the clients waiting patiently in a comfortable waiting room, while the barking of a hyperactive Labrador echo's through the white walls of my new hospital. Walking to the back of the building I watched the rain trickle down the pealing window panes as I tried to imagine technicians scurrying about working on pets in a bright treatment room; perhaps preparing them for surgery as I waited in my modern surgical ward, for my next anesthetized patient to be prepped for surgery. The kennels would go here, X-ray there, the pharmacy in the center. It was my vision of my hospital. I was confident, the practice was growing, the economy was good, and my idealistic snow globe was growing into a real-life dream. I placed my vision in the hands of this crusty, seven-fingered, octogenarian.

It took four weeks to finalize blueprints, secure building permits, and obtain zoning approval; Angelo's crew started demolition on June first. The plan was to gut the interior of the building and start from scratch. By June third Angelo's demolition crew had transformed the administrative office space into a cement basketball court-concrete slab ceiling to the cement floor, empty cinderblock wall to bare cinderblock wall; nothing remained. Angelo said when we started this project that, "We're not going to dick around here, we either do it right or don't do it at all." My reaction the first morning I saw his handiwork was shock and awe. The reaction of the landlord was more, "Oh shit what did you do to my building!" Her voice echoed off the bare walls as she spun around in dismay. No one else, in the fifty years since the erection of this building had anyone eviscerated the interior of her building like that grumpy old man. After she stopped hyperventilating, I assured her this was the plan all along; not to worry, after all,

I'm a veterinarian-trust me. She left that day and didn't return until long after the completion of the job.

However, significant changes were still to come. The building had one sink; I needed thirteen. Every window and door had to was replaced. They dug trenches in the concrete floor to accommodate the plumbing for the sinks, another bathroom, and kennel runs. They installed a redesigned HVAC system, and oxygen delivery system and electrical system. As frightening as it was to think we had dismantled an entire building, it was also exciting. The most fantastic revelation; all these people were scurrying around like worker ants because of my imagination and a whole lot of someone's else money.

I saw my plan rise from the crude pencil sketch I had drawn on white copy paper months before to the detailed architectural blueprints which magically appeared into a three-dimensional world I could touch. I marveled at every part of my creation; from the initial chalk lines, which rose into aluminum studs covered with smooth, sanded sheetrock to eight-foot ceiling frames with inlaid snow white, corrugated panels. I designed the structure; my wife designed the décor and the color scheme. We had no other choice; I had too much against me. I am a colored blind, straight man with poor fashion sense. If I had chosen the swatches at the Benjamin Moore dealer, my hospital would have plaid walls, checkered floors, and fluorescent countertops. It would have been a disaster, like a set from a Tim Burton movie.

Angelo used his sixty years of construction experience, his three-fingered hand, and unfiltered mouth to direct the team of contractors like he was directing a profane symphony. Electricians and plumbers, carpenters and framers, sheet rockers and tilers, painters and masons; they hammered and nailed, screwed and bolted, sanded and painted, clipped and cut, drilled cement and poured concrete, flushed pipes and stripped wires, to make everything "just right." Now on that blessed day when everything was "just right" something magical happened to that cantankerous, moldy, digitally challenged, soul deprived, fossil; something none of us would ever have imagined changed in that antique of a man. On that fateful day, as a heavenly light of the morning sun poured through the new treatment room picture windows onto his wrinkled, hairy white brow, Angelo proclaimed those angelic words like the Pope professing the good news at Easter service: "Time to call those bastards at the building department. We're getting a damn CO!" On that day for the first time, he smiled-if only for a moment and in that fleeting moment, the light reflected off his dentures in a way that reminded me of the vision of Halley's comet I had seen twenty years before.

Angelo finished the renovations in just under seven months. One week after New Year's Day, the inspectors filed in with clipboards in hand examining every electrical and plumbing fixture, every exit sign and emergency spotlight, and every oxygen outlet valve with the scrutiny of inspectors before an Apollo mission. Under Angelo's condemning gaze the last inspector scribbled his final approval and granted us a Certificate of Occupancy. Thirty minutes later I scratched my name on a final check to Angelo DiMaggio for seventy-five-thousand dollars-I believe I caught another glimpse of those fake pearly whites one last time, and he never once did he asked me to treat his sister's dog.

We scheduled our grand opening for Monday, January 21st- Martin Luther King's birthday. The week before we started to pack the old hospital while keeping regular business hours. I tried to reduce the impact of the change over by planning to move after Saturday afternoon hours. Twelve O'clock sharp every employee chipped in to move the entire hospital; every cage, box and bit of equipment into waiting cars and pickup trucks a mile down the road to the new facility. In a miraculous example of organization and hard work the employees, under my direction, moved the entire veterinary hospital in eight hours. I would be forever amazed and eternally grateful for those employees, and true friends, who sacrificed their Saturday to complete this task. I guess I had learned something from Angelo in the last seven months.

One week later I sat alone in the reception area of the new hospital with a glow that rivaled the gold paint on the waiting room walls-I felt proud and satisfied. After a week of working in a brand-new hospital, I was starting to believe this had all become a reality. I received accolades from clients and compliments from employees who began to appreciate the dream of that idealistic snow globe I had invented many years before. However, the gravity of this project and the weight of this new mortgage was already starting to dampen the joy of this victory. I had committed my life and my house to a mortgage five times my original investment. I had to believe our success, and the strong economy would continue forever. As that naïve thought lifted my sinking spirit, I stared over the counter at the midafternoon sun which cast a glow through the glass front door onto to the snow-white walls of the pharmacy. In that glow was my stenciled name in reverse like a credit on a movie screen. I didn't take it as a sign but as a reminder of how thankful I should have been to have survived this long journey from a kid watching kittens in the basement windows to this wonder built around me. I started to think back on how I had struggled in the first six months of opening the tiny office five years before; how it was just a blessing to get a client and a miracle to get them to pay, and how my future had been even more uncertain then, then it was today.

CHAPTER 10

TIME TO WEAR THE BIG BOY PANTS

"Don't let it be forgot, That once there was a spot.

For one brief shining moment,

That was known as Camelot!"

- The Movie: "Camelot" (1967)

(Five years before Angelo's rapture)

I had to laugh, thinking about last night's episode of *Everybody Loves Raymond*. Ray was in trouble with his wife Debra, and he was trying everything to get back in her good graces before date night. Oh, my goodness, how many of us haven't been there once or ---.

"Do you think this is funny? Do you think this letter was cute? Get that smirk off your face."

"No," I answered as I was shocked back from my daydream into the red cold reality which stood before me. "Actually, I didn't write it to be cute. I wrote it deliver a message, and I wasn't laughing at ---"

"Shut up," shot back a middle age red-head named Julia Reston. She stood in front of me waving a crumpled letter I had written a week before. Ironically the letter was written to another woman named Gloria Johnson. "What's the message that I don't take care of my dog? This letter says I'm irresponsible. This says I refused to pay my bill. I never even got a bill."

"Well, you got four bills which include the initial statement Ms. Johnson gave you the day we first saw your dog. Which by the way that visit was four months ago." I was standing across a Formica exam table in the exam room of my first new hospital. Ms. Reston was leaning over the table with a clenched fist and angry freckled cheeks which were quickly becoming the same color as the bright mauve exam table. "Ms. Johnson said she gave you the bill. I've spoken to her several times---"

"How dare you talk to her about my dog or me," she interrupted. "It's none of her business."

"Well, she did bring the dog on that day. She was the responsible agent who authorized treatment. So, in the end, if you don't pay the bill, she would be legally responsible."

"It's my dog, not hers. What makes you think you can make these accusations? You shouldn't be allowed to bully people. Who do you think you are?

Writing letters like this?" She squelched, as she slammed the crumbled letter on the table. "I want to knock that grin off your face. Here's your money, you greedy bastard. Choke on it." She then flicked the folded check at my forehead which bounced off my chest and landed on the floor. Almost before it hit the ground, she was out of the front door, trailing a stream of profanities that would shame a Navy Seal.

I walked into the reception area aware the employees had heard the entire battle royal through the thin wooden door. With everyone's eyes bulging in anticipation they waited for a response; maybe with defiant words of profanity, or perhaps with tears of surrender. I calmly handed my head receptionists the $132.00 check and said, "See, that's how you get a client to pay their bill."

Four months before, a young groomer named Gloria Johnson had brought a two-year-old Pit Bull mix, named Joshua, in for a severe ear infection. Ms. Johnson was pet sitting the dog for a friend, Julia Reston, who was on vacation in the Bahamas. The treatment was simple and uncomplicated; the bill was a reasonable $132.00. Ms. Johnson wasn't prepared to pay the bill at the time but did assure me Ms. Reston would take care of the charges as soon as she returned. I trusted the groomer's story and sent the dog home with medications and a bill for Ms. Johnson. After three months of ignored invoices and unanswered phone messages, the bill remained unpaid. So, I turned to Ms. Reston's pet sitter for assistance. She called me a day later with Ms. Reston's response, "She hadn't brought her dog to me; she hadn't authorized the treatment, so she wasn't paying the bill." The pet sitter was both embarrassed and disappointed in her friend.

So, the pet sitter had an idea. Write a letter addressed to the sitter, threatening to take the pet sitter to court if she doesn't pay for the charges on her friend's dog. Ms. Reston certainly wouldn't want her friend sued, so when she saw her friend threatened, I would guilt into paying the bill. I sent the pet sitter a certified letter to that effect. I also included a minor inflammatory statement: "I'm sorry Ms. Johnson that it has come to this. I'm sorry you are being penalized for the apathy of an uncaring pet owner."

One week later I was faced with a screeching redhaired medusa, letter in hand, fist in the air threatening my manhood. How could I write such a letter when she was going to pay her bill when she got around to it? When both she and I both knew the truth, why she was standing before me; that awful letter she crushed between her sharp talons. In the end, it was faster than sending her to collections. A grin both of satisfaction and amusement shot across my face. Oh, that Raymond.

I was struggling in the first year of practice ownership. One of the greatest joys of this brave new world was getting people to pay you for your services. I had started the practice in July, exactly six months before Ms. Reston's surprise visit. I would worry about everything; every debt, every client, every unpaid bill. Now the daily pressure was immense. The difference between working for someone and owning my practice was the difference between strolling on a garden path with a light jacket on a bucolic spring day and hiking with an eighty-pound military pack, up Mount Everest, in a blizzard. Every Friday afternoon I would count the appointments for the next week to see if there was enough business to make payroll. My wife was pregnant with our second child, and I was gestating a two-ton business loan. Statistics show that eighty percent of all small businesses fail in the first year, and eighty percent of those who survive meet their demise by the fifth year. Experts also point out that it takes a minimum of two years to see a healthy profit. So, in those years two things are critical to the survival of a veterinary practice; getting clients and getting clients to pay. When I first opened my practice, I was hungry, I saw everything and did almost anything, I did not have the luxury to turn clients away. However, this often trapped me in a compromising position-taking unnecessary medical risks and in the end not getting paid for my trouble.

People can be dishonest. Some clients were subtle in their deception; paying with rubber checks that days later bounced down the nearest sewer or writing bad checks on closed accounts. Some used the "I forgot my wallet in the car" excuse, then exited the front door, never to return. While others were less subtle like the patriotic man, who falsified everything in his new client paperwork, if I had been more observant that day, I may have noticed some oddities; his name was Frank Benjamin, his current address was 1776 Washington's Crossing, Philadelphia, Pennsylvania. Even his dog's name, Handcock, was a bit of a stretch. I guess in 2003 I wasn't in the bicentennial spirit or I would have suspected foul play. Now at that time, if he had said his name was Adam Hussein from al-Qaeda court, New Egypt, New Jersey, and his dog's name were Benji Laden I might have picked up on it.

Some others took a bolder approach. Some of the greatest joys we experience as veterinary professionals are the puppies and kittens, we see in our hospitals. It is the reawaking of the idealism of youth. Even better are the rare times we perform Cesarean sections and bring new life into the world. Whether they are piglets or puppies, it is always a joy. The technicians also loved these cases as they take the emerging fetus and clean, message, and perform CPR to bring them alive into the world. Most of us would work overtime to have this rare satisfaction. It is in those moments we are reminded why we chose this profession.

Such was the case on a slow Friday afternoon in my first year of business. Cleopatra was an oversized two-year-old mastiff in true dystocia. The owners rushed in after the dog had been in active labor for almost twenty-four hours. She had produced one dead puppy four hours before, and nothing since-this was twice the two-hour window considered safe for a normal birth. Radiographs revealed three more oversized puppies, too large to be born naturally. I advised the owner that an immediate cesarean section was necessary.

"Sure, whatever she needs," he boldly stated. "After all I've got a couple of buyers already. I've already lost one; I can't afford to lose another. I can get a good $1500.00 a piece for these guys."

I printed a surgical estimate as the techs prepared the dog for surgery. The dog had been put under anesthesia just as the owner looked at the $1,200.00 estimate and said, "OK let's do it, but I just want to let you know I'm can't pay for it."

"Oh, this is going to take about an hour, so you'll have time to get to the bank. Get your checkbook, whatever. You can pay when you take her home," I said.

"No, you don't understand I'm not going to pay anything for the surgery. Not a cent. I don't have the money."

"When can you get the money?" I asked, hopefully.

"Never."

Now as my eyes started to bulge, and my face began to ripen I knew I only had one option; to perform the surgery and rely on the owner's human decency to pay the bill when he held those precious new pups in his greedy little hands. It would be medically unethical to wake the dog and send her out in her condition.

I walked into the surgical suite shaking my head and wringing my sterile hands, subduing my anger long enough to concentrate on the C-section. Sixty minutes later the mother was groggy as her three healthy puppies fought for the first available teat. In the afterglow of the successful surgery, I almost had forgotten the frustrating back story which brought me to this table. I lost my last glimmer of hope for humanity when I heard my wife, the office manager, ask for even a small crumb to put towards his bill. To which he responded, "No, I don't have anything. You know what, you can take me to court, and you can see what that gets you. Good luck!"

A month later we started to get our bills back as, "Not deliverable as addressed." We never did take him to court. Dr. Klein used to take everyone who cheated him to court, to prove a point. Most of the time they didn't even have the respect to show up. The court would issue a warrant, and they disappeared in the system. I once filed a police report on a client who wrote a check on a closed account. The duty officer stated, "This was a waste of time, like pissing in the wind," he gleefully stated. After much debate, I decided not to take this gentleman to court; I wasn't a fan of golden showers. Fifteen years later Cleopatra still holds the record for the highest unpaid bill. I hoped the puppies fetched a good fee on the open market; that scam netted him an impressive one hundred percent profit. This is a reasonable profit margin for someone who probably never took a business course.

Three weeks later I was in the middle of a routine dog castration when my receptionist June presented me with a question, "I have a guy on the phone who says his dog has a creamy red liquid coming out of her vagina."

"What kind of dog is it?" I asked.

"Sir, what kind of dog do you have?" June asked. "He said she is a six-year-old German shepherd."

"Has she been spayed?" I asked, as my instinctual voice whispered the apparent answer.

"Sir, has your dog been spayed?" June quickly relayed the message. "No. No, he didn't spay her because his other vet told him not to spay her, he told him to let her go through some heats."

"Has she been vaccinated? Is he a client here?" I asked as I liberated the last testicle from the scrotum of the golden retriever lying on the table.

"Have we seen your dog here," June asked, as her face seem to express his answers without saying a word. "Uh ha, uh ha. I see. No, no I understand." June started to grin as she placed the phone on hold for the fourth time. "He said he's never been here. In fact, his dog hasn't been to a vet since he was a puppy; six years ago. He also said the reason his dog hasn't been to a vet was because someone told him that the vaccines are not good because they weaken their immune system."

"Who told him that? Let me guess. His next-door neighbor, a nurse, told him."

"No, it was his brother-in-law. A chiropractor."

"That figures. The last chiropractor I saw cured my sciatica, but I don't remember him advising me on my dog's vaccine schedule. Here's what you need to do. Please give him a surgical estimate, include hospitalization, X-rays, and bloodwork, and tell him we need half down and the rest at discharge. Then see what he says and let me know." I finished the castration by placing the last drop of skin adhesive into the small incision and removed my surgical mask and cap. Then I sat and started to contemplate my future with a difficult pyometra surgery-if this man agreed to my terms.

A pyometra is a bold condemnation of the irresponsible pet owner because it is an entirely preventable disease; by merely spaying the dog. An intact dog has two estrus cycles yearly, roughly six months apart. These hormonal changes alter the interior of the dog's uterus which can create a large amount of intrauterine fluid which can predispose the organ to bacterial infection. This bacterial infection creates a pus-filled uterus which in some cases leaks out of the dog like strawberry yogurt. The condition is life-threatening and warrants immediate ovariohysterectomy. The surgery not only is much more complicated than a routine spay, but the situation can lead to anemia and organ failure. The uterus in a pyometra can swell from the average size of a drinking straw to a fragile, friable tube the size of a knockwurst. In a worst-case scenario, they do not drain and rupture causing fatal peritonitis. That is why I'll charge about four times what a regular spay would cost. This shepherd would be a real challenge.

During my seven years of working in a weekend emergency clinic, I had performed many of these emergency surgeries. One which continues to trouble me was an old Chow Chow. A few years before I saw a sweet Chow Chow dog on a Saturday night who had a large pyometra. This kielbasa shaped uterus topped the scales at almost six pounds. The problem was the dog had been sick with this infection for so long it had become septicemic-the toxins had significantly damaged the dog's kidneys. I spayed the dog and sent it to a specialty practice for continued treatment. The dog expired one week later from kidney failure. A survivable disease, but the dog was too old and too sick to fight. Struggling to pay the bills I had to accept this new challenge; I couldn't turn over a fifteen-hundred-dollar surgery to a surgical referral practice. Thus, I sat and contemplated my fate.

"I just gave him the estimate," June reported. He says he doesn't want to spend that kind of money. So, he's going to call around for a cheaper estimate."

The news gave me mix feelings which oscillated between disappointment and relief. I had just dodged a critical surgery but had lost much-needed income. I knew the dog would not survive while the owner shopped around for the profession's best prices. Then June asked me a question which echoes the public's unreal expectation of veterinarians.

"But what happens if he doesn't find someone who would do it cheaper? If he calls back what do I tell him? Would you still do surgery on the dog even if he didn't have the money?"

"No, of course not. First, this is a complicated surgery, with many possible complications. If we hospitalize his dog for more than one night his bill could be higher than the original estimate. He's already told you he's doesn't have the money to cover that. Secondly, he is making his problem, my problem. If I'm going to be up to my ears in a pus-filled uterus, he can at least figure out how he is going to pay the bill. Besides he has alternatives, he could go to a practice with medical financing or a payment plan. He has one other alternative; he could choose to euthanize the dog instead of letting her suffer until she dies of septicemia."

"That seems a little cold," June responded.

"No, it's not cold; it's realistic. He has lived with a carefree dog for six years. Absolutely, no medical expenses. Believe me, the story about the chiropractor is bullshit, and a vet never told him, 'not to spay the dog.' His decision to save the dog will depend on where he intends to spend fifteen hundred dollars, here or at the crap tables in Atlantic City."

We never heard from him again. June called the owner a day later and left a message which went unanswered. In my experience, the man probably took his dog to another vet a week later; her stomach bloated with pus and her organs failing. I'm sure he told a sad story that made it sound as if he didn't know she was sick. "How did this happen so quickly?" He would say. The only path for that was euthanasia-after all he knew she was suffering because she was too weak to lift her back legs out of the bloody, putrid discharge pouring out of her body. "By the way," he would sob, as he left the hospital. "I wish someone had told me to spay my dog when she was a puppy. Maybe then she would still be alive."

In the first year of business, I spent as much time focused on empty appointment slots in the schedule as I did on appointments. I was willing to do anything to gain clients. I would place flyers in local malls, announcements in the newspaper, and attend pet fairs. I even had one of the most substantial adds in two phone books, each costing about eight hundred dollars a month. This was a time before Facebook, and other sites were readily available to the average business. Social media would have been helpful and saved me a great deal of money. It took months to finagle approval for my sign, but even that wasn't enough to fill my appointment slots. I had another idea to stimulate business which seemed smart at the time. If I could solicit some of the local rescues, I could bring in some income and satisfy my altruistic side while stimulating some needed presence in the town. Besides, it is what they always talked about in vet school. "Give back to your community."

I garnered a local cat rescue, a dog rescue, and a large shelter in the next town. They would bring in a fair amount of spays and neuters, and they would refer clients who adopted pets to our hospital. The downside was two-fold; they sometimes took months to pay their bills, and I had to offer generous discounts for my services. I would do four and five surgeries a morning and charge about two hundred dollars for four hours of work. The shelter was known for presenting large breed dogs for a challenging one-hour surgery -that was a sixty-five dollar spay. A washer repair man gets more for an hour of work. After a year, these business relationships started to sour as I did one evil thing which sealed my fate; I raised my prices by ten whole dollars. After one week, I received a call from the director of the dog rescue who asked how I could do something as callous as raising prices when they counted on me to provide cheap services. How could they could keep their costs down when they had to pay such high prices for veterinary services? It was hard to imagine why their losses were so high when they charged over four hundred dollars for each adoption. In two months, the shelter just faded away. I later called the shelter director who merely stated, "We're no longer in need of your services." They found someone cheaper, or perhaps more desperate. Eighteen months later that shelter built a million-dollar addition on to their modest facility. It had two wings, and neither wing was named after me. Six months later the cat rescue eventually followed suit and sought cheaper services. The director made her dissatisfaction known throughout the town; I heard on multiple occasions how, "That greedy doctor we used before was dreadful. We'll never use him again." So much for giving back to the community.

This cat rescue advocated a policy which utilized an accepted animal control program throughout the country called "trap, neuter, release." I call it a "trap, neuter, and condemn an animal to a lifetime of want." The object of this program is to capture feral cats, have them neutered, and then release them back into the community. In my opinion, this solves one problem while ignoring another. These cats will no longer breed, but they still can spread feline diseases like feline leukemia and feline immunodeficiency virus, and zoonotic diseases like rabies and intestinal parasites. In a suburban area, it doesn't make sense to release feral cats back into a populated area to struggle through harsh winters and dry, hot summers living behind a local strip mall, eating out of dumpsters, while avoiding abuse and aggressive wildlife. Euthanizing these cats when captured would solve both problems and drastically reduce the stray cat population. I believe it is a humane alternative. To be given the same drugs which are used for general anesthesia as would be used for euthanasia. These cats feel nothing, they do not suffer, and they have no conceptual awareness of their fate. The people who run these programs have flawed logic; they are naïve, albeit good-hearted people who place the value of the cats above the safety of the community.

 I started to focus on more profitable contracts, including three branches of a national pet care franchise, three municipal animal control contracts, and both the county sheriff and the community police dogs. However, my real goal was the municipal shelter contract. This jewel was worth over thirty-five thousand dollars a year (the equivalent of more than two hundred and fifty clients). This contract was under the exclusive control of the Pinetree Veterinary Hospital for over twenty-five years. Dr. Murray Blevins had a tight grip over the shelter as he did over the cantankerous geriatrics who worshiped at his feet. I was the first to challenge and win the shelter contract since its inception. I would have loved to have seen his son's face when I fired that shot over his bow. I was letting him know I was still there.

However, even with these contracts, the practice would die without a regular client base. Conventional business wisdom states that twenty percent of the clients produce eighty percent of the income-these are our best clients; the remaining eighty percent range from moderately loyal to genuinely expendable. These are the clients who show up only when their pet has a problem; they ignore years of vaccine reminders, they demand a diagnosis while declining diagnostics, they refuse hospital medications because they can get it cheaper at a local megastore pharmacy but complain when they cannot get an appointment two minutes before closing. They are expendable because they tend to take up more time for less money and create greater headaches. Inevitably the will to take their pet to the quack down the street because he offers coupons for more "affordable veterinary care."

Dr. Klein would caution that most clients were loyal to a point, pass that point and they will, "Sooner stab you in the back as look at you." I would often wonder if this happened to human doctors, dentists, or the neighborhood mechanic. Were these expendable clients just disrespectful to us or were they habitual offenders and caustic to the rest of the world? When I was working for someone else, these complainers would challenge the owner. Now I was the owner-now the directed the complaint at me, my business, and my reputation. I had to answer for the complaint whether it was the fault of the receptionist, the technician or the doctor. Usually, it was the fault of the client. In the medical profession, the client is not always right, regardless of how they may think otherwise. Sir Richard Branson, the founder of Virgin Airlines, once spoke of putting the employees first, to treat them well and then they will, in turn, treat the customers well. In many industries, the client is not always right. Many veterinary professionals lack self-esteem. I can hear praise from a hundred clients in a week and can be devastated by one complaint.

One client typified Dr. Klein's great law of loyalty. She had been coming to me for over ten years, following me from hospital to hospital. Her twelve-year-old springer spaniel had a suspicious illness which pointed to lymphatic cancer. Preliminary pathology results suggested further diagnostics, and I referred her to an oncologist-she refused. Opting for conservative, affordable care, she requested a steroid trial. (Steroids are one of the cheapest medications in our profession- a one-month supply is about twenty dollars). The dog responded well; in fact, six months later she was still alive; that's where the trouble started. I suggested she wean the dog off the medication to see if the dog relapses. If it did, then it would point to the original suspicion of cancer. Our conversation made the argument with the red-headed medusa seem like an excellent first date. It went something like this: (Please be cautioned, she loved the word frigging. In her urban dictionary, it is a noun, a verb, an adjective, a pronoun, a preposition, and I think on one occasion a gerund).

"Hi, this is Dr. Cimer I am calling about Lacey. I wanted to see if she is doing well."

"She's doing great, no thanks to you. What the frig you people doing over there? No one knows what the frig is going on. I stopped by to pick up more medication, and they tell me she shouldn't be on those frigging pills. It costs thirty frigging dollars a month for the pills you put her on. What the frig is wrong with you people."

"I want to see if she relapses when she comes off. After all, the steroids could be masking the true signs of her illness. Like I said six months ago, the only way to diagnose this is by doing a biopsy. However, if she relapses, it's not a good sign."

"You frigging told me not to do a biopsy. You said I didn't have to do a biopsy. Now you want a frigging biopsy?"

"No that's not true," I interrupted. "I did tell you to do a biopsy at that time, and you declined."

"Are you calling me a frigging liar?"

"If you're saying I told you that, I am. Read the file, it doesn't lie, I noted it six months ago, 'Owner declined further workup and referral.'" (Ahaa, CYA)

"That's frigging, not true! You're the frigging liar! You said she would be dead and she's not dead. Worse I've been frigging spending forty dollars a month to keep her alive. Now you want to take her off and your frigging telling me she could get sick again. Why did you put her on pills which could kill her?"

"Those pills may be keeping her alive. However, without a biopsy, I just don't know."

"See what I mean. You don't frigging know what's going on. I don't want to keep her on the pills if she doesn't frigging need them. I am not spending money on a biopsy because you don't know what the frig is going on. You don't know frigging anything. Nobody there knows frigging anything. The receptionists are frigging morons, and the technicians are frigging idiots. I called your office, and your frigging receptionist tells me you're on a two-hour lunch. Your lunch hours are frigging ridiculous. Who has a two-hour lunch? Now you ask me if my frigging dog is doing well on the frigging medicine. Now you want to stop it. What is the frig wrong with you? I can't keep spending that kind of money every month."

"Then it's the perfect time to wean her off slowly."

"Are you frigging crazy you're the one who put her on it. What if she gets sick? I can't keep spending sixty frigging dollars a month on medication that should cost a few frigging cents each. I want a copy of my records. I'm not coming to you anymore. It's all about the frigging money with you people, so I'm going to the guy down the street. His office call is five dollars cheaper, and he has a coupon for a free first visit. It sounds like he knows what he's talking about. I'll bet he's not a money hungry bastard like you. If I find out you were wrong, I'm going to get a lawyer to sew your ass for all the money I've spent on those frigging pills. It has got to be over a thousand dollars." When she slammed the phone in my ear, all I could think was she would have been great on *The Real Housewives of New Jersey*. I would TVO that season.

At the heart of many of these complaints beats the sound of money. The money they've spent, or the money you are asking them to pay, or the refund they want to make it all better. Many go from one veterinarian to the next unsuspecting vet and are truly never satisfied. These chronic headaches came from other hospitals to land on my new doorstep. The big clue is multiple records from multiple hospitals filled with hints like "owner declined workup," "client refused treatment," and the less subtle abbreviation P.I.A. (pain in the ass). I am a glutton for punishment, I tried in vain to make my troubled clients recognize their deranged logic. However, this frustrates me and never changes their opinion: "I don't know what I'm frigging talking about." After one of these conversations, I always ask myself: If they are so unhappy with our services why don't they just quietly go elsewhere? Instead, they bring everyone in the hospital down and succeed in ruining my day. Some are verbally abusive while some are so angry that they write letters for posterities sake.

Mrs. Ethel Schwantz was a seventy-year-old woman whose oversized Lincoln crashed on my doorstep on one humid Monday morning in August. She brought two items with her; a stack of records from four separate hospitals and a fifteen-year-old Chihuahua named Rudy. When I saw Rudy, he resembled a trout struggling to breathe in polluted New Jersey lake. His chest was full of fluid from a failing heart; each beat sounded like a Kenmore washer on a spin cycle. He was cyanotic with purple gums and could only breathe with his mouth fully agape. He was suffering from congestive heart failure due to mitral valve regurgitation, a common condition in old Chihuahuas. Medical records from eight-months before suggested a diagnosis and a recommendation for medical therapy, which the owner declined. Many cases of heart failure have a life expectancy of six months; without treatment, it can be much shorter.

I placed him into an oxygen cage and gave a myriad of multiple medications to help him breathe. He made minimal progress, and two hours later he started to decline rapidly. I called Mrs. Schwantz to notify her of Rudy's condition and advised her to return, thinking if she saw how poorly he was doing she would consider euthanasia to end his suffering. She arrived sobbing and appeared visibly traumatized as she saw him struggling to stay alive in pure oxygen. It took me about fifteen minutes to convince her to put Rudy down; she had great difficulty accepting the truth that he was dying. There was nothing more I could do. Only the oxygen was keeping him alive. She finally signed the authorization to give the final injection which ended his struggle. She left in tears without another word.

Two weeks later I received a hand-written letter which stated:

* * *

"I want you to know how much I miss my little Rudy he was everything to me, he was my life. I am so angry that you killed my Rudy. Rudy was a happy, friendly puppy who was perfectly fine until I brought him into your office…When I saw him in that tiny oxygen cage struggling to get out, I had to ask how you could be so cruel as to put him in there in the first place…Don't think I don't know what you did. You made him look awful, so I would agree to put him to sleep, that removes the blame from you. You made up that story about him dying so I would sign the form that killed my dog so that I couldn't sue you, but I know what you did…He has been my friend since my husband died ten

years ago, and you have taken my only friend away. Vets are supposed to help animals. I hope you can sleep at night knowing what you did! I hope you can live with yourself...Sincerely, Ethel Schwantz (Rudy's mom)."

* * *

Mrs. Schwantz was one of those clients who was convinced her dog's death was someone else fault, to alleviate her guilt. Was she ignorant, or was she a genuinely selfish, bitter, old woman? She probably told her friends how her dog died in a positively dreadful hospital which offered nothing to comfort her in her last hours. Mrs. Schwantz will also add that none of the vets she had seen were any good and she wouldn't give a plug nickel for any of them. These are the clients who leave permanent scars even though my conscious was clear. I was starting to pine for the days of pig pens and horse auctions.

All clients don't bring us down; some are there to provide comic relief to a stressful day. Mrs. Faccini was a petite senior citizen; she was the type of client whom my clever associate use to refer to as "bat-shit crazy." She followed me from the Pinetree Veterinary Hospital where I had euthanized her aged Pug dog, named Joshua. She discovered my new practice and introduced me to her eight-year-old rat terrier, Butch. He was Satan in an eight-pound package. He would raise his lip and snarl from the safety of the arms of his five-foot tall owner. Every time I saw Butch, I had to examine him in her arms; uncomfortably close to

Mrs. Faccini's sixty-eight-year-old sagging bosoms, as I inhaled the mixture of baby powder and drug store perfume. She was a germaphobe and refused to place him on the exam table and never muzzled his shark-like choppers. Her tale of woe began the day the Pinetree Veterinary Hospital took Butch in the back for treatment and wrapped in a blanket from head to tail. When she took him from the technician's arms, she could tell he was in distress; panting and covered in doggy sweat. She wrote a letter to the board, claiming negligence. That was that last time she would go to that place. Thank God, she found me, again.

Thank God indeed. Mrs. Faccini was a complainer. She criticized everything; our prices, the furniture, the music, the air conditioning and even the color of the waiting room. She would often bring a male companion, or prisoner, depending on the day. He was a fragile seventy-five-year-old man, who took the brunt of her complaints. She would speak loudly, to accommodate his failing hearing aid. "These walls are hideous. What color is that? Aren't these chairs uncomfortable Hal? If this starts my sciatica again someone is going to pay." Mrs. Faccini would scold this pathetic geriatric for everything from sitting in the wrong seat to asking questions while she was speaking. I always thought he looked like he was on a hunger strike to protest his inhumane treatment. On one September morning, she seemed exceptionally agitated as she paced in a crowded waiting room. Butch was in for a simple pedicure. My head technician was familiar with Butch, as well as, his cantankerous owner. She cautiously approached the snarling wonder, nestled deep in his mother's arms, and reached for the dog.

"Get away from me! Don't touch my dog."

"Mrs. Faccini, it's me, Robin, my startled technician, replied. "I'm just going to clip your baby's nails."

"Don't you touch him. You're the one who tried to smother him. You the one who wrapped him in a blanket in the middle of summer and got him overheated."

"Mrs. Faccini, I would never do that. I've been handling Butch for a year now. I would never wrap him in a blanket."

"Oh, I remember it was you," she yelled in a hoarse voice which started to become more threatening with each word. "That was the middle of summer, and he came out all sweaty. Get away from him, you blonde bitch."

I could hear this argument rising through the walls of my office. When I rushed up to the waiting room, I could see the other clients were backing into their respective corners, retreating as far away from this woman as possible. Mrs. Faccini stood menacing in the center of the waiting room holding her dog over her left shoulder as Robin put her hands out to ease her frustration.

"Mrs. Faccini, please calm down," I interjected. "You're frightening the rest of the clients. How about we go into an exam room and discuss this." I gently reached for her arm to lead her out of the crowded waiting room.

"Don't hit me, don't do it. Don't hit me; I'll sue!" She screamed as she slapped my hand away and stood to menace from the center of the room.

I couldn't tell if she was terrified or if she was daring me to take a swing. Regardless, I was stunned by her reaction. The other clients were in shock.

However, during the uncomfortable silent stand-off, I started to fantasize about a perfect world where I would reply, "Sue, sue me for what? Ah hell, it's worth it." Instead, I just looked over her shoulder and ordered Robin to call the police. Mrs. Faccini then gave me a quick penetrating stare that I could feel in my gall bladder; then she raced out the front door with the dog in one arm while giving me the bird with the other. Hal followed obediently and silently.

A week later I received a call from a colleague who offered a sarcastic word of appreciation for steering Mrs. Faccini into her direction. There she apparently wouldn't even finish the new client information sheet because she thought the questions were too intrusive. She screamed, "This stuff is nobody's business." Then she then got up from her uncomfortable chair, whined about her sciatica, and ordered Hal to drive her home.

I was sure we had heard the last of Butch Faccini and his eccentric mother. Then on the first day of spring the following year I was scanning the police blotter from the local newspaper and I came across an interesting headline:

✸ ✸ ✸

LOCAL ELDERLY WOMEN CHARGED WITH ASSAULT

"On Saturday, a sixty-eight-year-old woman, Mrs. Columbia Faccini was charged with assault and battery. In the early hours of Saturday, March 19th, neighbors reported a disturbance at the home of Columbia Faccini. When they arrived, investigators reported a horrible scene in the kitchen. A seventy-five-year-old man, Hal Malena was found unconscious in a pool of blood on the kitchen floor. Mrs. Faccini admitted to beating Mr. Malena into unconsciousness with a frying pan over a dispute over undercooked eggs. Mr. Malena is in serious but stable condition, and Mrs. Faccini is being held on fifteen-thousand-dollars bail."

* * *

Butch had yet to be charged but was retained as a material witness.

Fortunately, those truly expendable clients are the minority. Many clients do show us the respect we deserve as real doctors. However, I didn't honestly feel the respect that someone like Dr. Murray Blevins received until I owned my practice. Now with the criticism came my share of praise. I would hear positive words spreading throughout my community. Clients were finding me after years of seclusion that had ended with the expiration of my restraining order with Dr. Blevins. One such client was my most loyal follower; Robert Whitehead and his dog Lucy.

It was just after Christmas in 1991 when Robert first brought his new eight- week old Labrador puppy which he named Lucy, into the Pinetree Veterinary Hospital for a routine checkup-he adopted her a couple of days before, and she had problems. I noticed she was not the vibrant, bouncy puppy like most eight-week-old labs; she laid motionless on the exam table barely able to lift her head. Loose stool stained her tail and fluid dripped from her nose with each deep cough. Lab tests revealed profound anemia, radiographs exposed bronchopneumonia, a stool analysis exposed four types of intestinal parasites, and a microscopic skin sample revealed a skin parasite called demodectic mange. Lucy was a classic example of a pet shop dog purchased from a puppy mill in Northern Missouri.

I recommended he return the dog for a refund; however, he was already in love with the puppy and that was not an option. He knew if he returned the dog to the pet shop its survival was uncertain. The State of New Jersey offers protection to pet owners in this situation with a pet lemon law. The pet shop is liable for treatment expenses up to twice the purchase price of the dog-it is always a fight to get the money, but they are legally responsible. Regardless of the cost, he wanted to try and save the dog- Mr. Whitehead honestly had a good heart. I hospitalized the puppy in intensive care through the New Year. Seven days later Lucy went home a pound heavier with a noticeable bounce to her floppy ears. Months later she was finally free of all her parasites and became an extremely hyperactive young adult Labrador. Lucy was five when I left the Pinetree Veterinary Hospital; a situation which made Mr. Whitehead extremely unhappy.

Mr. Whitehead was one of those clients who refused to be denied, constantly badgering Ken Blevins to find where I had gone. He even would pressure my wife to give him just a clue to my whereabouts. She would remind him she was restricted from divulging that information but would give him hints like, "Did you try that new restaurant across the street from the new supermarket, they have an excellent new cook, I know you would like him" (Dr. Klein's practice was across the street from the shopping center). Eventually, Dr. Ken Blevins released him into my care without repercussion. I believe he became sick of the constant third degree. After a year of frustration, Mr. Whitehead finally got the hint and found me. Every time he came into the hospital, he would reenact the same dramatic story; he preached like a Baptist minister evangelizing from the pulpit. It didn't matter who was listening; the receptionists, the technician, or an innocent client trapped in the waiting room.

"When I bought Lucy, she was weak, cold, riddled with every parasite known to man. Her lungs were drowning in her fluid; she could barely breathe. So anemic, her blood count so low she did not have the strength to lift her head. Then I brought her to this man, this selfless doctor who laid his healing hands on her and filled her with every manner of medicine. Almost a week she was with him, fading in and out of life. On the sixth day, she ate again, on the seventh day was cured, and on the eighth day, she returned home to me. This doctor saved her life."

Dr. Klein soon tired of hearing his sermon. I think he was jealous. "That guy thinks you walk on water, it's damn disgusting," he would say.

To that, I would boldly respond, "A veterinarian is not without honor except in his clinic." Given he was Jewish, I think he missed the sarcasm. Still, I was ill at ease with public praise as it brought me unwanted attention; ironically, I was much more comfortable with criticism.

Ten years later, now in my own practice, Mr. Whitehead was still telling his tale, and Dolly was still bouncing into my office, both happy to be alive. He was one of my first clients in my hospital. However, by the time she was twelve, Lucy's pace slowed, and her muscles atrophied as the curse of poor genetics, and degenerative arthritis ravaged her joints. Mr. Whitehead gave Lucy analgesics for almost two years until one day she could no longer stand; we both agreed it was time to end her precious life. So, on a hot day in July, lying on the floor of her master's kitchen she drew her last breath with the entire Whitehead family at her side. Mr. Whitehead was too distraught to speak, but his son expressed gratitude on behalf of his father. He was only a teenager when his dad first brought Lucy home Christmas Eve almost fourteen years before. "My dad still talks about the miracle you performed that year you saved Lucy. Deep down he knew it was time to put her down, but he wouldn't agree to do it until he heard the words come out of your mouth. Thank you for being there for Lucy all those years." Now I was speechless as my German iron shell was starting to crumble. I shook his hand tightly as I turned and followed the stretcher that carried Lucy's body out the front door.

Three months later, on a chilly October day, Mr. and Mrs. Whitehead stood in my waiting room with a new friend, Barney, a one-year-old Wheaten Terrier. "I had to do something," Mrs. Whitehead said. "Robert needed something to cheer him up; he has been so depressed since we put Lucy down."

This wasn't Lucy, but he was indeed a reasonable facsimile. Mr. Whitehead had to retire because of poor health and Barney was his new companion. He was a friendly, energetic dog and Mr. Whitehead was beaming with joy again. "He's no Lucy," Mr. Whitehead would say. "But I still love this little guy."

The years went by quickly, and I saw Barney a few times a year for routine wellness visits and minor scrapes and scratches. There was never a time when Mr. Whitehead didn't mention Lucy's' name. She would always be first in his heart, but Barney was a close second. In the spring of his ninth year of life, Barney started to show obscure signs of illness. Lethargy, lack of appetite, occasional stiffness. Because he had significant tick exposure through the winter, I suspected a simple case of Lyme disease. Bloodwork was positive for two tick-borne diseases, confirming my suspicion. Two weeks later Barney started to improve on antibiotics; he was himself again.

However, in early June Barney conditioned worsened; his neck stiffened, he cried in pain with each movement. This time another round of antibiotics didn't help. I performed more blood work and took radiographs, but I still didn't have a diagnosis. I started to suspect something more than a tick-borne disease; I began to think about a spinal disorder. I began to think about cancer. I began Barney on steroids and narcotic analgesics in the hope of alleviating his pain. He would feel better for a day or two, and then he would become painful again. I spoke with Mr. Whitehead about the need for an MRI at a local referral practice-each time he would listen to the option then would ask me the same question, "Can't you give him something to stop his pain. He can't sleep at night; he's in constant pain." I doubled the dose of steroids twice, each time with the hope that we would see some progress. A week later I would receive another call, "Barney was good for a day then he went right back to standing with his head against the wall, too painful to move." I could hear the growing frustration in his voice.

Then one afternoon in late July I saw Mr. Whitehead standing at the front arguing with the receptionist. His hands were flailing in the air. He was distressed. In the twenty years I had known him, I had never seen him so angry. Our eyes met, and I motioned him to the back. He walked through the door carrying Barney in his arms, Mr. Whitehead's hair was disheveled, and his face was pale. Barney wasn't moving. He placed the dog on the ground, and I stood aghast at Barney's condition. He stood with his head against the wall, eyes tightly closed, ears back swaying slowly from side to side. Sporadically, the dog would have head tremors which would radiate down the back of his neck.

"Look at my Barney. He's been like this for two days. I've been up all night with him." He faced showed the agony of the long night. His voice cracked as he continued, "Dr. Cimer, I don't understand, I've been giving him both pills you prescribed. We keep raising the dose and raising the dose, and he seems to get worse. This is a nightmare. Why can't you tell me what's wrong with him? I've been bringing him here for two months, and I still don't get any answers. Listen if you can't help him then send me to someone who can. Be honest, should I go to one of those specialists? Would they be able to tell me what's wrong with him? I would be willing to go there if they could help Barney get better?"

I had known this man for over two decades. Most of those days he worshiped the ground I walked

Time to Wear the Big Boy Pants

on-but not on this day. I placed my damaged pride in the drawer with useless pamphlets and began to speak.

"Mr. Whitehead I will be honest with you. I have suspected for some time that there is something more going on with Barney that probably can't be treated with medicine alone. When you consider the dose of steroids and pain relievers we are using, and he keeps getting worse, that is a sign that this is something very, very bad. Look at him. You can see Barney is in so much pain. It must be very severe neck pain. It's hard to imagine how bad it must be. Look if you do take him to a specialist, they'll do an MRI, maybe a myelogram to diagnose him. They may even add some meds to make him comfortable, but there are no guarantees. If he does need surgery, there is no guarantee for a cure, and if it is a tumor, it may be inoperable. Listen, Robert," I continued, as now my voice started to crack. "I've known you for a long time so that I can be honest. If Barney were my dog, I wouldn't take him to a specialist. Don't get me wrong it's not about the money. He's in a lot of pain and to put him through additional testing and then maybe a surgery with a questionable outcome seems cruel to me." Then in the second time in our professional relationship, I had to fight to hold back my years. "I had to give my mom advice when I was in vet school years ago, about my dog, and I think she knew what she had to do. I think you know what you must do. You know he's suffering..." My rising emotion and the lump in my throat prevented me from voicing my final thought.

Mr. Whitehead's continence changed from frustration to calm acceptance. "I can tell by the tears in your eyes you're telling me the truth. I'm going to ask you one last question. Should I put my dog down?"

"Yes."

"Dr. Cimer, you've been treating my dogs and my son's dogs for over twenty years. You saved Lucy's life, and in the end, you put her to sleep in my kitchen. You're a part of my family, and I trust your judgment. I know you are right. If you say I must put Barney down, then I have to put Barney down." He then shook my right hand tightly and placed his left hand on my back in a comforting manner like he was trying to ease my guilt for Barney's failing health.

I left Mr. Whitehead and Barney to return to the privacy of my office. I sat down at my desk and put my head in my hands. There I wept. A few minutes later, I said a short prayer, regained my composer and I returned to treatment and my technician's inquisitive eyes. "Mr. Whitehead is putting Barney to sleep," I whispered as the words stuck in my throat. Ten minutes later we put an end to Barney's suffering and Mr. Whitehead's nightmare.

Robert Whitehead adopted a new dog six months later, a two-year-old Border Collie. Of course, with each visit, he often speaks of his dog's Lucy and Barney, but he is genuinely in love with Max who is a close third to the originals.

With good clients like Mr. Whitehead, the practice grew beyond original projections. The primary driving forces were not flyers, rescues, and expensive phone book adds but good, old fashion word of mouth; a reputation fostered on compassion. The clientele doubled in the first two years and was beyond the client base of Dr. Klein's twenty-year-old practice in only three years. I was alone, working six days a week and was competing with one of the largest practices in the county. A couple of factors contributed to the success of the practice. The buyer of Dr. Klein's practice had to take a medical leave after his first years and would eventually close the business. The Pinetree Veterinary Hospital was purchased by a national corporation which was in sharp contrast with our family owned, old fashioned approach. Our whole persona was an intentional attack on the larger impersonal hospitals taking over this profession. Our logo was Noah's ark, our name was "Calling All Creatures Veterinary Hospital," and our hospital motto, was "We're your neighborhood vet for your family pet"; all conveyed a more personal approach to pet care-and it was working.

In addition to hiring Angelo to build my expansion in 2007, I hired a full-time associate and doubled my staff and dramatically increased my operating budget. However, I was confident there was gold in "them there" Retrievers. In 2007 the economy was booming, the stock markets were bull, and the housing bubble was inflating. Who knew that bull would turn into a bear, that bubble would burst, and that golden rush would soon be over? If that wasn't bad enough a storm was forming, and that storm had a name, and her name was "Sandy," and she would be a bitch.

CHAPTER 11

MADAME, YOU HAVE CATS IN YOUR MATTRESS

"It's a madhouse...A madhouse!"

- The Movie: Planet of the Apes (1968)

I can remember growing up in the early '70s when I was still an impressionable young teenager watching episodes of *Marcus Welby, M.D.* To clarify to those millennials, it was not a reality show about a sex therapist who counsels mob housewives of New Jersey. This was a medical drama about an old-fashioned family doctor, played by the distinguished actor, Robert Young, who treated his patients with empathy and common sense. He had a young, handsome associate, Dr. Steven Kiley, played by James Brolin. Dr. Kiley sported a tailored suit, a well-groomed beard, and rode a cool motorcycle-he was the original Dr. Mc'dreamy. I was most impressed when Dr. Kiley would travel to house calls riding his Triumph Bonneville through the streets of his small town to attend to the medical needs of desperate women in their bedrooms. I wanted to be that doctor, but not to treat desperate women; I wanted to treat the pets of desperate women in their bedrooms. I never dreamed reality would fall so short of fiction.

When my wife and I developed our mission statement, we wanted to resurrect the myth of a small family practice built on a foundation of empathy and common sense. The house call was one of the cornerstones of that foundation. When I opened in 2003, there were few standing practices which offered this service. Twelve years later there would be multiple hospitals offering competitive house call services. It always was a great practice builder; the house call was a valuable brick in the foundation which supported our rapid expansion. It was a vital link to the local senior citizen villages which had grown like dandelions throughout the county. Many owners prefer house calls for their pet's euthanasia-it creates a comfortable environment for a pet's last moments. However, entering a stranger's home to treat their sick pets opens the door to a unique, entertaining, and sometimes shocking experience-rarely is it sexy. One of my competitors who started an exclusive house call practice proudly announced on Facebook, "House calls are my passion." Now that is dramatic hyperbole. That veterinarian should find an exciting hobby like panting pants on little toy soldiers.

About half of all house calls visits end in euthanasia. These are heartfelt events, solemn and serious, usually proceeding without complication. I feel honored to be able to help these cherished pets painlessly leave this world in the arms of their owners in familiar surroundings. Many of my clients voice the same opinion, "I wish when it was my time someone would do this for me." Most end with the client thanking us for the service; some with a handshake, some with a comforting hug. We place the pet on a stretcher and quietly leave the family to their own private, emotional embrace. Often, I am touched as I witness the client's face as it flashes the grim realization that tonight their home will be empty for the first time in years; they have lost their friend, forever. We all take this part of our job seriously. However, sometimes, in some instances, not being serious is a smart way to avoid the painful reality.

I worked with some qualified technicians. I usually take the best on my house calls as these appointments are so unpredictable. In first the two years of my practice I employed a thirty-year-old man named Fred. He was the best man at my second wedding, a good friend and a talented technician. He had a dry, sarcastic sense of humor, and was a consummate pessimist; and he was beside me during most of the memorable house calls during the early days of my practice.

One summer afternoon, Fred and I were on a call to a home in the seedy side of town. It was no-frills euthanasia; afterward, we were to leave the body. We pulled up in the late August sun to a home more typical of a back-water Missouri town than a New Jersey suburb. A dilapidated two-story framed home with splintered shutters and crumbling shingles. Fragile, broken wooden steps led up to a tattered screen door attached by only one hinge. Before I could find solid wood to knock, I was startled by the voice of a young man who ordered us to come inside. In a depression era kitchen stood three shirtless teenage boys who surrounded an emaciated Rottweiler who laid, splay-legged, panting on the cracked tile floor. Behind them sat a plump, middle-aged woman who reluctantly claimed to be their mother. Her overflowing ashtray was piled high with the day's spent cigarettes.

After a brief discussion about the dog's pathetic condition, the woman agreed to sign the euthanasia authorization form. The youngest two boys started to sob, while the oldest of the three boys raddled off a set of profanities. In a profound tirade, the mother scolded her oldest boy using what I can only assume was his Christian surname: Worthless Willie. As in "...shut up Worthless Willie," or "...get away from the dog Worthless Willie," or "...honest judge Worthless Willie will never sell drugs in that schoolyard again." With the dog lying on the kitchen floor, mom at the table, and kids huddled behind us I gave the final injection. I then thanked God the euthanasia was over, and we could end this poor dog's miserable existence and our nightmare on Elm Street.

"Bam! Bam!" We were shocked by what sounded like two gunshots from behind our heads — two rapid explosions in succession. Fred and I immediately looked at each other expecting to see blood spurting from our foreheads. We then looked back. Worthless Willie still had his fist clenched in the air bright red from punching the old wooden kitchen cabinets behind him. "Do it with honor," he said as he gave us the most menacing stare since that Brahma bull charged me in vet school. "You better put him down with honor. Do It!"

I looked in Fred's eyes, he stared back at me, and we both silently mouthed the same words, "What the hell does that mean?" With that thought, we heard another loud clap. This time it was the mother's paddle- like hand slapping down on the kitchen table which flipped the ashtray and three packs of cigarette butts onto the dog's lifeless body. She then turned around and swung a left cross which slapped Worthless Willie in the back of the head. The momentum of her hand propelled him forward as he fell through the screen door and down the wooden stairs. Fred and I agreed it was time to leave. This family needed some alone time.

"I'm sorry about that Doc," the mom said. "He's just like his daddy; I had to slap him once or twice you know."

I assumed she was talking about Worthless Willie, Sr. AKA, Worthless William. I had no reason to doubt her story; the last time I saw a left like that it broke Mohammed Ali's jaw. We briskly walked back to the car looking back expecting to see junior welding his father's shotgun screaming, "I said with honor!" While speeding back to the safety of my office that afternoon we agreed we were lucky the mother was there, she may have been crude, but she was a voice of reason in a volatile situation. She certainly controlled the unstable son. "You know what they need in that madhouse," I said, as we pulled up to the hospital. "They don't need a vet they need Dr. Phil."

Two days later, with the memory of my afternoon in *Deliverance* still fresh in my mind, I received another request for a house call euthanasia.

This time it was from a local wealthy Italian family from the money side of town. The husband had a reputation, he was rumored to be connected, and when you're from Jersey connected doesn't mean you work for ATT. They had a ten-year-old Bull Mastiff named Sonny who had been failing for months. Now they called me to end his suffering.

I didn't know what to expect. What if the euthanasia did not go smoothly or individual family members still were not ready to put the dog down? Given what happened at the last house call I wondered if the kids in this family were as unstable. If they were loopy would I get slapped in the back of the head, or worse? I had seen every episode of *The Sopranos*. Fred and I would watch new episodes every Sunday night; we had a thing for mob movies. We knew what happens when the boss gives you a job to do and things don't "go so good." It was with that vision that Fred and I drove out to the Domenici estate (The breeds have been changed to protect the innocent).

We pulled up to the eight-foot pillars and through the rout iron gate, then up the winding cobblestone driveway that arched around an enormous cascading granite water fountain. A topless lady in the center was pouring water from ceramic vase over the edge of the top tier which cascaded down two more levels. We walked up the granite stairs and stood in front of a large oak double door with elegant stain glass windows. The three-story house had wings which stretched to the north and the south. The south wing had a connecting four-car garage; larger than my modest two-story colonial home.

After a short conversation on the house speaker, the Spanish maid brought us into the house. We stood

Madame, You Have Cats in Your Mattress

in a large open foyer, in the center stood another naked lady fountain. This one had a vase in each hand and doves on her shoulder.

"Nice jugs," Fred quipped, as we started to walk past the double curved staircase towards the back of the house.

"That must be her sister out front," I whispered. "Who has fountains inside their house?"

"People who lend money to other people and then break their legs when they don't pay."

"Shut up before you end up in the footing of their next fountain."

On the back-marble deck, we met the man of the house. Michael Domenici was a handsome middle age man dressed in a powder blue sweat suit and white sneakers. He had jet black hair with white wings along each side. He pleasantly thanked us for coming and pointed to the back yard. We could see people gathered at the wood-line at the back of the property, behind the pool house, past the oversized in-ground pool, and beyond a third fountain. "Sonny's lying back there with my wife and kids. We've already dug a hole. He's so big I figure we can do it right there to make it easier."

When I approached the dog, the entire family were in tears. Each of the four teenage boys kneeled and kissed Sonny on the forehead then shook my hand in a sign of sincere appreciation. Mrs. Domenici followed with a hug and in a strong North Jersey accent gave her heartfelt thanks. We euthanized Sonny next to a meticulously dug five-foot deep hole; custom made that very morning. In between sobs, Mr. Domenici firmly grasps my right hand in gratitude and placed five one-hundred-dollar bills in my left hand.

When I reminded him, the charge was only three hundred dollars he gave me a compassionate look, squeezed both my hands around the money and mouthed the words, "Thank you." This time we left without the fear of being pursued by a shotgun-wielding maniac.

"They have more fountains than I have bathrooms," I remarked as we got into the car. "But they seem to be nice people. I feel almost guilty thinking they were the typical mob family. Their great people and the kids are certainly respectful."

"Yes, they made us comfortable. However, to be honest, I started to get worried when I heard Mr. Domenici had already dug a hole. I was hoping it wasn't big enough for all three of us,"

"No, I wasn't worried about that. Now if they had dug three holes, then I'd be worried."

"Think about it if you didn't get that vein the first time, we'd be digging our graves right now." Fred added, "After all, they always make the poor slob who screwed things up to dig the holes."

"Not always, when they clubbed Joe Pesci and his brother to death in *Casino*, someone else already dug the holes. Do you remember they stripped them down to their "tighty-whities" and beat them to death with baseball bats in the cornfield?"

"Yes, but that was because they planned to whack them. When it's a planned whacking, they dig the graves before they do it to save time. That's why there was only one hole today."

"So, what's your saying is if I had screwed up, we would have been forced at gunpoint to dig two holes, ten feet behind their Rainbow swing set and

Madame, You Have Cats in Your Mattress

then shot us to death, burying us next to their beloved Sonny?"

"I'm just saying when these people get pissed off people start dying. Do you remember in *Goodfellas,* when Joe Pesci shot Christopher from *The Sopranos* in the chest during the card game just because he told Joe Pesci to go screw himself?"

"Are you forgetting when that mob guy who told Joe Pesci to shine his shoes which pissed Pesci off so bad that he and De Niro beat him to death in Ray Liotta's bar?"

"Yes," Fred answered. "That's right, and then they drove to Scorsese's mom' house and ate spaghetti and meatballs, the whole time the guys rattling around in the trunk."

"I thought that old woman was Joe Pesci's mom."

"Yes, in *Goodfellas* but in real-life it was Martin Scorsese's mom. My point is that Joe had to dig that hole too because it was an impulse kill. It's like a penalty for killing some guy on a whim."

"First, Joe didn't dig a hole in *Eight Heads in a Duffle Bag* where he was running around with a bag full of heads? Secondly, don't you think you a little guilty of stereotyping?"

One, *Eight Heads in a Duffle Bag* sucked. It was easily his worst movie. Second, I'm just saying I was a little concerned because they dug such a beautiful hole before we got there. You have to admit someone in that family is good at digging graves."

"Maybe their uncle Paulie is an undertaker. I don't know but let me ask you something. Do you remember in *Goodfellas* when Pesci stabbed that Jewish toupee salesman in the neck while he was sitting in that

Cadillac? Then they took him to the Italian deli and chopped him up in the meat slicer."

"Yes, the bald guy with the big mouth who did the bullshit wig commercials."

"Well, the Domenici's had a Cuisinart on the kitchen counter. Weren't you afraid they were going to chop you up and put you in their meat sauce?"

"Shit. You know what? I didn't think of that."

"Do me a favor, Fred. Remind me never to invite you to dinner at my mom's house. She's German, and I don't want to know what you think she would do to you. Maybe she would put you in the…?"

"Don't say it. Now that's racists… Shit!"

"What now?"

"When you killed the dog, I missed my cue. I should have screamed, "Sonny is dead Michael!""

"That's *The Godfather*, and that would have gotten us whacked."

Fred worked for me for about a year after the Domenici house call. A short time after leaving he was found dead in his apartment of unknown causes. His life had changed dramatically, and we had grown apart. After he quit, he and I had a dispute based on a business decision which he felt was unfair-ending a ten-year friendship. However, the years as his friend, the hours we spent on Sunday nights watching *The Sopranos*, and the memorable days we spent together going on house calls will always define our relationship.

Eventually, I would always take two technicians at each house call. The unpredictability of these calls required skilled and experienced assistants. If I were to place an ad for a house call technician it would ask them to be sympathetic and compassionate, to be adept at packing a house call bag, to be able to improvise, to be able to decipher confusing Google directions, to be able to see in the dark, and to be willing to chase and wrangle nasty cats from under beds and from behind dryers. No one person could fill all those criteria, but Robin, Candace, and Dave were close. Robin was a survivor of over twenty-five years of servitude under Dr. Klein-a major feat as I lasted only six. Candace was a Pinetree Veterinary Hospital convert, and Dave was a young man who virtually grew up in my practice. He started with us when he was fifteen-years-old.

Robin, Dave and I had just arrived at the final house call of the day in another senior village. It appeared to be a typical simple euthanasia. Even though a client does not say the words "put her down" it is easy to read between the lines. They usually say, "She's an old cat, she been sick for a while, she hasn't eaten for a week, and I don't want to see her suffer." Such was the call from the sister of an elderly cat owner in a gated community called Happy Acres. In those cases, we always bring the euthanasia solution in case the owners decide to put the cat down; more than not our instincts are correct. This was the reason I wanted Robin's on these house calls. She could use her experience and sensitivity to encourage these owners to make the difficult decision to put their sick pet to sleep.

Three senior citizens met us; Mr. and Mrs. Seitz, and the woman who called us, her sister Alva. They directed us to the sunken living room where the nineteen her old cat Trixie was lying motionless on a blanket. Three feet away blared an episode of the *Dr. Phil Show* on a thirty-two-inch flat screen television.

"She seemed fine yesterday, I can't imagine what happened," said Mrs. Seitz. Her voice barely audible, over Dr. Phil's opening monologue.

Her sister's facial expression caught my eye as I gazed over Mrs. Seitz's paper-thin frame. Alva stood with a deep frown, shaking her head, and mouthing the words, "No, No. Not true."

I could easily see that Trixie was dying. She was thin, dehydrated, and had infrequent shallow breaths. The cat didn't respond as her temperature barely registered on a rectal thermometer. I pulled up the cat's lip and exposed gums which were as white as the Seitz's living room walls.

I approached Mrs. Seitz's-she was as fragile and skinny as the cat. "Trixie is very sick, Mrs. Seitz. We can do bloodwork to put a name on her problem, we can take her back to the hospital and start her on fluids and medications, but honestly, I don't think it will help."

"What do you mean, I can't imagine she is that sick. She was fine just a few days ago."

"I understand how you feel, but cats hide their illness. By the time they stop eating they are already very sick and believe me Mrs. Seitz Trixie is very sick. She is not even responding to us, she is hardly breathing, and she is cold."

"I can turn the heat up," replied Mrs. Seitz.

"No, see when cats get sick and when they start dying their body temperature gets very low because her metabolism gets very slow. I want to help Trixie, but if I take her back to the hospital, she most likely will die alone in a cage. I know you don't want that."

"What are you saying?"

"I think you should put her to sleep."

"Herb," she cried to her husband who had been sitting at the kitchen counter behind her. "The doctor wants us to put her to sleep."

"Why, is she that sick?" He responded.

"He says we can't help her. When should we do it?" She asked as her voice began to crack.

"Can't you help her?" Herb responded. "Can't you give her a shot to make her feel better?"

'No, there is nothing I can give to make her better. If there were something, I would use it. Listen I'm going to let you and your wife talk about it for a bit. We're in no hurry." However, we were in a hurry. I had to be back at the office for my next appointment in about thirty minutes. In these euthanasia cases, it's not business, as usual, I try to be patient and empathetic during this process-the people deserve the courtesy to make their decision. While we waited, I spoke with Alva. She explained that her sister had no idea the cat was so sick. Her husband virtually ignored the cat, and she knew her sister couldn't make the final call; Mrs. Seitz had difficulty making even simple decisions, so her sister called us.

Now, I knew it was time for Robin, whom I referred to as my closer. I call her the closer because she can help close the book on these sad cases where the owner has difficulty making the right choice. She helps these clients feel comfortable about their decision in a way that is more empathetic than I can. I see so many cases where the owner cannot make the final call because of the guilt of ending their animal's life. Robin appeals to their compassionate, logical voice. She doesn't just explain the grave condition of their pet, but she will gently speak of the pet's suffering, their poor quality of life, and the owner's responsibility to end that suffering by showing them the final act of love. Sometimes it is the hard-fact most pet owners don't want to admit; keeping a sick animal alive just because they don't want to let them go, is not only selfish but also cruel.

In the case of Trixie, the cat, it was not just our time limitations which concerned me it was, more importantly, the cat was failing fast-they needed to decide in the next few minutes. I could tell we were close, so Dave and I opened the house call bag to prepare for the euthanasia. I noticed a strained look on Dave's face as he came close to whisper, "There's no Euthasol. Robin must have forgotten it."

"What," I shot back. "Shit, what are we going to use now?" The Euthasol was the solution we gave intravenously to stop the animal's heart. We needed to end the pet's life, and we didn't have any drug to do it. Three ideas raced past my mind; I could speed back to the hospital and pick up the solution, but that would cost us another thirty minutes-far too long-the cat could expire by that time. I could I take the cat back and euthanize it back at the hospital? That's fine, but they wanted to be present when she died. I started to panic. Lastly, I could inject her with something to sedate it, then I could wrap it in a blanket and take it back to the hospital. Maybe I could fool Mr. and Mrs. Seitz, but not her sister. Besides, I did not feel comfortable; that was deceptive not to mention unethical. I thought of any drugs we would carry which could humanly stop the heart. "Check. What do we have in the bag?" I ordered as a bead of sweat dripped off my forehead.

Dave fumbled through the bag removing one bottle after another, spilling gauze and cotton tip swabs on the blanket next to the cat. His frustration mirrored mine as we looked back; the Seitz's still had not decided. "Wait, we do have a bottle of Telazol." Telazol was a tranquilizer we used to sedate the animal before euthanasia.

This could be the solution; maybe we could overdose the cat on the injectable Telazol, and that might stop the heart-as sick as the cat was it might stop the heart-it might work. Although if it didn't then, I might have to go to plan "B" and take the poor cat back to the hospital for euthanasia. Then, a terrible thought struck my mind; what if they wanted to bury the cat in their yard. I could envision the cat waking up, as they watch their beloved Trixie spring back to life as they lower it into a hole next to their daffodils.

Finally, Mrs. Seitz agreed to sign the form to end Trixie's life. Robin came back fully satisfied she had been successful. "You forgot the Euthasol," I whispered as we kneeled next to the cat.

"What, are you kidding? I'm sorry. Damn you're right," she mumbled against her chest, trying to be inconspicuous. "What do you want me to do? Do you want me to go back and get it?

"No, we don't have the time. We're stuck. I'm going to overdose with Telazol," I answered. "It better work." I drew up one milliliter, ten times the dose we would have used to sedate the cat. "This should do it," I added as I prayed it would indeed, do it. We all held our breath.

"Wait a minute," Robin interrupted.

"What now," I said.

"I think her heart stopped already. I don't hear a heartbeat. I think she's gone."

This was one of the few times I was relieved to hear the phrase, "I don't hear a heartbeat." She had died just as I was pulling up the Telazol into the syringe. I picked up the stethoscope and listened for a heartbeat. Robin was right; the cat was dead. I looked up at Mrs. Seitz and softly said, "Trixie is gone, she's passed."

"What? Are you kidding?" She was genuinely surprised. "I don't understand I didn't think she was that sick. She was just fine a couple of days ago."

Mrs. Seitz put her head in her hands and started to sob. Her sister pulled her back to the kitchen and hugged her. She had forgotten our entire conversation. She was grieving again for an emotional decision she had already made. A harsh reality she had already accepted.

They had agreed to send Trixie back for cremation. Dave wrapped the body in a blanket and prepared to take the cat out to the car. Now came a sensitive part of the home euthanasia; getting paid. This is an uncomfortable procedure; one of the few times I personally collect the money from a client. I briefly cut through the sorrow of their recently deceased pet to gently ask for payment. Many already have a check written, a credit card ready, or cash in their hand. However, it is that uncomfortable moment where I stand alone in a stranger's living room waiting for them to return with some form of payment. Hoping they do not view me as a simple mercenary collecting my pay for a job well done. Mr. Seitz was paying this bill. There was one problem; no one told him.

I walked over to Mr. Seitz and handed him the itemized bill. His hand vibrated as he held the paper.

He read it like he was examining his will. "What's this?"

"Those are the charges for Trixie," I replied. "I didn't charge you for the euthanasia because we didn't have to do it."

"Is she dead, already?"

"Yes."

"Are You taking her back with you?"

"Yes. We are."

"What do I have to pay? This amount?'

I pointed to the total at the bottom of the page and shook my head. Mr. Seitz walked back to the kitchen and placed the bill on the counter. He then returned to the living room and started conversing with his wife and sister-in-law. I stood baffled, with each passing minute it got closer to the time of my next appointment. I tried to lessen my anxiety by watching the *Dr. Phil Show*. He was counseling Danny Bonaduce on his troubled life and failing marriage. It was hard to muster sympathy for a spoiled child star who was rich before he reached puberty. He was born in Philadelphia, and he was my age. I could have tried out for that part. I would have loved to have played Susan Dey's brother, or anything else with Susan Dey. Damn, a commercial, I wanted to hear Dr. Phil's advice. I had to deal with my issues, Dr. Phil wasn't going to get Mr. Seitz to pay the bill any faster. I walked up to Mr. Seitz and reminded him that I would take a check or credit card for payment. He looked at me, then looked at his wife then back to me again. Finally, Alva tapped him on the shoulder to remind him he needed to pay the bill. He turned and took a stroll into the kitchen, picked up a medicine vial, turned and walked back out to his sister-in-law and started talking about his cholesterol medication-apparently, he missed this morning's dose. I began to cross my limited patience threshold as I realized the time from my first appointment of the afternoon had arrived, we had to get back to the office. Alva noticed my agitation and again told Mr. Seitz to get a check to pay the bill.

"Oh yes, I have the checkbook in the kitchen. Let me get it." He then started the ten-foot pilgrimage back to the kitchen. Upon arriving at the counter a few minutes later, he turned and asked his sister-in-law, "What did I come up here for?"

"The checkbook Herb." He then cupped his hand behind his ear and shook his head. "The checkbook to pay the doctor," she shouted as she pointed in my direction.

"Oh yes, it's right back here where I left it. How much is it again?"

"Three hundred and eighty-five dollars," I replied trying my best to control my angst. I could tell Mr. Seitz didn't fully hear, so I repeated the amount and added, "I circled it at the bottom."

"Oh, OK. I'll be just a minute. Flo, do you have a pen that works? This one doesn't work."

"I have one," I quickly shouted out in a tone the dead cat could have heard, and it was in the car. I stood on the other side of the counter as he signed his name and slowly filled in the amount. I could imagine portraits painted at a faster pace. "I'll fill out the top for you" Finally with the check in hand I gave my final condolences and hurried out the door. I was already thirty minutes late for my first appointment as I started the car and backed out of the driveway. "Shit. Mr. Seitz kept my pen."

292

Madame, You Have Cats in Your Mattress

"Do want to go back and get it," Dave asked from the back seat.

"That's OK. I'd sooner stick a needle in my eye then endure another ten minutes in that geriatric black hole."

Not all house calls are frustrating appointments with unhappy endings. Many are frustrating appointments with comic book endings. One example was a routine cat vaccination-the easiest of all house calls. "Fifteen minutes max. Let' do it," I proclaimed as Robin, Dave, and I walked up to the door of a simple looking ranch in one of the older senior village developments.

Mrs. Mildred Transom greeted us at the door. She was a seventy-three-year-old woman who called us to vaccinate her female cat, Mary. We entered a house typical of the old Spartan retirement villages with one large open combined living room, dining area, kitchen with two small bedrooms, plain white walls, and a thirty-year-old carpet. I was struck, not by the scant décor, but by the scent in the air. The house hung heavy with the smell of old urine and moldy carpet; yellow stains spackled the rug. We walked into the dining area and met Tonto a black and white mixed breed dog. Mrs. Transom directed us to the door of the far bedroom where she had confined her cat, Mary. I could see in the shadows of the other bedroom sat an old man in a recliner whose silhouette was illuminated by the glow of a small television. We opened the door of the far bedroom and one by one we slowly squeezed through the opening. We had learned during these cat appointments how to keep the cat inside and the owner outside.

We entered a small bedroom with a queen size bed, one bureau, and a standing light. The closet had classic nineteen seventies mirrored sliding doors. The smell of cat litter was everywhere. We stepped on dry cat food pellets embedded throughout the carpet.

"You know guys," I said, as I slid one of the closet doors to the left. "There are three litter boxes in here. That's an awful lot for one cat." The boxes were full of feces, and the litter was spilling onto the tan carpet. I didn't see the cat anywhere, so I asked Dave to check the bed.

As he kneeled, I could hear his voice echo from under the bed, "There a couple of them under there. I can see them hiding in the box spring."

"Great. Let me make sure which cat it is," I said, as I quickly stuck my head out the door and called to Mrs. Transom. A minute passed before I got a response. "She says it's the female tabby. Can you grab her?"

After a few minutes of bed shaking, floor-slapping, and stretching under the bed, Dave realized all he was doing was getting covered in cat hair. "I can't get any of them."

"All right, here's what we'll do, I'll lift the bed and Dave will shush them out and Robin, you can catch the tabby. Ready?" With my crew standing ready I lifted the bottom of the box spring and mattress over my shoulders. "Get her."

What we saw next startled all three of us. Six cats flew out from under the bed like tennis balls shooting out of a cannon. Dave almost fell back as one jumped towards his chest and then bounced away. Robin, wearing a pair of large leather restraint gloves, didn't know which direction to dive. She looked like a goalie trying to block six pucks at once. One jumped into the litter box knocking it over onto the rug, and another bounced head first into the mirrored door and back under the bed. One leaped onto the bed, towards me and over my shoulder. Then onto the bureau into the lamp and smacked into the closed window. The light hit the floor, the curtains fell to the ground, and the cat leaped back under the bed. If we weren't laughing so hard, we would have been in shock. In thirty seconds, every cat was back where it started.

"Did you see the tabby?" I asked as I laid the bed gently on the ground.

"I saw a couple of tabby cats," Robin said, unable to control her laughter. "I think the one that bounced off the mirror, oh, and maybe the one who jumped over your head onto the window sill."

"I didn't know she had more than one cat. All right well, this time let me get the vaccine ready, so if you catch her, I can give it a shot."

I lifted the bed one more time, and again the cats sprung out of the box spring like they were in a malfunctioning pinball machine. Finally, after two minutes of mayhem, Robin trapped a tabby cat against the bedroom door. I slammed the bed down and raced over to the trapped cat who was rolling like an alligator as Robin held it down with the leather gloves. I quickly gave it the distemper vaccine in some unrecognizable part of its body and told Robin to let it go. It was impossible to examine the cat as claws, teeth, and urine spun through the air. The room was a disaster; the bedspread had fallen to the ground, cat litter was everywhere, the window was bare, urine covered the mirrored closet doors, and cat hair was still cascading from the air minutes later. In seconds, every cat had disappeared back into the bed.

"How do we know that was the right cat," Dave said as he packed up the bag and we got ready to leave the bedroom.

"Are you kidding me, the old woman probably doesn't know one cat from another. Let's put it this way; it's like a fifty, fifty shot that we got the right one."

"I don't know I thought a saw a third tabby cat flying around there," Robin sarcastically remarked.

"You know what you can stay here and look for it, and we'll pick up your body in a couple of days. It'll probably in the box spring with the cat shit." I joked as I opened the bedroom door.

Robin and Dave left the house quickly to escape the odor coming from the soiled rugs. I was left alone again to collect payment. Mrs. Transom was sitting at the dining room table, checkbook in hand, ready to oblige-but first she told a story.

"Clarence and I moved to this house eight years ago," she began. "That's Clarence in the front bedroom. He has end-stage Parkinson's Disease; I must do everything for him now. We originally lived in southern New Mexico on an Indian reservation. Clarence was a Methodist minister; he ran a church for the Native Americans for almost twenty years. He also has a degree in psychology. He counseled hundreds of them; they trusted and loved him. When he retired, they threw a wonderful memorial. They gave him so many gifts. You can't believe what they made for him. So much stuff we had to have it shipped out here and put in a storage unit. He helped so many of them; now he can't even feed himself."

She paused to fill in the blanks in her Native American custom bank checks. I started to feel great sympathy for her plight. Between the old dog in the living room, the six cats in the bedroom, and her invalid husband she was far beyond her limit. She didn't intentionally neglect her cats; they were just left to fend for themselves. She and her husband had led an exciting life. We spoke of the movie *Dances with Wolves*, which honored the heritage of the proud Native Americans. "Mrs. Transom," I said. "I hate stereotypes. I know you must hate stereotypes too because you lived with those people for so many years. You know what I mean, like the one that portrays the Native Americans as alcoholics."

She reached up and handed me the check. Then she proclaimed bluntly, "Oh no, they are drunks. Alcoholism is everywhere in Indian society, and there is also a major unemployment problem. However, the problem is alcohol. That's why my husband had to council so many alcoholic Indians. Their nice people but they love their whiskey. They call it firewater. Between you and me that's why it was so easy for us to take over their land. They were always drunk, probably fell off their horses. Yep, Firewater that's what they call it, firewater."

I wanted so badly, to say to good old Mildred, "Damn that Kevin Costner. What the hell does he know anyway?" However, I just shook my head and placed the Navajo designer check in the clipboard and ended the conversation. I couldn't believe it. This sweet old woman was a racist; I was talking *Dances with Wolves*, and she was talking *Blazing Saddles*.

When we arrived back at the hospital, I instructed Robin to call the local Health and Humans

Services. I was still concerned about Mrs. Transom's ability to maintain her cats in a healthy environment. I didn't know if they could help, but I had to try for the sake of the cats.

The following spring Mrs. Transom asked me to examine Tonto; he was starting to have trouble walking. I looked at the dog and prescribed medication for its worsening arthritis. While Mrs. Transom held a quick seminar on Indian burial grounds, I snuck to the back of the house. Her husband was lying in the front bedroom on a bed lite only by the rays of a mid-afternoon sun. I peaked in the cat room I could see the rugs were clean and the litter boxes lined up, neatly positioned along the bottom of the bed and the food bowls were on plastic kitchen mat. The windows were bare, and the bureau was gone. I couldn't see any cats, but I assumed they were hiding in the inner recesses of the box spring.

When I returned to the living area, I complimented her on the cat room. She informed us that an official from senior services had inspected her home, then they appointed a nice young lady to come in and clean the room three times a week. The poor old woman didn't have the energy to do it anymore. I could only smile and say, "God works in mysterious ways Mrs. Transom. Mysterious ways indeed."

The following fall I was called to her home for the third time to put Tonto to sleep. When I arrived, Tonto was lying on his side, panting heavily, lying flat, with a barely perceptible tail wag at our greeting. The smell of urine and vomit saturated the living room. Mrs. Transom was ready; she knew it was time to put Tonto down. While we were waiting for the tranquilizer to take effect, I walked over to the bedroom to check on the cats. Before I opened the door, I glanced through the entrance to the front bedroom and was surprised to see the television was dark and the shades were drawn low with slight points of the dim morning sun spraying yellow sickles of light on an empty twin bed.

Mr. Transom had passed in August. Now his wife would be alone with only semi-feral cats to keep her company. She was getting frail and seemed at times confused. I suspected her life in that home would also soon be ending, as well as, the lives of the six cats who lived in a box spring, under the bed in a typical ranch house, in another senior village of New Jersey.

On another house call, three blocks away in the same senior village I was greeted by another long- term resident, much smaller and infinitely more aggressive than Mrs. Transom. I could hear Tommy's yapping the moment I rang the doorbell. I knew he was a scrappy little terrier just from his bark. If Tommy's bark didn't scare me, Mrs. Pasteli's flowered house dress certainly gave me a fright. Isabella Pasteli's was a seventy-two-year-old Italian widow. Five foot nothing and ruffled hair she wore a blue plaid house dress that barely covered her knees. Below those gems, her calves resembled the knotty bark of two mighty oak trunks growing out of two worn bright pink slippers. Mrs. Pasteli scooped Tommy up in her arms a split second before he bit my ankle; when she bent over, I saw far too much-weathered cleavage for a man of my age. She invited us into the kitchen of a nicely decorated senior ranch home. A framed picture of Pope John Paul II hung above the sink. We were encouraged to sit, but there were only two kitchen chairs; one for her and on the other laid a soft hand sewn pillow, with a bold "Tommy"-embroidered on the face; that seat was taken.

Mrs. Pasteli was as scrappy as Tommy, but because of their petite frames neither was genuinely threatening. When Robin tried to grab Tommy, he would hide under Mrs. Pasteli's hanging house dress, squat between her legs, and snarl. Robin was a sane person and was not about to tempt fate and reach for that dog under that plaid curtain-who knows what treasure she would find. We knew we couldn't get a muzzle on his little jaw; Mrs. Pasteli would have to hold him in her lap and squeeze his snout as we examined the dog. With each growl, Mrs. Pasteli would scold him with a harsh reprimand; degrading and laced with personal insults.

"Shut up, Tommy, you little Bastardo," she would scold. "Don't you know this doctor could end you? Behave, or I let him do it."

We had several calls through the years to Mrs. Pasteli's ranch home; with each visit, we began to develop a special relationship with this old woman. We became immune to her insults and started to understand her sarcastic sense of humor. However, we began to feel sorry for little Tommy.

"Tommy, you're such a little bastard," she said through his growling. "He's just like my husband. He was a little bastard too. I think that's why I adopted him after my husband died."

"Where is Mr. Pasteli?" I asked. "Did, you kill him. What's he buried in the Pine Barrens?"

"No, I didn't kill him, but I wanted to, many times. We were married for forty years. I don't think a year went by that I didn't want to kill him."

"How long has he been gone?"

"He's been dead for ten years. He was my big Bastardo."

"What, did he run around on you?"

"No, he had better not. Then he would have been gone a lot sooner. Besides he had a good time with these," she said palming each breast. "He didn't need to go anywhere else for a good time. These were his own personal fun bags."

"I can see what you mean," I said shaking my head. I didn't know whether to laugh or to gag. Trying to change the subject I asked, "What did he do for a living?"

"He was in waste management, up in Paterson. We always had money. We went on so many trips; he took me to Italy three times. He would buy me expensive jewelry. He bought me a mink coat, but I told him to take it back, I would have looked like a whore. Besides I wasn't going to wear anything that growled or purred. It would be like making a muffler out of Tommy. Then when he died, I moved here. I couldn't afford to stay up there; the house was just too big. He was actually a pretty good man but now he is gone, and I'm stuck with the rest of these dying old people. Nothing ever happens in this town; I call it the waiting run for death. Most of these people are in bed by six. No one even comes out during the day. I don't drive, so I can't go anywhere. Up in Paterson I could walk to the butcher, or baker, or get my hair done. Here there's nothing. All because that bastard died on me."

Often Mrs. Pasteli would offer us pastries, or cookies, or even a glass of red wine. I would politely decline the wine, but it was impossible to leave without an Italian cookie, or a fresh cannoli-that would have been a personal insult. Mrs. Pasteli was not a hateful woman. She adopted that nasty little dog because she found a ten-pound version of herself. She covered the regret of losing her life and her husband with a thinly veiled shroud of insults and sarcasm. Tommy cowered under her dress and growled at the world because what he feared most was that he would lose his down pillow and his homemade dog treats-maybe even in his worst nightmare he would be taken back to the shelter. Both characters were comical, as well as, tragic, but both were harmless.

"Doctor," she would say at the end of every visit. "Here's what I will do, I'll pay you half of this bill now. The rest I pay in a month." Each time I would remind her we don't do business that way. We require full payment when services are rendered. "You can trust me doc. I'll pay it." Then she would grudgingly agree and write the check for the full amount, the whole time grumbling about how doctors were so greedy. Such was our lesson until the next visit. I may never get to Italy, but I could count on fighting her for that money every time. It was a sure bet, like Tommy barking at the door every time I rang the bell.

A year passed before I saw Tommy again, he pranced in our office with a young woman trailing behind. He was calm, quiet, and well behaved, this time he didn't need a muzzle to examine him. His new owner told me Mrs. Pasteli was admitted to a nursing home that spring and was forced to give Tommy away. He wasn't the ornery little terrier we had grown to love. He never even lifted his lip when we cut his nails. I would never know if his new owner had exorcized his demons or he had just fed off that disagreeable old woman. Either way, he was a new dog. Mrs. Pasteli called an hour after his visit to check on his progress. She assured me she would soon be out of her nursing home and back with her best friend "Her Tommy, the little Bastardo." Of course, Mrs. Pasteli lived out her life in that nursing home and never again reunited with her surly little friend. Was Tommy happier with his new owner? I think so when I saw him that summer afternoon, he didn't complain.

Most calls to the senior village follow the same script: No air conditioning, poor ventilation, dim lighting, and disappearing cats. When we answered the next call, we encountered some new obstacles unique to the home of eighty-two-year old Emma Fleming; aluminum foil, an oxygen tank, and a broken couch- sounds like ingredients on a MacGyver episode. We had been summoned to perform a simple rabies vaccine on a middle-aged female cat. In such visits, we always instruct the owner to confine the cat before our arrival; an order they usually ignore. Thus, we typically chase the cat from under a couch, or from behind a washer, or more commonly from under a bed. In fifteen years of house calls, I have spent a great deal of time rolling around in the sack of mature older women looking for their cats (don't even think it).

We walked into a front sitting room to the peculiarity of aluminum foil covered living room furniture. The sofa, the love seat, even the end tables, and coffee table had an unwrinkled covering of Reynold's wrap. I thought it was modern art or perhaps protection from solar flares. I would soon learn it was foiled covered to prevent the cat from jumping on furniture. We were led into the second living room by a Jamaican day nurse. This room had a small television and an old slipcovered sofa. At one end sat Mrs. Fleming, a frail, almost translucent woman with thinning white hair. I could see a nasal tube which wrapped around her face and down her side and continued along the floor to a suitcase size box on the opposite side of the room. Every five seconds I could hear the low swoosh of the compressor pumping oxygen across the room into Mrs. Fleming's nose.

After a brief discussion between the nurse and Mrs. Fleming concluded they had no idea where their Siamese cat was hiding. The search was on. Under her bed, behind the bureau, in her closet piled high with clothes-some of an older intimate nature. Robin even checked behind the toilet and in the tub-no cat. I suggested we check the freezer; maybe the cat was wrapped in aluminum foil behind the frozen Tilapia. Then Dave noticed a motionless ball of fur under the sofa; the cat was under Emma's butt, the last place we suspected or ever wanted to look. However, as Dave leaned on the back of the sofa to try and get a better position to grab the cat, the leg of the couch broke dropping the couch and Mrs. Fleming to the ground. Strangely, neither the cat nor poor old Emma moved a muscle.

The dilemma was obvious; if I couldn't get this old woman to move off the sofa, how was I going to get the cat. Well, I had been around enough senior villages in my day to know how to move a stoic, old woman on a couch. I stood opposite Mrs. Fleming and motioned to Dave to get ready to grab the cat. In mindless obedience, he assumed the position of a baseball catcher. With a grimace, I lifted the far end of the sofa to my chin. Emma just sat rigid as her night slippers rose off the floor; she handled the forty-five-

Madame, You Have Cats in Your Mattress

degree tilt with ease, still focused on her soap opera. Dave snagged the cat in a towel, and Robin held the syringe ready. I returned Emma to the Earth and in sixty seconds had examined and vaccinated the terrified cat-as Dave release the sofa the cat disappeared into one of the back bedrooms, most likely into the nearest box spring.

I stood in the center of the room, both proud and satisfied I had performed my duty without losing a man. Now to fix the sofa, Dave placed a phonebook under Mrs. Fleming to level her buttocks. The technicians began to gather the gear and said their farewells, as I started to calculate the bill. "Beep, beep, beep," the rapid, loud sound replaced the periodic quiet swoosh of the pump. Those annoying beeps were breaking my concentration. I assumed the nurse had something in the oven. I thought, "Somebody stop it I'm trying to think. Doesn't anyone else hear that? Why doesn't that nurse turn off that damn timer?"

"Pssst. Hay," Robin whispered under her breath. Then she repeated it again but a bit louder.

Annoyed, I finally raised my glance from my ledger, and mouthed the word "What?"

Robin motioned to the ground and pointed at my feet. "The tube, you're standing on her line."

I was standing on her oxygen line. The annoying beeping was the occlusion alarm. I don't know how long, but for a brief period I had personally stopped that life-saving oxygen from flowing past Mrs. Fleming's nose and into her scarred lungs. Like her magical sofa ride she seemed to handle the oxygen deprivation like a fighter pilot, she hadn't passed out, but she did turn a pretty shade of blue. However, as is my custom, when something embarrassing happens, I don't draw attention to the situation by apologizing. I ignore it, hoping no one notices. Mrs. Fleming certainly had no idea her life was in the balance. I made some quick closing remarks and left through the shiny foiled sitting room while Mrs. Emma Fleming's color returned to the white, pasty shade we had become accustomed.

"The next time," Dave joked as we headed out to the car. "You need to wait until she pays the bill before you cut off the poor old woman's oxygen supply." I was in total agreement as I pulled out of her driveway.

I grew to appreciate house calls. I escaped the confines of the office for a while, I met some interesting pet owners in their natural habitat and spent a great deal of time under a ton of some very seasoned mattresses. In fifteen years and hundreds of house calls, there is one lesson I have learned; how to improvise. I was like a farm animal vet without the hot sun and horse flies. Some clients saw me as a healer, some as a savior, and some as the grim reaper. However, none saw me as a bearded, sexy hunk on a cool chopper sent to treat their ailments and satiate their most intimate medical fantasies.

CHAPTER 12

DEFENDING THE INNOCENT

"God requires that we assist the animals,

when they need our help. Each being

has the same right of protection."

- Saint Francis of Assisi

In three decades as a practicing veterinarian, I have addressed a multitude of animal cruelty cases from neglected horses to tortured pit bulls. Those cases did little for my bottom line, but they did develop and mature an ethical philosophy that guides me down my moral pathway. I treated my first animal abuse case during my third year at the Pinetree Veterinary hospital in 1992. A four-year-old Siberian Husky was rescued by a police officer who discovered the dog tied in the back yard of a modest ranch house in the outskirts of town. When served with the citation, the owner swore the dog had been tied up for only a day; he also attested the dog had plenty of food and water. The dog was lying in a muddy hole filled with his feces tangled in a leash rapped inches away from a cold steel post. Six feet away was an empty food bowl, dried and crusty; licked clean of any nourishment. My examination revealed that the Husky was dehydrated, pale, weak, and unable to stand; over twenty pounds underweight. His head was down and dejected; I could see the struggle for life frozen in his pathetic eyes like the water in the ice puddle next to his doghouse. I performed a rectal exam and retrieved a sample containing almost entirely of fur-proof that the only nutrition he was getting for days was in the consumption of his own hair.

    I set an I.V. catheter, started the dog on fluids and placed his cold body on a warm heating pad. I offered him a bowl of water and a high-calorie moist dog chow which he quickly sniffed and then ignored as if the scent of food made him nauseous-he stomach was probably dry and constricted; unable to accept something so alien as real food. Two hours later the dog mercifully took his last breath. The next day I wrote a detailed deposition which would help convict the owner of animal abuse: his penalty, a modest fine and a proverbial slap on the wrist.

    The Executive Board of the American Veterinary Medical Association amended the Veterinary Oath in 2011 to include the phrase: "…to use my scientific knowledge for the benefit of society through the protection of animal health and welfare…" This would appropriately place the veterinarian at the forefront of animal welfare in America. This sphere of animal care has expanded to include the psychological, sociological, and physical stresses placed on an animal. It contains aspects previously ignored for generations: space, comfort, socialization, and playtime.

Veterinarians witness many forms of abuse; from ignorant neglect to gross animal cruelty. In minor cases, the animal control officer encourages the owner to surrender the animal to avoid prosecution- the real focus is to save the animal not punish the owner. The shelter authorizes treatment in the hope that another, more deserving family would adopt the dog. Many are simple neglect cases like dogs and cats unvaccinated, unneutered, undernourished, or largely ignored. In these cases, this evidence was enough to remove the animal from this environment and place in another home. Veterinary corroboration and documentation proved the crime of abuse. This case with the Husky was rare; obtaining a judgment against the pet owner is difficult. However, this would change as the AVMA, answered the growing public concerns in animal welfare.

Certain dog breeds have a higher potential for abuse. In the last ten years, the most prominent dog breed surrendered to our local shelter was the American Pit Bull. Many were fighting dogs. Their ears are cropped short to the forehead, their body is covered in poorly healed and callused scars; their teeth are worn and broken. Most are intact females with sagging teats under an emaciated frame which were a testament to a long, torturous life as a breeding bitch. In Michael Vicks conviction of 2007 for "cruel and inhumane treatment in the running of a dog fighting ring," the inhumane sport of dog fighting rings was exposed; most involving the American Pit Bull.

A decade before, I would often see Greyhounds transported from southern dog tracks. Rescues had obtained these dogs after the trainers had relinquished these beautiful animals after a few years of service; their profit potential exhausted. Their physical injuries were far less than those of their fighting counterparts, but their psychological scars were far more profound. Many were nervous and firmly attached to their new owners; afraid of loud noises and sudden movements. These majestic animals would often refuse to sit; even anesthesia took far longer to take effect than other dogs. They would fight the effects, wobble, sway, and reluctantly fall to the ground. A specialist explained this behavior as a trained psychological response to their life at the dog tracks where they were punished for just lying down.

I believe there are three types of abuse. The first I refer to as soft abuse. This abuse is neglect due to owner ignorance or simple frugality. In the opinion of one instructor at a recent veterinary seminar; obesity was the most common form of animal abuse. She was referring to those owners whose never-ending buffet turns their pet Labrador into a fur-covered hassock, or the cat owner who grows a striped tabby into a monster that resembles an overfed raccoon from a Disney movie.

Such was the case with Sandy Katz an eight-year-old beagle who had already seen three other veterinarians for the same problem; she had trouble breathing. A typical beagle averages about twenty pounds; Sandy tipped the scales at just over fifty-six pounds. Its legs bowed under the stress of the weight of another dog and a half as it waddled across the exam room. It struggled to get air through dilated cheeks, a swollen dewlap that compressed the trachea, and a chest that filled with an oversized beating heart encased in fat. She panted with any attempt to perform mild physical activity and coughed with each labored step. The previous veterinarian had taken X-Rays, performed an ultrasound, and even did a bacterial culture of the trachea-all results were negative. Sandy had been on a myriad of antibiotics, corticosteroids, bronchodilators, and even a trial on common heart medications. Still she struggled to breathe; still, she coughed, and still, her owners ignored the obvious. Now they were looking to their fourth veterinarian to find the elusive answer to Sandy's condition.

I stood speechless, reading through twenty pages of previous records dating back almost two years. Each entry had one common denominator: a weight issue. Each recorded chronological body weight incrementally heavier than the last. With a sigh and a guarded query, I asked, "Mrs. Katz, did the other vets ever mention her weight problem?"

"No, not really. I took her in for coughing. They seemed to think it was an infection, allergies, or maybe her windpipe was a little flaccid."

"When you gave these medications, did any seem to work?"

"Oh, the cough stopped for a day or two, but her breathing problem never went away. Besides, I think she started to put on weight after she was on those pills. She used to be so thin."

I led the dog back for an X-ray already knowing what I would find. The radiograph looked like a negative of an engorged tick. It was obvious; the reason the dog wasn't getting better on medication was that it didn't suffer from asthma, bronchitis, or heart disease. It was just too damn fat! This was a sticky situation. Mrs. Katz was at least three hundred pounds and fought her own struggle to breathe. Mr. Katz was slightly smaller. How does one tell obese owners their dog is too fat? Very carefully.

"Mrs. Katz," I started, as I switched the lightbox on to show this aberration of nature. "I don't see anything abnormal with the lungs, heart, or trachea. I don't think another round of antibiotics or heart medication is warranted. I honestly believe, now this is my opinion," I continued as I tried to focus on the dog instead of the delusional owner. "She is not sick. I honestly think Sandy is just too fat to breathe. One of these hot summer days she is going to be in such respiratory distress she could quite possibly pass out and die."

Mrs. Katz's raised one eyebrow reminiscent of Mr. Spock. "Thank God. You're telling me she doesn't have cancer, she doesn't have diabetes, she doesn't have heart disease? See herb I told you, the doctor says she's not dying."

"Yes, well no, that's not what I'm saying. What I am saying is if you don't get Sandy to lose weight, Sandy is going to have trouble staying alive; frankly, all the medication in the world is not going to save her."

"Even antibiotics?"

"Yes, even antibiotics," I answered. "Unless you want the bacteria in her body to lose weight." Now, I knew why I was the fourth veterinarian to attack Sandy's problem. I started to curse those other three doctors for putting me through this frustrating nightmare. However, deep down I knew it wasn't their fault. I knew the other vets had told her the same thing. After a while they probably grew tired of reciting the same mantra and eventually just gave up and handed her medication, to pacify her. It was all over the files: "Grossly obese!' Discussed weight loss. The owner declined diet food! The owner declined to start a weight loss program.' "Listen, what do you feed Sandy? What type of dog food do you feed her? Do you feed her any table scraps?"

"Oh No, doctor she won't eat dog food. She doesn't even eat table scraps; she eats the same food we eat. Her favorite food is macaroni and cheese. She has pizza every Friday. Don't worry doctor I take off the onions because I know they can be poison. Every night I boil a little chicken and mix it with string beans, so she gets her vitamins. My husband and Sandy share a midnight snack of liverwurst and cheese sandwiches. She is so cute. Listen you don't need to worry about her getting over-heated on summer days because we take her to Dairy Queen when it's hot; she has a vanilla cone. It cools her right off. Oh no, do you think she coughs because she is lactose intolerant? I think I read on the internet dogs are lactose intolerant."

In the last few years, I started to adopt a nervous tick much like I had seen in Dr. Hershey twenty years before; I would fiddle with the rim of my glasses during those times when I started to lose my patience; this was one of those times. Now I polished the edge of my glasses like a piece of fine silverware. "Mrs. Katz, the cough has nothing to do with food allergies. Her diet is all wrong; it is making her too fat. Her obesity is killing her, and frankly, you are killing her with kindness. Now, I'm not giving any more useless drugs, but I am going to recommend she get on a weight loss program with a very restrictive diet. Oh, and that's dog food, only. No table food. Ever."

"Even ice cream?"

"Especially ice cream!"

With my stern message, a prescription weight loss diet, and limited caloric feeding schedule, Sandy and Mrs. Katz both waddled out the front door-never to return. I can only assume the fifth veterinarian will have the answers she had been seeking for two years.

Abagail suffered from a different form of soft abuse. She was a six-year-old Chihuahua who was growing a golf ball size mammary tumor on the right side of her abdomen. Mrs. Clair Dozer brought the dog in because the tumor had ruptured and was bleeding all over her bed sheets. I told her at every visit for six years to spay Abagail. Each time she refused to have the procedure done as she didn't want to put her through such a "painful surgery." Now she had no other choice.

I removed the tumor and finally spayed the dog. Mrs. Dozier was exuberant when the dog went home after the successful spay. However, Mrs. Dozier was not so happy when the tumor grew back three months after the surgery; one month later, cancer had spread to the lungs. Then we had to euthanize Abagail. Logic would dictate Mrs. Dozier had learned a valuable lesson. Apparently not, Clair, her next female Chihuahua is now three years old and is still intact, ignoring my recommendation to spay the dog. Is ignorance cruel or is cruelty ignorant?

Recently, I examined a ten-year-old Golden Retriever who was mostly hairless. A small tuft of hair on the top of his head was the only proof he once had fur. The skin on his legs and abdomen were black and course resembling the leathery skin of an elephant. The eyelids were black and crusty. It was apparent the dog had been suffering from this severe skin condition for months, if not years. I was brutally honest with the man, explaining the severity of this condition suggested abuse. I told him that if I were to report this to animal control, they would take the dog, and he most assuredly would be charged with cruelty. He then explained he recently was granted custody of the dog, as well as, two children from his ex-wife who was now in prison for drug abuse. I proceeded cautiously, without judgment. I recommended diagnostics and treatment. The man agreed and continued therapy for two months; the dog improved growing much of his hair back. I did not report this case to the animal control officer because he followed through with the therapy and the dog did improve. Sometimes it takes cautious trust to be fair to the dog and their owner.

Whether the cause of animal suffering is ignorance, stupidity, carelessness, or domestic disharmony the animal still suffers. In soft abuse cases, even when the outcome is disturbing, they rarely lead to a punishable offense. However, some cases may seem clear, but facts can blur the lines of logic.

In the spring of 2015, a seventy-five-year-old man carried the lifeless body of his fourteen-year-old black Labrador Retriever into the local shelter. His voice was hoarse, his words sincere as he slowly explained what had happened to his beloved Charlie, just a few hours before. Charlie was recently diagnosed with terminal kidney failure. Since that diagnosis, he saw his dog progressively worsen; Charlie was lying around, unable to stand, vomiting constantly; yesterday he even refused his morning donut. The owner knew his dog was suffering, and he also knew it was only a matter of time. Today he awoke; like every morning he drank a cup of black coffee, ate half of a glazed bear claw, then finished his morning cigarette. However, today, unlike other mornings, he didn't offer Charlie the other half of the donut, and he didn't take Charlie for a walk through the senior village park. Today he carried Charlie to his crate in the garage, covered the cage with a green leaf bag and attached the bag to a rubber hose which was connected to the tailpipe of his twenty-year-old Dodge pick-up. It took only a few minutes for Charlie to succumb to the toxic carbon monoxide of the HEMI V-8 engine's exhaust.

The public prosecutor did not press charges on the dog's elderly owner. Initially, this may seem like a cruel act by a genuinely cold-hearted and ignorant man. However, it is important to look at the man behind the action before casting judgment. In his youth, many pet owners put their pets down in what I call "The Old Yeller method" of euthanasia. He honestly did care for his dog; he truly did want to relieve his suffering. Maybe the method is horrific to some, but to this old man, the act of euthanizing his old friend with the same toxic gas some choose to end their own life seemed humane-better than a twenty-two-caliber bullet to the head his father would have used half a century before. He honestly believed the end justified the means.

However, in the court of public opinion, many believed he should have been convicted of animal cruelty. Perhaps slapped with a hefty fine or even a few months in county jail. They felt his antiquated logic was no excuse for his dog's suffering. The dog could have been euthanized using a more human method.

That is one of my most important responsibilities, as a veterinarian. However, to place a seventy-five-year-old man in jail for just trying to end his beloved dog's suffering, as misguided as he was, would also be cruel.

Today, an increasingly more common cause of soft abuse is the psychological disorder of hoarding. Pet hoarding presents two vital questions to animal control officers. Do you convict an individual who has no malicious intent because they have chosen to collect pets like other people collect baseball cards? Then, how to rehabilitate and relocate those animals, confiscated from these homes. In a recent hoarding case in a central New Jersey over sixty dogs were discovered in varying degrees of medical need, living in the filth, cramped into small cages in an average size range home. This case physically strained the county shelter. In this case, the local rescues were indispensable in finding homes for many of these desperate animals.

The second type of abuse is what I call hard abuse — intentional, malicious animal cruelty. Like the Husky I had seen in the early nineties it usually results in derangement or death of the animal. Last year the local shelter was called to a home where a young Dachshund was dead on the scene. The women believed her estranged ex-husband had abused the dog. My initial examination of the dog didn't reveal any external wounds, but it did reveal a more profound trauma; when I palpated the neck, the spine crunched like a bag of corn flakes. Radiographs showed the fragmented bones of the cervical spine. I shaved the dog's neck, and I could easily see the bruised outline of a shoe print on her right side, from her jaw to her shoulder. Someone's foot had crushed the dog's

Almost A Real Doctor

cervical spine. It was apparent what killed the dog; however, who killed the dog was still a mystery. Following an investigation, the husband cleared due to a lack of tangible evidence.

Divorce and domestic squabbles are a common excuse for animal abuse, like the case of a jilted boyfriend who drowned his girlfriend's cat in a bucket of water. Then the case of the girl who in a jealous rage threw her fiancé's Chihuahua out of a three-story window just over the half-naked body of his new lover. However, one hot summer day in 2015 I witnessed a new category of animal abuse.

The local animal control officer walked into my air-conditioned, sweet-smelling office with a large, plaid blanket that carried with it an odor worse than death. "You've have got to see this," Miguel proudly exclaimed as he placed the rolled blanket on the treatment table. "I found this on the beach this morning. You better get a mask and put on some gloves," he added as he slowly unrolled the blanket.

The putrid stench which crawled under my surgical mask was unbearable to my nose, but the sight of the contents of the blanket was an offense to my eyes. Steven King could not have imagined this in his worst nightmare. It contained two exsanguinated chickens, the severed heads of four roosters, along with their amputated feet, yellow corn, black beans, squash, and finally a varied array of coins adding up to one dollar and eighty-three cents. "What the hell is this?"

"The best I can tell is that they used this as some prop for witchcraft or a voodoo ritual," Miguel answered quickly.

"Are you telling me this is like a black magic blanket? Like a ritual to bring zombies back to life?" I asked.

"I don't know about zombies, but voodoo is my best guess. I've seen shit like this when I lived down in the islands," Miguel replied.

"Yes, but this is New Jersey, not Haiti. I wouldn't be surprised if you found a bloated mob guy wash up on shore, but this, no way. Do you have any idea who did this?"

"Well, not really, they didn't leave their business card," Miquel quipped. "I'll report this to the police and will see what happens. I doubt we will find out who did it. However, let me know if you see any of the walking dead coming in with a sick rooster."

"Oh, I'll let you know, after I shoot them in the head," I joked. The pungent odor hung heavy in my treatment room for two days. Miguel was correct; they never did find one clue as to the perpetrators of this bizarre crime. However, for a good two weeks, I would often look over my shoulder, as I walked to my car in the warm summer twilight. I would listen for the telltale sound of a dragging foot, and the occasional grunt of a mindless, hungry flesh-eating zombie.

The third class of animal abuse is what I call, abuse for profit. When I was in farm animal medicine block in Missouri, I spent a day on a swine farm which doubled as a puppy mill. They were breeding dogs which only remotely resembled Yorkshire Terriers. They housed about thirty dogs; each kept in a wire cage the size of a toaster oven suspended three feet off the muddy ground; exposed to the harsh winter winds and the scorching summers. Each morning pigs would eat the excrement from underneath the cages. The dogs were only released from their wire prison to breed and whelp their puppies. The farmers would vaccinate, deworm, and medicate their dogs using drugs they would obtain from pharmaceutical supply houses; rarely under a veterinarian's supervision. Years of inbreeding produced puppies with poor conformation, congenital abnormalities, and inherited defects. Then these puppies are sold to pet shops in the Midwest and throughout the country.

Twenty years later one of these "puppy mill" pet shops opened a half mile from my practice. The proprietor would sell a pathetic facsimile of a myriad of breeds from Golden Retrievers to Yorkshire Terriers. He obtained these puppies from puppy mill farms in Oklahoma and Missouri for about seventy-five dollars; he then would sell them to the dog-loving public for over two thousand dollars. I would see these puppies a week after their adoption by naïve, compassionate owners who couldn't understand why these dogs were sick. Many had intestinal parasites, mange, ear mites, viral infections, and bacterial pneumonia. Some suffered from poor hygiene, dietary insufficiency, and stress-related illness. They all had poor confirmation and genetic diseases, such as canine hip dysplasia which were ticking time bombs ready to destroy the lives of these dogs as they matured- long after the owners had formed a tight bond with their pets. It became almost a weekly exercise to document the puppy with multiple abnormalities; it became far too common to sign a "certificate of unfitness." This document and the New Jersey State Dog Lemon law gave the owners legal recourse against the pet shop. They could either return the dog for a replacement, but many people had already fallen in love with these dogs, or they could seek reimbursement for medical bills; up to twice the cost of the dog. However, the pet shop owner didn't always honor these requests; he would deny culpability by claiming my medical opinion was unsound misguided by prejudice; thus, not his responsibility. In many cases, they had to pursue legal means to obtain compensation.

In one case, an owner paid eighteen hundred dollars for a six-month English bulldog named Rocky- he had more things wrong than were right. In three veterinary visits, I diagnosed two skin parasites, four species of intestinal worms, a massive underbite, and hips so far out of their sockets that the femur was not in the same zip code as the pelvis; the dog could barely climb the three stairs to get in the woman's house. They met her complaints with resistance. "That vet doesn't know what he is talking about," he would say. "Besides, that guy has a personal vendetta against me. After all, I 'm just trying to earn an honest living."

She called an attorney. I called a special friend at the New Jersey state SPCA. I first meet this man during a procerus set of events a year before. The local shelter was under investigation for an incident involving two Pitbull dogs who had escaped from their yard and attacked two men jogging down the road; one was a police officer. The director of the shelter captured the dogs and appropriately humanely euthanized the pair. Unfortunately, the dog's owners and a local Pitbull rescue thought the action unwarranted. They expeditiously filed a complaint with the state SPCA; this challenged the fundamental rights of the dogs, versus the responsibility of the shelter to protect the public. They accused the shelter of euthanizing these dogs without legal or ethical authority. I had not put these dogs to sleep, but I had worked with the shelter for almost ten years. I was guilty by association; they had questioned my ethics. The one contract I had worked so hard to obtain was threatening my reputation.

The state officer flashed his shiny gold badge a few seconds after entering the front door. He shot the serious dead gaze of a state trooper as he approaches your window wielding a Mag flashlight and asks for your license and registration. A fifty-five-year-old, seriously burly man wearing an official looking vest and hat introduced himself. "Donald S. Jacobs, deputy New Jersey SPCA. Doctor, can I have a moment of your time?"

"Sure, sure come on in." I was glad he had told me who he was because I didn't look at his badge. He could have been a meat inspector for all I knew. We walked back to my office, and he shut the door behind me as I sat, proudly in my black vinyl desk chair.

"Before I tell you why I'm here I want to let you know up front, we can do this, one of two ways. Either you can be forthcoming and give me the information I need today, or I can come back tomorrow with two state troopers and a warrant, then you will be forced to give me what I need."

Immediately, my confidence scurried under my desk as my disappearing freedom flashed before my eyes. I had visions of sitting in a six by eight-foot concrete cell carving small pocket pets out of a bar of soap while enjoying a committed relationship with a three-hundred-pound felon. So, of course, I screamed at the fears dancing in my head, "I'm too young and pretty to be in prison. Orange is not my color!"

However, outwardly, I said just one word, "Absolutely!"

"Good, let me also tell you," he stated with a calming smile. "I am not looking to implicate you or this hospital. I know you have a clean record. There have only been two complaints in the last ten years. One was a false claim, and this current claim is going to find you blameless."

Two months before I had prescribed a twelve-year-old Labrador a non-steroidal anti-inflammatory drug for arthritis; the dog died two weeks later of heart disease. She asserted, the medication was poison and killed her dog. I couldn't believe this gentleman already knew the result of a case, still being reviewed by the state board of veterinary medicine; I had been agonizing over this complaint for over a month. He knew everything about my career, where I had graduated, where I had worked, and even references obtained through personal interviews.

"I'm looking for a pattern. I'm looking for a pattern of abuse at the shelter; which in some cases was approved by the director. They have been accused of taking a cavalier attitude when it comes to euthanizing pets — performing unwarranted euthanasia. So, what I want is a detailed history of the euthanasia's performed at this hospital, which was sanctioned by the shelter, for the last two years. I need names, dates, and the reasons for these animals were put down. If it seems there is a pattern, as with the two Pitbull dogs who attacked the men a week ago, then we have a problem. If there is not a pattern, then we don't have a problem. Then you don't have a problem. I would appreciate this information by Friday afternoon."

I submitted the information by the end of the week. I couldn't have been more cooperative. I felt like a rat like I was squealing on the shelter, and you know what they do to rats at the shelter. I had a big fear of sleeping with the fishes, but I had a bigger fear of sleeping with a guy in cell block "C" they call "Piledriver."

Three meetings and a month later the case was closed. Officer Jacobs found no evidence of inappropriate or unethical treatment with the shelter, its director, or with me. I breathed again, oh the sweet smell of freedom. During our time together, Officer Jacobs and I, developed an excellent professional relationship. He would call to consult on possible abuse cases throughout the state. I would offer my opinion and even wrote a few depositions that hopefully would lead to convictions. I was willing to help him, so when I called him about this degenerate pet shop owner, he was happy to help.

My complaint was not the first to reach his desk. In the twelve months, this pet shop had received ten complaints documentary various egregious acts of deception; defective, sick and dying puppies sold to naïve people for a two-thousand percent profit. The officer new a great deal about the puppy farm industry; he also knew a great deal about this gentleman. The pet shop owner had owned a similar retail puppy shop in Northern New Jersey and had been driven out of business two years before. Now he was trying again; he was either arrogant or stupid, even using the same business name, Perfect Puppies.

I told my wife the night after I met with the state officer, "I don't know what I must do, but I swear to you I am going to make it my life's mission to drive

Defending the Innocent

that man out of business." I continued to report each new sick puppy I examined from the less than perfect puppy shop. The shop owner fought each case; rarely reimbursing the pet owners for their medical bills. Many just gave up, content to love their challenged puppies through the rest of their troubled lives. By the end of the following summer, under mounting public pressure, Perfect Puppies closed its doors, forever. The following week the public health department inspected the abandoned eight-hundred square foot shop. Among numerous violations, the inspector found ten frozen puppies in a small Kenmore freezer. Those dogs did not live long enough, or were fortunate enough, to be adopted by one of those loving, naïve owners who would have saved them from this abuse for profit tragedy. Like Mr. Whitehead's yellow Labrador two decades before they were the victims of the irresponsible puppy mill industry. However, unlike his dog, they never made it to a veterinarian who swore the day of graduation, "…to protect animal health and welfare…"

Although many larger chain pet shops have either gone out of business or stopped selling puppies, there is still a significant concern with the sale of puppy mill puppies. I routinely see mixed breed puppies, now called designer breeds, bred at puppy mills in Pennsylvania, Ohio, Missouri, and Oklahoma. These mutts are sold for thousands of dollars by small pet shops which use words like professional, breeders, and purebreds, to sell to a passionate and naïve public. Many have poor confirmation, parasites, and congenital defects. Pet owners still face resistance when seeking reimbursement for these medical issues. Unfortunately, neither the AKC nor governing bodies of those states have applied much-needed pressure to prevent these abusive, deceptive sales practices. In 2017, New Jersey governor, Chris Christie, vetoed a bill which would have restricted the sale of puppies from puppy mill breeders. The governor affirmed this bill would have limited free commerce and would adversely impact small business. The impact on small puppies is incalculable.

Veterinarians must be the guardians of animal welfare; our experience, knowledge, and unique perspective give us the credibility no other professionals possess. However, this ethical responsibility involves much more than identifying potential abuse cases and casting judgment, it also requires considering the circumstances and exhibiting some degree of compassion for the owner, as well as, for the animal. Every case is unique, thus, requires careful consideration before indictment. Animal welfare and animal rights are not interchangeable. The scope of an animal's rights is debatable, not so with an animal's welfare. Many non-professionals confuse welfare with an animal's inalienable rights; pets are still property in fifty states and thus legally do not possess the rights of their human owners. It is this personification of animals that can lead to radical agendas which do nothing but cloud the real issue of animal welfare. Whether it is a good-hearted pet rescue, an ignorant owner who overfeeds her beagle, or a hopeless old man who regrettably chooses to euthanize his best friend, it is our moral obligation to examine each case with compassionate, informed contemplation.

In 1988, when I stood on that stage with seventy-five other graduating students the words,

"…the protection of animal health and welfare…" had yet to be included in the official veterinary oath. The profession has developed these principles and concepts incumbent to this oath over the three decades spanning my entire career. Like this oath, my professional view has grown to address the essential concepts of the humane treatment of animals and my inherent responsibility to protect the welfare of all my patients.

CHAPTER 13

KNOCKING ON HEAVEN'S DOOR

"God's finger touched him, and he slept."

- Alfred, Lord Tennyson

I am often asked two questions about euthanasia. Clients frequently ask, "How do you do it? I always wanted to be a vet, but I couldn't put animals to sleep." By understanding the meaning of my oath; by knowing I have done my job. Each case is unique. Some cases are much more stressful than others; some clients are devastated, some are relieved, some like many senior citizens are in a state of quiet consolation, some owners are hysterical, some will feel eternal guilt like my mother. My hope is they will understand it was the right thing to do. The most mindful part of this process is to have the professional experience and personal confidence to look directly into another person's eye, regardless of their mental state and say, "It is time to put your pet down." Then later to know, unequivocally, you gave them the correct advice. That is an incredible responsibility.

The second question I am asked, "What would you do if this were your pet?" All of us in the veterinary profession have made that decision with our pets. In twenty years of marriage, I have made that choice ten times; six dogs, two chinchillas, one mouse, and a parakeet; I euthanized all of them. I know what it feels like to put a pet down and later ask myself, "Did I do the right thing?"

I draw from a lifetime of my sorrow and my torment. When I was eight-years-old my father bought my brother and me two rabbits; not surprisingly I called my rabbit Bugs, and my brother's rabbit was Peter. We kept them in my Grandfather's chicken coup for over three years. One summer they contracted a virus which affected the central nervous system causing seizures and eventually coma. A veterinarian advised us to put them down immediately. In the '60s methods of euthanasia were less humane than today, people were less likely to spend money on something they could do themselves. I can still envision my father lifting my grandfather's old shovel high over his head and clubbing the rabbits to death. I knew then they had to be put down, I could see they were suffering; I also knew I would always remember that horrid scene in my grandfather's hen house. Today's methods of humane euthanasia are quiet and painless. However, with each euthanasia, I still ask for

God for three things in prayer; an uncomplicated euthanasia, comfort for the owner, and a blessing for the soul of the animal.

Personally, the most challenging pet to lose was a twelve-year-old Golden Retriever mix named, Shakin. He was named after a nineteen fifties song, "Shake" by Sam Cooke. His name became his trademark. He had one major fault, a horrific and sometimes violent reaction to thunderstorms. Upon hearing the virtually imperceptible vibrations of the approaching thunderclouds, he would stand and reverberate with tremors that started in his jaw, undulated along his back and down his back legs. When he was confined, he would become so unhinged, he would fight his way out of his cage or out of a closed room. He would chew through his cage destroying and bending the metal bars like a canine Hercules. During one storm, while confined to a small bedroom, he ate through the frame of a glass window before jumping through the jagged glass so he could get to safety under a backyard deck. The bedroom looked like an NCIS crime scene with the blood from his mouth spattered on the bedspread and curtains. He suffered no long-term effects, but he did teach us a valuable lesson, that we could never confine him again.

We all have weaknesses, and we all have our strengths. Shakin's strength was his unwavering loyalty and pure dedication to my wife. He would follow her twenty-four hours a day; standing alongside her during every activity. He could sense the approach of her car before she pulled into our driveway. He was her protector and our watchdog for the first ten years of our marriage. If any dog would have given his life for their owner, it would have been Shakin. When I worked an overnight shift at the emergency clinic, I knew my wife would always be safe with Shakin at her side. I grew exceptionally found of this skinny, gentile dog laying at the foot of our bed.

Then one day in his thirteenth year I noticed a firm lump over his left hip. The next week I surgically removed an ugly black grape-like mass which extended deep into his hip joint. Three days later the pathologist reported it to be a very aggressive, malignant nerve sheath tumor. Shakin started to feel better for a short time; we were hopeful. Then two weeks after surgery, he began to limp. A few days later his leg was paralyzed. He was in such pain that he would stand, leg held to the side, panting. He tried his best to follow my wife throughout the house, but he was unable to climb the stairs to our second-floor bedroom. We spoke briefly about amputating his leg but just couldn't put him through the pain of that surgery-we knew we had to end his agony. The last night of his life I carried him up the stairs and laid him on the foot of our bed to guard my wife one last time.

In the morning, I euthanized Shakin on our kitchen floor, on the small rug where he would often lay as my wife cooked dinner for my oldest son. He laid motionless, cradled in my wife's arms as I injected the final overdose of barbiturate into his vein. With tears running down her face she asked, "Are you sure we are doing the right thing?"

Unable to speak I nodded my head in confident affirmation. Shakin wasn't the dog he once was; in his condition, he could no longer protect her, he could no longer sit by her side as she fed our baby, he could no longer stand patiently waiting for her to come through the door after her call pulled into our driveway. I remember the final expression on his face which seemed to say, "It's all right, you've got to let me go. It just hurts so much." When he took his last breath, I listened for a heartbeat in his silent chest. I turned my head and started to cry; in my silence, my wife knew his life was over.

My five-year-old son was present during the whole procedure. I always wanted my children to appreciate life and respect death, so I didn't shield them from this reality. I wondered how he would react to the loss of a dog who had been there since he was born. His had a tear in his eye as I wrapped Shakin in a blanket and placed him in the trunk of my car. I then transported him to the hospital for cremation. Two weeks later my son asked me a question, "Dad, when are you going to take Shakin out of the trunk? You know he doesn't like small spaces." I think he handled the whole death issue, as well as, most adults.

All graduates from American schools of veterinary medicine swear an oath which includes, "…the prevention and relief of animal suffering…" Unique to our profession is the relief of suffering by elective euthanasia. This is a tremendous responsibility. It is one I approach with sober consideration based primarily on the condition of the animal; whether it is a dog or cat, a raccoon or seagull. If the animal is suffering and recovery is unlikely; I recommend euthanasia. I use the word recommend because that decision lies, except for wildlife, ultimately with the owner. That decision rests on a clear understanding of the pet's condition, cost of treatment, and the prognosis for recovery. In a moment, they will be asked to make the most critical decisions in their pet's life; this is an end of life choice.

In these cases, I bring a lifetime of influences, both professional and personal; these influences combined with my religious beliefs, my ethical obligation, and my moral compass guide my approach in the act of euthanasia. It has matured through twenty-five years of practice. My approach may differ from other veterinarians, but we all struggle with this most sensitive aspect of veterinary medicine. My job is to convince a stranger to put their beloved pet to sleep. Then I must go home that night with the confidence I have led them done the right path.

On the contrary, many clients have already decided to put their sick animal down before the walk into my clinic. My responsibility is to listen to their needs, without judgment and offer some basic treatment or diagnostic options. Sometimes it about reading their faces, understanding their concerns and respecting their wishes. However, ultimately, I must support their choice because I know the agony of making that final decision. They already feel guilty; they think they are solely responsible for killing their pet. I assure them I understand; I assure them I would be making the same choice if it were my pet. Finally, I encourage them to look at it this way, "You have given your pet a long, comfortable life. Now she is in pain, and it is now our responsibility to relieve that pain. It's time to let her go."

Some owners are unaware or unwilling to recognize the severity of their animal's condition. When it is usually evident on a physical exam that their pet is critically ill, or when lab work is irrefutable, and I can identify an accurate terminal diagnosis these owners are blind-sided by my recommendation to euthanize their animal. They honestly thought something was wrong but not "that." Understandably, they often ask if they could take them home, for a night or just for the weekend, to spend some time with the family, and then they will be back to put them down. That time spent with their pet not only acts as a final farewell, but it solidifies their ultimate decision. "You're right Doc I can tell she's in pain, once I looked at her, I could tell she is not the dog I once knew. My wife and I can't stand to see her suffer any longer."

Then they can return with the resolve to perform the humane act they had not been prepared to do a few days before-it's an essential process of realization and acceptance.

Some will walk into the office with the quick disclaimer, "Let's get one thing straight. We're not putting her to sleep, no way." Then when I explain how sick their pet is truly terminal, they reply, "Then I'll let her die at home." Many of these pets present in the worst condition; emaciated, unable to walk, or they stand leaning against the wall, panting, drooling, and in obvious pain. It seems obvious that it is time to euthanize the pet. The owners have various reasons for their refusal to put their pet down; they don't believe in it, they want her to die at home, so they don't have to make the decision, or in one case, "Before my wife died, she told me never to put her down, no matter what."

This is selfish, foolish reasoning. My oath is first to the pet, "To prevent and relieve animal suffering." However, the pet owner makes the final decision, as these pets are their property, and more importantly, their family; I can't force them to euthanize their pet. It becomes a delicate task which sometimes turns into a battle to change their view of euthanasia, and their responsibility to do the final act of love and end their pet's agony. Finally, is it logical to believe a departed spouse would want their beloved pet to remain on this earth in mortal agony? When clients say, that they do not believe in euthanasia, I can only answer with two words, "I do." I have dedicated my life to a profession whose ultimate duty is to relieve the pain and suffering of pets regardless of how illogical an owner may be.

My approach starts in a sensitive plea for the client to look at their animal, see the signs of pain, realize she is no longer functioning as the pet they once knew, and then to understand the finality of her condition. I point out that a dog who can longer walk has lost fifty percent of her joy in life; Playing, eating, and sleeping are the three daily goals of a house dog. If they can't do these things, they cease to be living things, and they cease to be pets.

Cats are unique; they linger-sometimes for weeks. Evolution has blessed them with the stoic peculiarity, to hide their illness. They stop eating and drinking, lose weight, dehydrate, and quietly find some cold, dark hiding place to die. Cats linger until they die.

Some of these clients choose treatment on terminal cases with the unrealistic hope of survival-many times I can only ask, "To what end?" To put their animal through stressful procedures, chemotherapy, surgery, or long-term hospitalization, just for a few more days or weeks of life. They need to be fully informed before they make their choice. Of course, veterinary surgeons and oncologists save and extend lives every day, but pet owners need to think realistically about the path they are taking. An example is the pet owner who had his West Highland Terrier's lower jaw removed to remove a cancerous melanoma. Following surgery, the dog attempted in vain to suck down enough of a dog food gruel to provide nourishment to stay alive; after four weeks of watching this daily struggle, the owner elected to put the dog down-vowing never again to put a pet through that kind of procedure. Dr. Klein would often ask, "Should we do, just because we can?"

There are some who want pain medication, and so they can take her home to die. This decision is naive, cruel, and self-serving. Some want to get their pet through Christmas, or the holidays, to imply these animals are consciously holding on until their next milestone. Animals don't know what is around the corner, and they do not plan. They feel comfort or anxiety, pleasure or pain. When they are in pain, they want it to stop.

In one frustrating abuse case, I reported the client to the State SPCA because the owner had refused treatment and euthanasia for their Rottweiler after it had suffered from a radial fracture from end-stage bone cancer. Bone cancer is a terminal disease which can cause weeks of agonizing pain long before it kills the dog. Limb amputation can relieve the pain but still doesn't cure the dog. I guilted them into finally euthanizing the dog; his hellish nightmare soon ended. I had done my job.

When I started to offer house call services, I didn't realize that over half of those visits would be a call to euthanize a pet. These emotional experiences are sometimes as hard for us as they are for the owner. They don't just end a pet's life; they can also end a long professional and personal relationship.

Euthanasia was far from our minds when we first entered the home of Mr. J. P. Foster for the first time; we were there for routine healthcare. Mr. Foster and his wife, Claire, owned a very friendly, grossly overweight, middle age, male, black Labrador, named Chief; his name was Mr. Foster's rank in the Navy; he was a chief petty officer in the Korean War.

When we first walked into his oak-paneled, suburban ranch house we were immediately struck by the dark, thick smoke cloud hanging at eye level and not in a sultry, back alley, New Orleans jazz club kind of way. It was more like a moldy, basement poker game kind of way; Mr. and Mrs. Foster were seasoned chain smokers. The room was always dark because Mr. Foster was legally blind; he didn't need illumination or obviously, ventilation. They were a throwback to the fifties; she was a frail, white-haired, woman in her mid-seventies, Mr. Foster was a year or two older who retained his jet-black hair and a donut shop full of carbs which he proudly stored in his ample midsection. She would scurry around tending to his every need, while he sat entrenched on their old plaid couch smoking pack after pack of filtered cigarettes. Chief had one other roommate a yellow and green budgerigar, named Gunny.

When I first met Gunny, he was sitting motionless in a small dining room bird cage-I thought he was dead-rigor freezing him on his perch. Many birds squawk loudly when an unfamiliar face enters their room. Gunny didn't move or utter a sound. I wondered if it was because he couldn't see us through the low hanging fog or because he was living in oxygen-thin air closer to the surface of Mars than a house in Central New Jersey. I also wondered if that was his natural color or he had been turned yellow by smoke like the dining room curtains and Mr. Foster's old t-shirts. Slowly, I wondered back behind his cage and whispered a question, "Gunny want a CPAP?"

We did house calls to the Fosters for about four years. Every time we entered their home before we even looked at Chief, Mr. Foster would ask, if there any ladies present. Each time I would reply, "Well, I have two women with me, but I can't tell you if they are ladies." He would laugh and then ask if we wanted to hear a joke. Each story he told, was what his generation called, blue humor. They usually involved some combination of a nurse, a navy seaman, a priest, and a lifeboat. With the delivery of every dirty punchline his wife would meekly scold him, "Now, John Paul, these girls don't want to hear your dirty Jokes." He would then reply, "Oh, mind your own business, Honey. I'll make you wait in the car." Every time we went to J.P.'s house we were eager to find out two things; the punchline of his next dirty joke and if that poor Budgerigar, Gunny, was still alive.

In the spring of the fourth year of my practice, Mr. Foster called for another annual wellness check on Chief. The clouds of smoke still hung heavy in the dark living room, and that bird still sat speechless on his perch. Mr. Foster again asked if there were ladies present and then he told his dirty joke of the day. However, something was missing; his wife's gentle reprimand. Claire had passed away over Christmas. He reminded us, "She would have scolded me if she were still here." Then for the very first time, he told us how he met his wife: "She was a Navy nurse, and we met while on leave in Japan, over fifty years now. She couldn't resist my humor," he added, with a childish grin. He for the first time had tears in his cloudy eyes.

Six months later we diagnosed the twelve-year-old Chief with renal failure and chronic arthritis; Mr. Foster chose to put Chief down, "To let him be with my wife," he said. "I want him to die with dignity in his own home. Not like Claire who died in a cold hospital bed on Christmas day." When we left with Chief's body that late afternoon in October, Mr. Foster had tears running down his cheeks for the second time. Gunny still said nothing.

The week after Christmas, Robin, my head technician noticed a familiar name in the local obituary column: "John Paul Foster, 80, died on Christmas day, of respiratory failure." A year to the day after his wife's passing, he was reunited with Claire and his dog, Chief. Recently, I passed by The Foster's home on the way to another house call in his old neighborhood, and I wondered if that poor bird, still sat motionless on his perch silently waiting for someone to open a window.

Senior citizens deal with the loss of their pet with sober, acceptance. It may be that the longer the years one lives, the more one accepts the inevitability of death; or maybe they don't want their beloved pets to experience the slow, painful decline they encounter every day. Many seniors have told me they wish euthanasia were legal option to end human suffering.

Mr. David James brought his nineteen-year-old cat in because he "wasn't doing well." The orange male cat was skin pulled over bone, dehydrated and weak. The cat's light brown eyes were sunken deep into their sockets, his mouth hung open as drool dripped down onto the table. Mr. James was in his mid-eighties; he wore thick glasses which outlined his own sunken eyes. His bald head was speckled with tiny irregular liver spots. After a quick discussion, he finally said out loud what he knew for a week; it was time to put his cat down. He adopted the cat almost twenty years before as a Valentine's Day present for his wife; she had died last month. In just five minutes we granted his wish. After his cat was gone, I shook his cold, leathery hand and patted the boney shoulder of his ninety-pound frame. He had loved and lost for the second time in three months; today he knew he did the right thing.

Young people tend to be less pragmatic and more emotional; for them, death seems to be a long way off. When I recommend euthanasia, they dismiss it as just an excuse to give up. Some become stubborn, and angry-some will even punch a kitchen cabinet. Sometimes the young people try to take control until their parents order them to leave the room. However, in one instance the parents were not even in the same country, and that made my job much more difficult.

Thomas Lent was the proud owner of three unneutered Cane Corsos; each was a hundred and fifty pounds of purely unbridled testosterone. The owner muzzled them so that we could walk in the exam room. The oldest was a precious gift of inbred genetics, appropriately named, Lucifer. He not only had to be muzzled, but he also had to be sedated just to touch the tip of his tail-my mother would have said he was rotten to the core-he would fight the effects of the tranquilizers for almost an hour before he crumbled to the ground in a deep, gurgling, growling mass of evil.

One summer morning I saw the name Lucifer Lent in bold letters under my ten O'clock appointment slot. It said, under complaint, "Not getting up." I knew then that sunny morning was going to turn stormy. Lucifer came in just before ten, not with Mr. Lent but with his three teenage sons. They carried him into the office on a stretcher; Lucifer was unable to walk. Mr. Lent was out of the country, vacationing in Cancun, Mexico. Now his three sons, each a gurgling, growling mass of indolence, were in charge.

The was the first time in his eight years of life I was able to perform a complete exam without giving the dog a date rape drug. He was weak, bloated, and his gums were almost pure white. Radiographs revealed what I had suspected: a softball size splenic tumor which had already ruptured and bled into the abdomen-he bled so much his hematocrit was half of what it should have been-he had almost bled to death.

Most tumors of the spleen are hemangiosarcomas, cancer which usually leads to the death of the dog within six months. In Lucifer's case, he was already in shock. If an attempt were made to remove the tumor surgically, he would be a poor anesthetic risk, even with a blood transfusion and intensive care. I often see this disease in large breed dogs, and a favorable outcome is uncommon. I owned a Golden Retriever, named Ashley ten years before with the same type of tumor. I performed a very difficult and very bloody splenectomy. She barely survived the initial procedure only to suffer the ravages of metastatic cancer five months later. I euthanized her on the same throw rug on my kitchen floor where Shakin took his last breath. It was then I vowed that I would never put another one of my pets through that type of surgery to gain only a few months of life. I knew this disease very well.

The Lent boys had two options: immediate transport to a surgical referral practice or euthanasia. With their reaction to that ten-letter word I now knew where the dogs got their temperate. Jeff the oldest, screamed, "No frigging way!"

The middle boy, Brian, added, "This sucks!" The youngest boy, twelve-year-old Tommy, just started to cry.

"Why can't you just take out the tumor, now, and save his life?"

"It's not that easy Jeff," I said. Even if he lived through surgery and I removed the tumor is will most probably eventually kill him. You can opt for surgery, but you need to make that decision today, or he certainly will die."

"I better call my dad."

During the next thirty minutes, I spoke with Mr. Lent in a three thousand mile call over a tiny flip phone. I worked hard to convince him that Lucifer was dying; his only real option was euthanasia. The entire time I spoke I stood at the head of a dying dog and three emotional teenagers. I had known Mr. Lent for about ten years, that trust was essential to convince a man a continent away to put one of his prize dogs out of its misery. I believe I galvanized his decision when I told him I was kneeling next to him with my hand in his mouth and he wasn't even growling. He knew that wasn't Lucifer. His affirmation was not taken well by his three sons. He addressed their anger with an order to leave the room to allow me to do my job. They left me alone with the speakerphone and Lucifer as I put the dog to sleep. Mr. Lent was grateful I had ended his dogs suffering-his sons were not as complimentary-they slammed the front door on the way out, hurling obscenities as they left. Even with a dog, we had considered evil, I still empathized with his owner and had sympathy for the dog. I euthanized Lucifer because of the same reason I had euthanized my dog Ashley ten years before, except, I don't believe they went to the same place (I think you know what I mean).

The most difficult euthanasias are not those performed in front of senior citizens, or even those done in front of agitated teenagers, the most difficult euthanasias are those done in the presence of children. Jonathan Youngblood was a survivor. He was a boy born with a rare congenital disease with a mortality rate approaching ninety percent. Abnormal development of the ventricles of his brain caused hydrocephalus and delayed neurologic development which can lead to seizures, coma, and death. He was now eighteen-years-old and had just survived his twentieth surgery. He still had occasional seizures, and still could not wholly function on his own-forever relying on his parents compassionate, unyielding care. On his third birthday, his parents bought a little white Maltese he named Twinkie. (He named the dog after his favorite lullaby: Twinkle, Twinkle, Little Star).

I first diagnosed Twinkie with an early renal disease when the dog was fourteen. He did well, Jonathan took complete responsibility for his care and medication. His mother always said that little dog was support for Johnathan through a decade of surgeries and medical setbacks and felt obligated to be there for Twinkie. However, now a year later the dog was suffering from end-stage renal disease, he was failing, despite Jonathan's constant attention to Twinkie's medical care.

I received the call on a Sunday morning. Mrs. Youngblood didn't think Twinkie would live through the day and asked if I could euthanize Jonathan's dog, humanly and quietly in their home. My wife and I arrived just after noon. Mr. and Mrs. Youngblood led us to the rear sunroom where Jonathan sat on a sofa holding Twinkie in a light blue baby blanket. The dog laid motionless with short, barely perceptible, shallow breaths. We gave Jonathan and Twinkie a final five minutes together as Mrs. Youngblood spoke quietly about the connection, he had with his dog over the last fifteen years. She couldn't remember the last time Jonathan slept in his bed without that little dog laying under the covers sleeping by his side. They even brought Twinkie to the hospital during Jonathan's frequent stays in rehab. I asked her if Jonathan knew what was going to happen and she replied, "Absolutely, he even told Twinkie someday he'll see him again when Twinkie's kidneys would be working again."

Jonathan held Twinkie wrapped in the blanket as I gave the final injection into his front leg. Twinkie took his last shallow breath just as Jonathan kissed him on the top of his head. As I turned to give Mrs. Youngblood a nod of final affirmation, I could hear Jonathan's high voice from behind quietly singing a familiar lullaby: "Twinkle, Twinkle, little star, How I wonder what you are…" My German shell crumbled once again.

What do I say when I am asked, "How do you put animals to sleep?" I have a loyal client whose, twenty-two-year-old son, Mark, was killed in a tragic motorcycle accident on a frigid winter night. They bought him a little King Charles Spaniel named Natalie for his eighth birthday. This past month the little Spaniel was failing; she was euthanized almost a year after Mark's death. His mother sent me a letter a week later thanking me for my help and stating, "Now Natalie can be reunited with Mark once again." How do I answer the question, "How do you put animals to sleep?" I do it for the animals, and I do it for the owners who love them. Each pet I euthanize leaves another small scar in my heart. I cover those scars with an emotional band-aid, and I tuck the memory of those pets in a special place. I occasionally visit that place and gently peel back that band-aid when I need to remind myself of the reason, I became a veterinarian.

CHAPTER 14

THE WORST-CASE SCENARIO

"For over a thousand years, Roman conquerors returning from the wars enjoyed the honor of triumph, a tumultuous parade... A slave stood behind the conqueror [in a chariot] holding a golden crown and whispering in his ear a warning:

That all glory is fleeting."

- Gen. George C. Patton

The highest peak of my early adult life was when I received my acceptance into veterinary school. This moment was quickly followed by the lowest valley of my early adult life when I realized I was accepted into veterinary school, and I had four more years of hard work before I could be called a "real doctor." When I was in vet school, I measured a triumph in a passing grade and a tragedy in a clinician's reprimand during grand rounds. When I entered practice, I measured a triumph in a thank you card from a grateful client and a tragedy in a verbal lashing from the boss. When I started my own business, I measured a triumph in a saved life and a good online review and a tragedy in a surgical mishap and an impending lawsuit. Thankfully, there are many more hills than there are valleys. Winston Churchill once said, "The price of greatness is responsibility." For those of us who are merely mediocre; every day in practice, every client we see, and every patient we touch affirms that responsibility. The weight of that responsibility excites me, humbles me, and terrifies me, all at the same time.

  Recently I read an excerpt from an opinion column of a well-known syndicated veterinarian which implied that veterinarians are money hungry professionals with big heads and bulging pockets. In my opinion, this characterization is unfounded. I have never been greedy, my ego has always been cachectic, and my head deflates with a tiny pin-prick. I can see ninety-nine clients in a week who are genuinely grateful for my services, offer praise for my expertise, and compliment my professionalism. Then I can have one client who complains about the bill, questions my recommendations, or criticizes my judgment-that one client poisons my week. I don't take compliments well; criticism I take worse. Perhaps I wasn't smothered in praise as a child, or maybe in the back of my mind echoes the old proverb: "Pride goes before destruction, a haughty spirit before a fall." In my experience, it is almost always true. I try not to let praise alone feed my ego or support my confidence. In respect of my good Christian faith I live by the motto, "First give the glory to God," for every success. Then the failures, well they are on me. Dr. Klein would constantly warn me to prepare myself for the inevitable fall from grace; he would often say, "Just wait, wait for the other shoe to drop."

We deal with peaks and valleys almost every day; this may be what initially attracted me to this profession. Mr. Whitehead is a perfect example of one of those peaks. The lives of his three dogs spanned over twenty-five years of my career. Some clients remind me how grateful they were when I came to the house to end their dogs suffering. When I put their dog down, they trusted my judgment and praised me for my honesty. These same clients returned two weeks later with a new puppy or kitten; another young life entrusted to my care. Some of the most straightforward cases garner the most praise. Like a routine surgery to remove a simple tumor, or a hypoglycemic puppy brought back from life with basic supportive care, or a simple skin problem heroically cured with steroids and flea control. Then there is the young child who sent me a hand-drawn thank you card to show her appreciation for spaying her new floppy-eared roommate, appropriately named, Bunny. The bible states, "Out of the mouth of babes…you have ordained praise."

I have given many hospital tours in my career; to Brownies, Girl Scouts, and local elementary school children. However, the most memorable was a recent tour I gave to a special needs group of young, special needs girls.

Eight Girl scouts and their parents arrived for a tour just minutes after closing on a Wednesday evening. When I came up to introduce myself, I could feel the energy in the room; they could barely stand still, raising their hands before I even began to speak. Throughout the visit, they continued to be attentive and inquisitive, far beyond most of the children in my tours. When I asked how many of them wanted to be a vet, three raised their hands and expressed their desire to help animals. One little girl with long black curls monopolized the conversation, asking detailed questions about the equipment and stated emphatically, her future career choice was veterinary medicine. Her mother pulled me to the side and whispered, "She's really interested; she picks up on things really fast." I was impressed, most tours I give to children consists of a barrage of unrelated questions and at least one student raising his hand enthusiastically to tell me his mother's cat had just died-which tends to kill the mood.

    I decorated my waiting room walls with many family pictures, one of which is a formal portrait of my daughter and me at her christening. These pictures portray a family-oriented atmosphere and impart a warm feeling to the waiting room. It was here the Girls Scouts enjoyed refreshments, and it was here I offered my final remarks. The head mother then had each child express their appreciation for our tour. "Everyone, thank Doctor Cimer for tonight's tour," she announced. Each expressed enthusiastic praise for the thirty-minute session.

    The eight girls bounced out the front door as energetically as they had entered thirty minutes earlier. Last in line was the little girl with long black curls. The picture of my daughter in her christening outfit and me in my tuxedo caught her eye, as she started to leave, she stated proudly, "Look Mom, it's Dr. Phil."

The mother whispered in embarrassment, "And I'm the one who said, she catches on to things fast."

I laughed and quickly replied, "That's ok, one of the fifth graders in my last career day thought I was that actor from the series *Breaking Bad*, and he played a drug dealer. Believe me, Dr. Phil is an improvement."

Three weeks later I received a thank you card in which each of the girls expressed their personal feelings. The little girl with the long black curls wrote, "Thank you for showing us some cool things." I guess she honestly does pick up on things fast. I was touched. That simple, well-worded act of appreciation can erase a week of ungrateful clients.

Sometimes, true satisfaction comes when you are forced out of your comfort zone. Of course, the client may never know where your comfort zone lies; they are grateful that their pet is alive. Moe was a four-year-old male Yorkie who developed bladder stones, a condition comparable to kidney stones in humans. When these stones have a calcium base, complete surgical removal is required, this is especially critical in males. Moe's owner, a twenty-two-old college student, reluctantly gave her authorization for the surgery under one condition; because she had limited funds, I had to streamline the estimate, reducing it by about half. I've done at least a hundred cystotomies; most done on small breed dogs are uncomplicated. I believed this eight-pound Yorkie would be no different.

When I examined the pre-operative radiographs, it was apparent that the dog had two small stones in the urethra. Male dogs have a bone in their penis called an os penis which can trap these stones and prevent emptying of the bladder. I warned the owner before I put the dog under anesthesia; if I couldn't dislodge the stone with a catheter the dog would need a more advanced procedure, called a perineal urethrostomy (p/u). Here the surgeon creates a permanent opening behind the penis, preventing another blockage. Ironically, this was the same procedure Dr. Jeffrey Goldblatt was performing on Sunday, the day I had volunteered at the emergency clinic in New Jersey when I was still in college. (Remember him? "What are you an idiot? When a cat freaks out you shut the door!") Yes, that Guy-I should have paid more attention to what he was doing before I escaped that morning. Twenty-five years later this is not a common procedure for the average practitioner-I had never performed the surgery. Therefore, we discussed the two choices if that happened, a referral to a veterinary surgeon, or one she was expecting, euthanasia.

When the dog was under anesthesia, I tried to pass a catheter, again and again with no luck. The dog is not like the cat where I can force the stone through a pliable urethra with brute force. These stones were trapped like a sea urchin in a rigid PVC pipe, and they weren't moving. I had my assistant call her with the bad news. I could hear the owner over the speakerphone, and she was sobbing. During the conversation, I kept trying to free the stones, as sweat started to drip down my cheek on to my surgical mask. My ability to remove these two stones would decide this dog's life. After five minutes, I realized they were permanently trapped. There was only one choice; she didn't have the three- thousand dollars for the referral surgeon. I could hear her mumble the words, "I better put Moe down." Then she started to cry.

'Wait, give me two minutes," I said as I removed my gloves, and headed to my office. There I called the closest referral practice and asked the attending surgeon one question, "Could you tell me in two minutes how to do a p/u?"

"Is she still on the phone?" I asked as I came back into the room. "Listen, I have never done this procedure, ever. However, I'll try it on, Moe. There are no guarantees, and if I can't get these stones out, I'll call you back. We have nothing to lose, but if I can't do it then we still may have to put him down; but if I can I promise to do the urethrostomy and the cystotomy, both surgeries, for the original price."

She gave her enthusiastic approval. Now with the help of my invaluable associate-she also had never done this procedure-we started the surgery. Sixty minutes later the dog was lighter by fifteen pebble sized calcium deposits, and Moe now urinated out of a tiny slot behind his penis. The owner wept as I gave her the news; Moe had done just fine; she could pick him up the next day. Four years later the little terrier is still doing well. The last time I saw him he was cradled in his owner's arms; all because she trusted me to give him one last chance at life. The beauty of that picture surpasses a little praise any given day. However, the real beauty may be that the owner never knew how close her dog was to being put down-that pressure was on me.

Sometimes, it's fun to play the hero. One broiling August afternoon the frantic owner of Brandy, a twelve-year-old overweight Pug dog whisked her through the doors in a panic. The dog had been trapped on a hot deck without water for two hours; now it was the equivalent of an unconscious Idaho baked potato with legs. When I withdrew the digital rectal thermometer, it read 108.1 degrees, the highest body temperature I had ever witnessed. I informed the owner there was very little chance of survival in a case of hyperthermia this serious.

I used every method possible to save this dog including; cold water enemas, ice cube baths, cooled IV fluids, intra-tracheal tube oxygenation, and a closet full of pharmaceuticals to treat this dog's systemic shock. Brandy was panting far too fast to count, her body spewing mucous and saliva from her lungs and out of the tracheal tube with each breath. Her head was so warm you could feel the heat radiating out of her ear flaps. Three full enemas later her rectal temperature reduced to a respectable 103.5 degrees. Slowly she regained consciousness, and she began to move, licking her tracheal tube and blinking. I had a suspicion if she did survive, she would have at the least, organ failure or at worst, brain damage.

Medical conventional wisdom implies core body temperatures exceeding 106 degrees usually prove fatal as the essential organs like the kidney, liver, and brain can cook leading to permanent damage. Fortunately, in Brandy's case, her recipe called for a much higher cooking temperature. She recovered fully, without any long-term effects. Two years later she survived a house fire which killed her housemate, another pug. She escaped the flames by fleeing onto the same deck which almost ended her life that summer day. She lived another two years after the fire to the elderly age of sixteen.

Some cases are frustrating; some are destined to fail before they walk through the door. Daphne, a six-year-old Cocker Spaniel, had been seen at the Pinetree Veterinary Hospital for a possible urinary tract infection. The veterinarian placed the dog on antibiotics for a month, and the dog was still urinating blood. The owner wanted a second opinion. Today the dog wasn't urinating at all. I palpated the abdomen of this gentle dog, and the bladder had the distinct feel of marbles in a leather sack; I could even hear the stones scraping against one another like chalk as I manipulated the bladder. As I stroked Daphne's ears I asked if they had taken X-rays at the former hospital; they had not. Two minutes later a radiograph confirmed what I had suspected; there was an uncountable number of stones in a bladder the size of a grapefruit. Small breed dogs commonly form bladder stones, so I routinely recommend radiographs in those dogs which present with hematuria or bloody urine-it was inconceivable the previous veterinarian had not taken one radiograph.

While we prepared the dog for an emergency cystotomy we were presented with a new complication; Daphne was in kidney failure. The stones had distended the bladder so much it had occluded the flow of urine and the increase in pressure had caused a condition known as, post-renal azotemia and eventually kidney failure. It was unclear if we could reverse the damage, but we had to remove those stones, so we immediately took her into surgery.

I removed fifty-eight calcium oxalate stones from an organ tortured by months of constant irritation; the bladder wall resembled a raw cube steak. The kidneys were swollen and pale; I started to doubt they would ever return to their full function. I was proven correct; Daphne recovered from the surgery but was euthanized three days later without ever returning home.

I sat at home that evening, thinking about that dog. Sitting in the middle of a thousand Lego's my boys had scattered throughout the living room, I tried to hold back my tears. I pictured the face of my own Cocker Spaniel, Susan, whom I put down a year before. "You know the worst part?" I asked my wife. "If they had just taken a simple X-ray when they first saw that dog a month ago, that dog would still be alive. If they had come to me earlier, I could have saved her life. Now all that work for nothing." The irony was that most people perceived that large hospital as the standard of care. They thought it was still the kingdom of Dr. Murray Blevins, but it wasn't. It was now the land of corporate America. They didn't benefit from the training I received from a true pioneer. They have so many doctors that the clients never see the same doctor twice. "It's amazing," I said. "If you look at their Facebook ad, they tout over one hundred and fifty years of combined veterinary experience. Bullshit, a fourth-year vet student, could have thought of a damn X-ray on a cocker spaniel with bloody urine!" The failure wasn't mine, but it hurt just the same, the real frustrating part was the first veterinarian who saw Daphne would never know how she had failed.

In the early nineties, when I worked at the Pinetree Veterinary Hospital, I had a small cartoon taped above my desk. I cut it out of a veterinary publication which occasionally offered satirical cartoons. It pictured a woman standing on one side of an exam table holding her dog, while on the other side of the exam table was a veterinarian with a befuddled look on his face. The caption read, "Are you going to spay my dog, doctor? You know I would do it myself if I had the time, after all, I am a nurse." This illustrates the dilemma veterinarians face when the public regards our advice like useless gossip on a tabloid news show. In my hospital, we recently diagnosed a toy poodle with a luxating patella, an orthopedic condition where the knee cap pops out of the joint causing the dog to limp. My associate confirmed my diagnosis, and we recommended surgery. To which the owner replied, "I'll have my physical therapist look at it first, thank you anyway." The dog never had corrective surgery.

In my practice, I follow the recommendations of the American Heartworm Society by recommending annual heartworm testing. This is a blood test to check for the proteins produced by the internal parasite forming worms in a dog's heart. Mosquitos spread the disease; it can take years to damage the dog's heart and scar the lungs. Clients frequently challenge my medical logic with the illogical statement, "My dog doesn't come anywhere near mosquitos" or more succinctly, "He's fine, I can tell by looking at him he doesn't have heartworm." Faced with that kind of naive thinking why do we perform diagnostics at all? I often wonder, are real doctors met with resistance at such simple recommendations.

Some problem clients can be harmless, like the Bichon Friese owner who swore that the fleas infesting her dog came off the waiting room floor or the client who didn't want a rabies vaccine for his cat because he believed New Jersey, "Never had and never will have, a rabies problem." After assuring him, I had personally diagnosed a rabies raccoon two weeks before-he responded by shaking his head in disbelief. These votes of no confidence insult my dedication, medical knowledge, and expertise. Sometimes I ask myself two questions: Why they come to me in the first place if they don't trust what I say? Then why do I even try to change their mind, is it just a waste of my time? (Sorry Dr. Blevins, I told you)

In my professional life, I have experienced three types of valleys in my career. The first is an aggravating mogul, as with the story of Daphne, the failure is not mine-I could have done nothing to change the regretful outcome. The second is a deeper valley; this is when a client casts blame where no blame exists. This one is hurtful and frustrating. Regardless of how intent I am at changing their opinion, their selfish logic shields them from their culpability. The final is an unexpected sinkhole, in which I have failed; this swallows my confidence and permanently effects my career. This is pure psychological pain.

Thankfully, in twenty-five years I have been reported to the governing state board of veterinary medicine for potential malpractice only three times. Every one of those cases was found, by the opinion of the board, without merit; of course, the owners will always think it was my fault. In the first case, a gentleman had a Cairn Terrier with neurologic disease. Following my evaluation, he took the dog to an elderly veterinarian who was convinced the dog had tetanus — this a rare condition in dogs; as humans are much more susceptible. The dog recovered without any laboratory work to substantiate his diagnosis. In the owner's eyes, I missed the disease, and if it were not for the pseudo-heroic efforts of the other veterinarian who prescribed oral antibiotics, the dog would have died. Expert testimonial and a good deal of intensive research supported my case-his dog did not have tetanus.

A second woman filed a complaint on behalf of her elderly Siberian Husky. The owner called one Friday afternoon to request a commercial non-steroidal pain reliever for its chronic arthritis. She was sure he wasn't sick, just painful; she refused my recommendation to do a complete workup to rule out any additional disease. I reluctantly prescribed the medication and cautioned her against assuming it was only the effects of arthritis. The dog continued to do poorly, went to another vet and who diagnosed with lung cancer, and she subsequently euthanized the dog- the condition was unrelated to the medication. She accused me of, "prescribing a drug that had murdered her beloved pet." She also blamed a major pharmaceutical company for, "making a drug that was killing dogs." Who did she not blame? Herself. In her own words, the dog had been failing for weeks. In this profession, we like to ask those types of owners: where's your responsibility in monitoring your pet? Again, the case was found to be without merit. These frivolous kinds of complaints require hours of the veterinarian's time to defend their integrity. Even after a lifetime of practice, these cases can still cause personal heartache and professional doubt. They encourage us to practice, not good medicine, but defensive medicine; medical logic based on covering your ass.

These cases muddle the day; selfish people who remind us why we prefer animals. The perfect example is a client whom I had seen for routine health care. She

Almost A Real Doctor

was already fuming when she walked into the room because she had sat and unbearable twenty minutes in the waiting room. My associate was in the middle of a very difficult large dog spay in the back surgical suite when she encountered a complication. I politely, excused myself to scrub in and assist. Twenty minutes later I returned to a now, irate women. "Do you have any idea how long I have already been waiting, just to get a shot?"

I was astounded at her petulance. "I am sorry you had to wait, but my associate had complications with her dog spay," I explained. "Now, if that was your dog on the table and something went wrong that would threaten her life, you would be upset if I didn't run back there to give her a hand. Especially, if your dog had died because some impatient owner refused to wait twenty minutes 'just to get a shot'." I couldn't tell if the expression on her face was one of infuriation or empathy.

Complications, such as a dog spay gone wrong, can ruin an otherwise average work day. They can shock us into the reality of the fragility of life. I think a line from *M*A*S*H* best illustrates it. In the episode, Hawkeye Pierce was grieving over a young soldier who died after a complicated surgery. Colonel Blake tried to place the tragedy in perspective, "Listen, Hawkeye, there are two rules about war. Rule number one, in war young men die. Rule number two, doctors can't change rule number one." We all take our responsibility seriously and deeply regret those failures. However, it is like one of my associates used to say, "Some owners believe we intentionally cause complications, that is not the case; they sometimes just happen."

The Worst-Case Scenario

I was on the other side of the hospital the day a young adult Chihuahua, named Binky coded on the preparation table during a routine procedure. My colleague tried everything his thirty years of experience could offer to revive the dog; CPR, epinephrine injections and shock therapy. Forty-five minutes later the heart still wasn't beating. The technician who was prepping the dog was devastated, blaming herself for a tragic anesthetic reaction. She collapsed on the floor, the tears flowing down her cheeks vowing never to touch another animal. I tried to console her, with words of encouragement through the mislaid cloud of guilt.

"Listen to me," I said. "This is not your fault. This could have happened to any one of us. The dog couldn't tolerate the level of anesthesia a puppy twice that size should be able to tolerate. This is the profession we have chosen. We're not fixing pipes or sewing sweaters; when something goes wrong it just doesn't leak or fray, it dies."

"I just keep seeing her eyes before I put her under," she replied. "I'll never get that out of my head. I don't know if I can do this again.".

"I know this may not make it any easier but in a lifetime of procedures something bad is bound to happen," I said as pulled her up off the floor. "You're too talented a technician to let it all go for one disaster. Go home, take a long weekend and I'll see you on Monday."

She was in still in shock, when her husband drove her home that Friday afternoon. She returned Monday and continued a long successful career. Necropsy results were inconclusive, and it was unclear why the dog could not tolerate the anesthesia; it was just one out of a thousand cases which ended in tragedy. That incident still haunts her two decades later. That day proved her sincere dedication to animals as she would always be a genuine, caring professional. The profession grows with new findings and safer procedures, and we grow as professionals with each close call and with each tragedy. We formulate more reliable protocols and institute better safeguards, perfecting the standards of care which we follow for future cases.

I learned the compassionate art of the bad-news call of bad news from Dr. Murray Blevins in my first years of practice. It is a delicate balance of sympathy, sensitivity, and medical professionalism. Express profound concern but do not imply guilt. It wasn't long before I had to make my first bad news call at the Pinetree Veterinary Hospital. I had just finished a front declaw on a two-year-old cat, and the head technician placed the cat in recovery. Thirty minutes later she called me on the intercom with the bad news; the cat had died. I had not administered the anesthetic nor was it my duty to monitor the cat post-operatively, but it was my responsibility to call the owner.

"Mr. Thomson, this is Doctor Cimer, I'm sorry I have some bad news about Winnie, she reacted to the anesthesia. She never woke up. I sorry to say she has died."

The response of a pet owner to the unexpected loss of a pet is unpredictable. It's understandable; it's horrific news-as challenging to give as it is to hear. Some are in shock, some in denial, "She's dead. No, it can't be; she didn't." Some people burst into tears; some become hysterical, unable to continue the conversation. Some relay the message to other family

The Worst-Case Scenario

members while we can hear their screams echoing in the background. Still others, like many of my senior clients, are calm, collected, understanding and supportive. , But my first call and my first anesthetic death had a different response.

"What happened?" he asked after hearing the news. "You killed my cat, didn't you? Listen, pal; I don't want to hear your bullshit excuses. I don't know if you are sorry, but I'll tell you something Doc you will be sorry when something happens to one of your family members someday, and I guarantee it will."

I awkwardly replied, "Again, I am truly sorry." I then hung up the phone in shock; I perceived it as a personal threat. I immediately approached Dr. Ken Blevins and explained I was not going to tolerate a client threatening my family over a cat whose death was not at fault; although I did understand in the eyes of the client, he felt I was ultimately responsible. Dr. Blevins spoke with Winnie's owner who had calmed down a bit, he offered a forced apology and gave an assurance his words were not a threat. Dr. Blevins consoled him by removing his charges.

I had some consolation knowing it wasn't my fault, but I did not feel vindicated. While I could pretend the cat's death didn't bother me, I took it personally. My mind was submerged in guilt as I drove home. Later that evening I took my wife to dinner, haunted by those words echoing in my head. I surveyed the parking lot for vengeful thugs waiting to exact their justice as I got out of the car. When we entered the crowded restaurant, I imagined the piercing eyes of every stranger pointing blame. I thought I heard the whispers of condemnation of people from across the room. I stared at CNN on the dining room flat screen T.V. expecting the breaking news of my deed scrolled across the bottom of the screen. I could barely tell the waitress my order; I could imagine her asking the question the entire restaurant was waiting to hear: "Aren't you the vet who killed that guy's cat?" I spent weeks getting over that guilt, hoping I would never feel that way again. Unfortunately, that is not a wish granted to most veterinarians.

When I started my practice, I didn't enjoy a buffer of an experienced, well-respected practice owner, to explain the tragedy away. I was personally responsible for the consequences of these events. It was hard to find a way to make a terrible situation better. My first tragedy as a practice owner was a routine cat spay which died under anesthesia. After making the faithful call, I consulted a cardiac specialist from a nearby referral practice. He told me the reason some younger cats expire after a routine surgical procedure is that they have underlying cardiac damage from previous bouts of upper respiratory disease, the kind seen in stray kittens. This damage is undetectable on routine health screening before surgery. Of course, this information does nothing to console a client with a lost pet; neither does it change their opinion about the real reason behind the pet's death. They had a false belief the cat had hemorrhaged during surgery or suffered an anesthetic overdose. In their eyes, I killed their cat. The husband's last words before he hung up were, "I should have taken my cat to the spay clinic; then she would still be alive." I may have had a clear conscience, but now I had a tainted reputation.

In most cases, veterinary professionals advised against refunding money as it implies guilt, especially when no guilt exists. However, charging clients in these cases can prove awkward. This theory would prove to be true in an unlikely species, the guinea pig. The pig was a nursery school project for three years. The teacher presented him because of bloody urine which I discovered was caused by a golf ball size bladder stone. I removed the rock in a successful cystotomy. Unfortunately, the little guy died two hours later-these species are very intolerant of stress and often succumb during many traumatic procedures. The problem arose when I presented the church administrator with a bill for one hundred-and-twenty-five-dollar surgery. It was returned unpaid.

The nursery school teacher personally apologized on behalf of the church; she had been informed that it was not church protocol to have a pet in her class, and not their choice to do the surgery. She promised to pay the bill. I thought it was unfair to force this working mother of three teenagers to pay for the nursery school class rodent, so I forgave the debt-I guess I was behaving more like a Christian and less like a church administrator.

In the life of a veterinary surgeon there is no sound more frightening, then the pulse alarm on a cardiac monitor, there is no silence more disturbing than the absence of a heartbeat in the chest of a pet on a surgical table. When this happens, the first thought is the administration of CPR, and medications to restart the heart. The second thought is the consequences if the animal's life ends on that table. Statistics show the success of reviving an animal which has coded during any procedure to be less than nineteen percent. This statistic slaps me in the face every time an animal's heart rate falls while on my surgical table.

One group of dogs which give every veterinarian an anesthetic nightmare are the brachiocephalic breeds: Pugs, Bulldogs, and Boston terriers. Their short faces, narrow nostrils, and long pallets make breathing difficult on a good day. Owners laugh when they hear the snorts and gasps as these little dog's fight for air. When they are anesthetized these physical defects combine to form a potential disaster- it's no laughing matter. These dogs can develop pulmonary edema, laryngeal swelling, and extreme respiratory distress. Through the years, we have developed custom pre-anesthetic protocols for preventing problems. We also keep intra-tracheal tubes in these dogs until they are fully awake; the average dog has these tubes removed at the first swallowing reflex following surgery. These brachiocephalic breeds are almost always overweight, usually aged, and extremely fragile. Even with special protocols, we have lost two Pug dogs while under routine general anesthesia. These tragedies are a constant reminder of the enormous responsibility we have every time we anesthetize someone's pet. It also reminds us that there are certain breeds of dogs poorly equipped to survive the stress the average dog can tolerate. I know breeds like the Bulldog are adorable, but I also know they are anatomical freaks of nature and make our job more precarious. When I remember these two loses, I think it is ironic that I could save the old Pug with heatstroke, minutes from death, and those two seemingly healthy Pug dogs couldn't survive a thirty-minute anesthesia.

However, even after the surgery is finished, the pet recovers from anesthesia, and the dog goes home the hands of fate occasionally reminds us that even veterinary surgeons are mere mortals. One memorable morning six years into starting my practice I had just placed the final suture in the abdominal incision of the second dog spay of the day. Both surgeries were uneventful. In twenty-five years, I had become a more proficient surgeon, confident and quick even with large dog spays; Shelby's was no exception. She was a six-year-old German Shephard who had been coming to my hospital since she was a puppy. The Ceniks had followed me from Dr. Klein's office years before with another Shephard named Aragorn. I had euthanized that dog a year before they had purchased their new dog, Shelby. They had initially wanted to have at least one litter of puppies but decided against the breeding because of an inherited joint disease called hip dysplasia. Shelby had her share of medical issues; chronic allergies, the early onset of degenerative arthritis, and a severe intestinal emergency which almost ended her life.

Eight months ago, she developed an intussusception, a life-threatening intestinal condition where a length of intestinal inverts into another, like a telescope. This can lead to the death of that segment of the intestine and eventually, shock and death. The Ceniks rushed her to the surgical referral practice just before Christmas thinking she had eaten some of Mrs. Cenik's heart medication; she was in shock and a great deal of pain. The surgeons corrected the defect and performed a surgical procedure where the small intestinal loops were sutured together creating a permanent accordion-like structure, thus preventing reoccurrence. Now eight months later they finally decided to have her spayed, trusting me to illuminate one less potential medical issue in her life.

The Ceniks were thrilled when Shelby went home that afternoon after her spay surgery; surprised she walked out only a few hours after surgery. They were expecting to carry her out to the car because after her last surgery she spent almost three days recovering from the surgery. However, today she had a routine operation, recovery is usually uneventful. Today she looked great; it always gives me a feeling of great relief to see my surgical cases walk out of the door almost as fast as they came in, playful and healthy.

"We were so concerned," Mrs. Cenik said as she tucked the discharge instructions in her pocketbook. "They told us at the referral practice there was a higher risk for a spay because of that last surgery."

"I know," I replied. "I spoke with Dr. Tobias last week. He was concerned about adhesions, scar tissue which could develop from the previous surgery. I didn't see anything like that when I was in there. What I don't understand is why they didn't spay her when they had her open."

"We asked Dr. Tobias the same question," answered Mrs. Cenik. "He told us they don't like performing both procedures at once, so we agreed it is best to wait."

"Yes, I guess that was their call, no big deal. Look at it this way; this was the last surgery she'll ever have to go through."

Robin, my head technician, called the Cenik twenty-four hours later for an update. Shelby was tired but was otherwise fine. The next day Mrs. Cenik called with a question. "Was it normal for her to be vomiting two days after surgery?"

I didn't think it was serious, but it did raise concern about the previous intestinal disorder, maybe the anesthesia had caused another intussusception or perhaps gastric bloat, so I instructed her to go back to Dr. Tobias if the vomiting continued-twelve hours later the Ceniks drove Shelby back to the specialist. The ultrasound studies identified abnormal intestinal loops; a surgical exploratory was performed just before noon to determine the problem; the preliminary diagnosis was another intussusception.

Robin has always been the bearer of bad news; she found the guinea pig dead in the cage after the cystotomy, she informed me she couldn't hear a heartbeat on the Pug who died in the middle of the dentistry a year before, and the Monday morning following the Cenik's dog surgery she told me Shelby had died.

In every patient who dies the first thought in every case is to recall that pets last visit. What did I do? What didn't I do? In Shelby's case, I quickly concluded it must have been the result of another gastrointestinal disorder leading to shock and death. The second thought is always to call the pet owner and offer condolences and find out the real story-I never got that chance. When I walked into the reception area, Mr. Cenik was waiting for me at the front desk-he had been there since we opened our doors that morning.

Mr. Cenik was a man who reminded me of my father. He was a forty-year-old, muscular, home builder. He words were blunt, his accusations succinct. In his blue-collar world, he wanted answers, not bull. He was visibly shaken, having spent almost the entire weekend in a referral hospital waiting to hear good news about a dog he had loved for nearly six years. He often spoke of "Cause and effect." How he wasn't a doctor but how even he could see that Shelby was healthy five days before, then she had surgery here, and now she was dead. They said something about an abdominal infection, implying that is what killed her. I calmly spoke of the success of her surgery, without one complication; how I had never seen a fatal abdominal infection from a routine spay incision. I reminded him that Shelby had multiple problems and there was a greater chance the gastrointestinal issue was the cause; not the spay. I was very confident the ovariohysterectomy went perfectly, and I urged him to be careful to cast blame when this entire episode could have been only a coincidence. He backed off a bit and agreed to wait on the pending necropsy for the final answer. I assured him that I would accept blame if the fault were mine. I would "stare him in the eye and admit it was my fault." He assured me if it was my fault that he would be staring me straight back in the eye expecting an apology and demanding an explanation.

Two days later I received a call from the founder and chief of staff of the surgical referral practice; I had known him for over twenty-five years, and I would trust him with my pets. Dan had personally performed the necropsy. Out of professional courtesy, he withheld the results from the owners until he could give me the report. "Bob, now that the necropsy is complete let me tell you what happened to Shelby. The actual ultrasound showed the spay ligations were fine, no bleeding, just some ascites. The abdominal tap showed diffuse peritonitis. We didn't know why. So, I ordered an exploratory. Just after anesthetic induction, she coded. We gave the owners the option of continuing, but they decided to euthanize on the table. When we opened her up, we found her abdomen fill of feces. Then we found a one-centimeter laceration in the ante-mesenteric surface of the jejunum which allowed GI contents to leak out into the abdomen causing the peritonitis. I'm sorry to have to be the one who has to give you this news, but you must have lacerated the intestine during the spay."

I slowly laid the phone on the desk. I couldn't believe what I had just heard. If it wasn't coming directly from a man I knew and highly respected, I would have questioned every word of it. I started to shake as the sweat dripped off my brow. I held my head in my hands and began to cry. I knew I had to call Mr. Cenik, and I had to do it immediately because by now he would also know the results of the necropsy. I made the call. It was a short conversation laced with humility, regret, and empathy. However, each word he spoke was a blunt knife stabbed into my chest, rhythmically eviscerating my soul. My final words assured him that my malpractice insurance would fully compensate him for all financial loss. Fortunately, the medical director at the referral practice, as a courtesy, forgave all medical charges for Shelby's entire treatment. However, I knew from Mr. Cenik's final words; it was not about the money; it was about the emotional trauma his family had suffered.

I sat at home shrouded in the dark as my wife returned home that evening. Through the lump in my throat, I spoke of what had happened. I summarized my day in four words, "I killed the dog." She was supportive, as always, but it did little to lessen the agony of my mistake. "I didn't become a doctor, to accidently kill someone's dog," I whispered falling deeper into a repugnant depression. When decades before, on the first day of vet school Dr. Bastian spoke of "imagining the worst thing which could happen, and then realizing it couldn't be that bad." This was "that bad." There was no other time, no other loss in my career which impacted my life as this mistake. Whether it was because it was preventable, or because it was all my fault, it would haunt me through every spay I would ever perform. I had done thousands of spays without a significant complication, and that day, Shelby became a permanent scar on my career. What made it worse was the fact that it wasn't a complication I could not even remember; it was a slip of the scalpel which went completely unnoticed. If I had seen the laceration, I could have easily repaired in five minutes.

There were times I blamed the previous surgeon for causing the adhesions, or for not spaying the dog during the first surgery, and there were times I wished the owner had taken my advice and spayed the dog years earlier instead of keeping her for breeding which never happened. I even asked God, as I did so many years before on that steel bridge in Missouri, why he had brought me so far; except now to kill someone's dog. However, most of the time I just blamed myself. Mr. Cenik had explained that his wife was truly devastated, and how his children would blame him for trusting me to do this surgery. Shelby would never again play ball in the yard or greet Mr. Cenik after another tough day at work. "My wife is sad," he added, "but I'm angry."

I often hear clients tell stories about this doctor or that guy who killed their dog or cat. Working at an emergency clinic for seven years you see mistakes and errors in medicine from others which eventually can lead to a bad reputation. Now, I was "that guy" which people speak of with harsh judgment and contempt. A year later I hired a technician who spoke of a family in her town who had an interesting story about my hospital. "I heard they lost their dog," she started. "They said they took their German Shephard into my practice for routine surgery and she died due to complications from a spay. They have a new dog now, and they certainly would never go back to that doctor who killed their dog." My last conversation with Mr. Cenik ended with one small consoling statement, "At least you stood up like a man to accept blame for your mistake." I guess that is at least one good thing I learned from my father.

Then in my twenty-fifth year of practice I found myself in a panic, sinking into my personal tragic whirlpool. Robin's face mirrored the desperation in my voice, "Get me another dose. Now! Keep breathing for him. Keep breathing. Again, every three seconds. Please no, God no!" I pleaded as I squeezed the soft, lifeless chest just one more time. Sweat trickled down my glasses as I stood staring at the lifeless body of my family's beloved pet bunny. Four times I injected a dilution of epinephrine directly into his failing heart, three times it started beating again only to slow after a brief few seconds into a dead, still silence which haunts the nightmares of every veterinarian.

We were unable to place an endotracheal tube or even an IV catheter; this is a tricky proposition even for the most experienced technicians. Would that have saved his life? Probably not. I knew the odds of reviving him were slim, but I did everything I knew hoping I could fool those odds just one time in my life. Later I spoke to an exotic animal specialist who confirmed my research; French lop ear rabbits have a propensity for a congenital cardiac anomaly called, cardiomyopathy which can lead to acute cardiac failure and death. A fragile animal was even more fragile than I had suspected. This may be an explanation for tragedy, but it wasn't an excuse, and it certainly was not going to ease the pain my wife and children would feel the moment they learned their bunny was never coming home again. It was my idea to neuter the rabbit, and it was also my idea to hide the surgery from the kids that morning so that they wouldn't worry. Now we had to tell them their bunny had died as soon as they got home from school before they saw the empty cage in the living room. It was with these thoughts that I finally said, "Stop, stop everything; it's over." My guilt was unbearable as I laid my face on his lifeless, grey and white body and cried.

If the agonizing five-minute drive home didn't intensify my guilt, it was the site of my sobbing wife cradling the rabbit in her arms like a lost baby, and yet the worst was yet to come-we now had to tell our three children. Our thirteen-year-old son would arrive at 2:30, our seven-year-old daughter at 3:15, finally my sixteen-year-old son would be home at 5:00-it was his birthday. My daughter had the most severe reaction; as could be expected, in near hysteria, crying eyes smashed in a pillow she just kept repeating, "Why? Why mommy is he not coming back?" My middle son, the quiet, silent sufferer, like his German father, refused to let that iron shell crumble. However, I knew it hurt him deeply, that rabbit was the last living thing he touched on his way out to the school bus in the morning and the first living thing he touched when he came home in the afternoon. My oldest son was sad but mature with the grim realization that he may forever remember his sixteenth birthday as the day his pet rabbit died. My wife spoke to the three children in private, reassuring them it wasn't daddy's fault. "Do not blame your father; it wasn't his fault. He did everything he could to save your bunny. He feels guilty enough, already."

The medical reason for his death was a logical explanation for "a real doctor," but it did little to ease the pain in a child's mind. They only knew their bunny was alive when they went to school on that ordinary Wednesday and was dead when they got home, and they didn't have a word in the matter. Their parents made the decision to keep him healthy; which would take the younger children years to understand. One of the hardest responsibilities of a parent is to explain death to their children; whether it is the loss of a grandparent or the death of a pet. They would eventually get a new bunny which they loved just as much as the first, but I know in their childhood memories they would remember the loss of their friend like the loss of the pets I can still recall five decades later.

I would also remember this loss forever, except my memory would be the vision of that terrible scene on that surgical table and the feeling of hopeless panic. I did do everything I knew to save that rabbit. Indeed, if he had a congenital heart anomaly, he was destined for a much shorter life. However, I also knew the only way I could have saved him would have been never to do the surgery; an operation I had done a hundred times before. I thought it was the right thing to do. This was Dr. Christian Bastian's worst-case scenario reemerging once again, in a personal sense, to haunt my sleepless nights. Minutes after my daughter broke down; I again started to question God as I had done many times before only to recant and remember the two-thousand-year-old biblical passage, "He causes his sun to rise on the evil and the good." Moreover, the other ancient axiom, "Death is a part of life."

However, I have a heavier cross to bear than most parents. Children at some point in their life are disappointed in their parents. A dad embarrasses his son in front of his prom date, or a daughter is disappointed she didn't get that yellow convertible at her sweet sixteen party. I will always be the dad who was personally responsible for killing their beloved pet bunny. A week later when I told my daughter we were getting a new rabbit she asked in her seven-year-old innocence, "Daddy, you're not going to do that surgery on our new bunny right? She then paused and added, "Or maybe I'll do it, so she doesn't die." What did Jesus say about the mouth of babes and praise? I guess that can be a double-edged sword which cuts both ways.

These personal tragedies remind us of the impact we have every day in the lives of our patients. Whether it is elective euthanasia or unexpected death, those owners retreat to a home with one less beating heart; a home which is missing a cat, a dog, or a French Lop-eared bunny. Then they must explain that empty cage, or that unused food bowl, or a silent squeaky toy to their children, or their husband, or their wife. A few days later my middle son put together a sixty-second video to memorialize the pet he silently mourned. In this montage set to music he followed his short five months of life titled: "The Years of Baby Bunny Foo Foo." I still find it difficult to watch the video without breaking down. I guess we all have our own way of dealing with loss.

CHAPTER 15

SHATTERED DREAMS

It was the best of times,

It was the worst of times,

It was the spring of hope,

It was the winter of despair.

- A Tale of Two Cities

Five days ago, hurricane Sandy was predicted to head northeast, out to sea, and continue over the Grand Banks, at most to deal us a glancing blow. Now Emergency Management ordered the closure of the Mathis Bridge, the primary artery between Seaside Heights and the mainland. Media posts read, "Mandatory evacuations of all waterfront and island residents." Now, this was no longer a glancing blow this was to be a Mike Tyson uppercut. Damn those weathermen! Thirty years ago, I was drawing stationary fronts with a number two pencil in meteorology 101 and today with two multimillion-dollar computer models they were doing no better at predicting one of the largest hurricanes in history.

I closed the hospital on Monday, October 29, 2012, at noon, just before Governor Chris Christie declared a state of emergency. Eighty-mile-an-hour winds soon toppled trees across the county; with downed power lines and blown transformers, the electricity failed just three hours later. Nine days after Sandy an early November nor'easter blew frigid winds onshore and dumped almost a foot of snow on brittle trees already damaged by the storm. Like a cruel gotcha joke, power was lost again to many homes which had just regained their electricity. High tides and flooding destroyed homes and displaced people across the shore area. Each day following the storm my employees and I would come to the cold office hoping to see a utility truck outside repairing our blown transformer-by Friday I had given up hope and left it to the utility Gods to decide when we could open our doors. It took over a week for those deities to restore power to the hospital, but it would be over four years before the county and at least a quarter of my clients would recover from the wrath of hurricane Sandy. Thus, in the ninth year of my practice, the storm surge from this October low would sweep my dream of building a legacy into the Atlantic Ocean with the outgoing tide.

Amidst political heavy petting and "Jersey strong" campaigns the depth of the damage was lost to most people west of the New Jersey Turnpike, and certainly to the rest of the country. Sandy damaged almost ten thousand homes along the coast. When hurricane Katrina pummeled New Orleans in 2005 many criticized the slow response to rebuilding the city. Four years after Sandy the houses at the Jersey shore or still being raised or rebuilt. Many believe the lack of similar concern for the slow revival was the belief that many properties are second homes owned by an affluent New Jersey and New York residents. "They are just rich people. So, who cares?" I care. First, many of those affected were average, middle class, single homeowners, and second, many were my clients who would no longer support the local economy, and or my hospital. The week after the hurricane I would lose tens of thousands of dollars; the next four years I would lose ten percent of my income-easily hundreds of thousands of dollars of lost revenue. Four years into our expansion Sandy blew away any hopes I had of clearing my mind and my ledger of endless business debt. She was a cruel beast which would put another crack in my perfect adolescent snow globe.

Sandy was just part of what I call my climatology curse (I don't mean that Al Gore scary bedtime story, "The Gingrich who stole the Climate"). This curse was real. My fate was sealed when in 1981 I changed my major and resigned from the meteorology club saying goodbye to meteorology forever, never to return. The meteorology Gods were sticking pins in a voodoo doll which looked a lot a skinny bald veterinarian from New Jersey. Since opening my office in 2003, the northeast experienced more snowstorms in the following ten years then in my entire lifetime. Some blizzards closed our office for days. Even the smallest snowfall kept the seniors out of their Hondas Accords and trapped in their leisure village ranch homes until the last snowflake melted. Each day closed was a financial whiteout, each snowstorm another green payday for another landscaper. During the winter, I would hold my breath during each weather report like I was counting down the seconds on a pregnancy test. Except this white bundle of joy always hurt my bottom line. When I was young, my father would say, "Whatever you do, don't get a job where you work outdoors, the winters can be a killer." The irony was that I worked in an office, and the winters were still killing me.

When the economy flourished these small setbacks have a minimal long-term impact on my business, but when the economy stalled, as it did in 2008 and remained flat for almost ten years, it was devastating. As my Italian barber succinctly stated, "When the business is doing great, owning a business is great, when the business sucks, owning a business sucks." He should know, he has owned a business for forty years and has more hair and more equity than I will ever have.

In early 2009, one year into our newly renovated hospital and twelve payments into our newly inflated business loan I started to notice something disturbing about my bottom line-it was beginning to bottom out. The following spring, I began to see a trend developing in veterinary trade articles which focused on the economy. The *VIN News* service published an article in April: "Economic downturn hits veterinary practices." *Veterinary Practice News* published: "How to stay busy during your clinic's recess." *Veterinary Forum* published an article in the summer: "What happened to 'the recession-proof practice'?" Recession? I didn't know we were in a recession. Quite typically for veterinarians, I was clueless when it came to economics, micro, macro, or whatever. I wasn't alone. Dr. Roman Wade, founder, and owner of a six-person veterinary practice in Southern New Jersey admitted, "I had no idea why my business was slowing. Until my accountant said to me, 'Hey, dummy, wake up, we're in the middle of a recession.' I ran a multimillion-dollar hospital, and I was the last to know what was happening." Eventually, the American Veterinary Medical Association and the American Animal Hospital Association addressed the crisis in studies focused on the impact of the recession on veterinary medicine.

    I had a chance to enroll in an economics course at Rutgers University; instead, I enrolled in some frivolous course on the history of Hollywood westerns. I could name every one of Clint Eastwood's spaghetti westerns, but I couldn't produce a monthly P/L statement if my business depended on it. In vet school, I learned the volume of semen contained in boar ejaculate, but they didn't teach me how much money to borrow to start a veterinary practice. Like it or not, Dr. Klein had a dramatic influence on my business philosophy; I wasn't greedy, I had a conscience, I didn't want to raise prices when people were always complaining about the cost of routine medical care; I refused to be a pricing whore. In good times, even the worst businessman can be successful. They can have a payroll far too generous, a budget far too high, and they can suck money from the business like a Dyson vacuum, and still, the company grows. I practiced this logic for five years before the recession hit the Northeast. Many of my clients who owned businesses in the service industry practiced this same faith; the local landscapers had two homes, and the neighborhood plumbers spent the weekends sailing on their yachts. However, our faith would fail us all by the end of 2010.

Every year before that crash our practice had tremendous growth; this allowed us to realize a four-fold expansion into a new state-of-the-art veterinary hospital. Practices everywhere were expanding their hospitals, adding additional veterinarians, hiring employees, buying new equipment, and increasing inventory. Banks were eager to lend large sums of money at obscene rates to tap into this exploding profession. In the winter of 2003, an article in a veterinary practice publication noted the default rate on business loans in veterinary medicine was one of the lowest of all professionals. In 2007 I acquired almost a half-million-dollar loan from a large commercial bank with a one-page application-and they came to my office to sign the note-I didn't even have to step into the bank. The pharmaceutical companies joined the game by extending credit terms and offering payment plans on large inventory purchases. I had a basement full of heartworm pills and flea products with tens of thousands of dollars of delayed billing. Even with adequate funds, it took restraint and proper budgeting to pay these bills on time. Dr. Klein would warn against foolish veterinarians who would blow their budget by spending their profits on family cruises, and later default on those agreements. These drug representatives didn't care; their job was to move their products and earn their bonuses.

When the housing bubble burst many in our profession didn't believe it would impact our businesses. At the start of the subprime mortgage crises, we thought little about our bottom lines. When the stock market plummeted, I mostly ignored the implications. However, then, I started to get hints, not from reports on CNN but complaints from our clients. Spikes in home foreclosures proceeded a mass exodus from prime New Jersey properties to a reasonable standard of living found south of the Mason Dixon Line. In a town where close to half of our clientele are senior citizens, I started to hear another grievance; they had lost much of their retirement and now had little to spend on their pets. Many younger clients in Central New Jersey had been laid off, losing their jobs because of major cutbacks for the tourist and service industries. They were avoiding wellness visits, delaying vaccines, canceling surgeries. Like my wife aptly stated, "When money is tight, and people must choose between buying groceries and vaccinating their pet, they will choose groceries."

The Obama administration handed out financial assistance to big banks like a rich uncle handing out gummy bears to fat, greedy children. The problem was that most of these banks were nasty bullies who not only didn't share but turned around and stole lunch money from the good kids. In my opinion, the American Recovery and Reinvestment Act of 2009 did nothing to help stimulate small business, and it was never intended to help the good kids. It was like saying to these poor, hungry kids: "Go out and play you'll be just fine, daddy's watching." While the federal government reached around their backs and waved the bullies on: "Have at it boys."

Before 2010 we were experiencing yearly growth in revenue of almost twenty percent; then the recession hit, and growth plummeted to zero for the next five years. Even for a fiscally challenged businessman can understand this is a formula for disaster. What I couldn't see was what to do to combat the loss. In the myriad of articles in publications like *Veterinary Economics* opinions were everywhere from payroll cutbacks to reducing prices, to a focused advertising strategy to bring in business. A local referral practice, employing hundreds of doctors, cut veterinary salaries to combat the decreasing profits. Doctors gave up ten percent of their salary to keep their jobs. I could not, with a clear conscience do what these larger practices did in tough times; cut hours and reduce staff. I hired these employees, and I viewed it as a betrayal to reduce their income to help the practice survive; in retrospect, a misplaced loyalty. However, then again, my college major wasn't business it was animal science. In the past, a veterinarian could maintain their business by sticking to one strategy; practicing good medicine at fair prices. This philosophy didn't seem to be the case anymore.

I recently attended a professional seminar which addressed this decade long dilemma of decreasing profits. The speaker made one crucial, disturbing statement: "Veterinary medicine has reached its financial ceiling; pet owners have reached their limit of spending on their pets." If this implies, we can't raise prices on procedures in the best of times, so what do we do in a recession? The speaker's unusual solution to the problem: "Do twice the work for half the price. In other words, perform four procedures for the price of two." Let that speaker ask the average United Auto

Worker member to work sixteen-hour days for the eight hours pay and see how "Tough" it would be to build a Ford truck.

In my town, there has always been a low-cost spay clinic; which is a no-frills, strip mall facility which offers spays and neuters at a quarter of the cost of a full-service animal hospital. I am always amazed by those pet owners who will ask me: "Doc I'm thinking of going to the spay clinic to spay my dog, Victoria. How is that guy over there? Is he any good?" I try to be the true professional, but I do remind them of the old saying: "You get what you pay for." While deep down I'm awestruck by their lack of respect. They are trivializing a major surgical procedure to save a couple of hundred dollars in the life of a dog; and then ask me for a recommendation which takes that money out of my pocket and hands it over to a Jiffy Lube of veterinary medicine. I always like to add a word of common sense, "He must be good at spays and neuters; that's all he ever does."

However, in lean times those businesses which provide low-cost services thrive like stinging nettles in a wilting rose garden. Competition from major pet supply chains and even local pet stores offer reduced vaccine packages which draw many regular clients away from hospitals who once garnered what old-time veterinarians used to call, "The bread and butter of veterinary medicine." In the veterinary school classes of the mid-eighties, they often warned of a profession headed for price wars like your neighborhood discount store. The Dean of the veterinary school would say, "We should have pride in what we know, charge for what we are worth, and laud what we do. If we don't," he warned, "we will be like every other service industry, except they did not spend eight years in school and hundreds of thousands of dollars to learn their trade." Years ago, it was unethical for doctors to advertise their business, now veterinary ads permeate the media, and the coupons flood the marketplace for "free exams to new clients." This trend is a sure sign we have accepted defeat, a sure sign we have abandoned quality veterinary care for affordable veterinary care.

What is not affordable is the cost of doing business, and especially the cost of doing medicine. Human resource management, OSHA requirements, and endless government regulation are making it too costly and too complicated for many veterinarians. Ten years after opening my practice I attended a seminar which explained changes in human resources laws and the risk associated with merely hiring or firing an employee. It was mindboggling and terrifying. I also heard of the horror stories of the second most nefarious agency next to the IRS, OSHA. All workers deserve a safe work environment but to threaten crippling fines to a small practice because of a mislabeled bottle of hydrogen peroxide is ludicrous.

When the recession hit the cost of pharmaceuticals and medical equipment were no less costly. It also became clear that these companies charge the same whether their product was intended for human medicine or veterinary medicine. Yet, we could not charge the high markup for these medications which most pharmacies charge. During the recession, the distributors extended less credit and less favorable credit plans. Understandably they may also have been struggling like many veterinarians who were reducing their capital investments. We build them up, and now it seemed they were only protecting their bottom line, such as, when they began to sell veterinary medications on the retail market. This policy essentially had the same effects as low-cost clinics; taking the money out of our porous pockets. I would hear from various pharmaceutical sales representatives of the ubiquitous nature of cash flow issues within the profession. Some large referral practices had outstanding delinquencies in the hundreds of thousands of dollars, dwarfing my small debt.

The year I developed my business plan there were some concerns about the direction of veterinary medicine. Like pharmacists a decade before, veterinarians were starting to sell their businesses to major corporations. Dr. Klein and I would often debate on the longevity of the small family owned practice; he believed they would soon be extinct. He would correctly point out that the profession was steering towards cheap marketing, competitive pricing, and overinflated services. I challenged that trend by starting an old fashioned, family owned hospital that practiced caring, compassionate, more personalized medicine. I had competed with a large corporate practice for years, but now in a weak economy, these corporations had two things my young, small practice didn't have; they had a large client base and equity. The Pineland Veterinary Hospital had over tens of thousands of patients-five years after opening I had about one thousand files. They also had capital amassed over fifty years, sizeable discretionary spending accounts, and the favor of local bankers. Combine these advantages with a multimillion-dollar national corporate base and these hospitals could weather the worst recession or the storm of the century. Then when one considers the cost of equipping a hospital with modern equipment like a digital X-ray machine with a price tag over seventy thousand dollars, it becomes apparent why the veterinary profession was changing from privately owned small practices to corporate juggernauts. I began to believe my logical voice which had said I could compete with these large hospitals had again been flawed. Another crack was forming in my perfect snow globe. I started to consider my options.

In the late eighties, trade articles made two predictions about the veterinary profession. The first warned of decreasing veterinary salaries due to veterinary saturation. Many schools reduced their class size to counter overpopulation. A decade later veterinary schools reversed this trend and increased class size. However, a recent study (sanctioned by both the AVMA and the AAHA): "Reversing the Decline in Veterinary Care Utilization: Progress made, Challenges Remain," did show a troubling decline in regular preventative health care. Pet owners were spending less discretionary income on visits to the veterinarian. A JAVMA study by Christine C. Lim, DVM et al. stated that the mean starting salary for new graduates in private practice was just over $67,000. The average practice owner made only one hundred and twenty-six thousand dollars a year; this is the lowest of all doctorate medical professionals; in contrast, educational debt increased to an average of $162,000 for veterinary school education; one of the highest for all medical professionals. At the same time, veterinary salaries lagged far behind dentists and human medical doctors. Our profession is speeding in the wrong direction.

The second prediction was the shift to women in the veterinary profession. The book: *The AVMA 150 years of Education, Science & Service* reports that in 1949 the AVMA identified only one hundred female practicing veterinarians in North America. In the fall of 1985 women outnumbered men in veterinary school for the first time. In 2004 the female-male student ratio was 3 to 1. In 2015 AVMA membership favored women by almost twenty percent. I believe this trend has two components; the public perception is that the female veterinarian is more empathetic and openly more compassionate-they seem to care more. Combine this with declining salaries, and it is easy to see why young males may be considering a career elsewhere. Low wages are driving men to other professions with greater spoils and less risk. A $67,000 salary and almost two hundred thousand dollars in student debt make it impossible to support a family, certainly as a sole provider. Twenty-five years ago, when I attended my first veterinary seminar in Cape Cod, the attendees were dominated by middle age men in ties and sports jackets. I would estimate they made up at least eighty percent of the veterinarians in attendance. In a recent seminar in Virginia Beach, I counted the heads in each lecture; the demographics had completely reversed-at least eighty percent of those attending my classes were women. These economic realities explain why men are leaving for more lucrative fields of dreams. I cannot blame them.

When I began to research a business plan, I studied several books on small business development and veterinary practice management. Each posed common queries to help the reader evaluate if he or she was cut out to be a business owner. One of the first questions was: Are you comfortable with debt? Because in business you are always going to owe somebody. The authors were correct. I was in debt every hour of every day and the answer; I wasn't comfortable-ever! I spent many a silent night staring at my dark bedroom ceiling imaging new horizons in creative financing. Even during the good times, with every debt up to date, with every bill paid, the next mail delivery brought another set of invoices, "amount due now." My business ledger contained a hundred payments a month-constant debt payment-with always an eye on the most significant debt in business-payroll. I once was asked by an accountant to show him my Quick Books; I didn't know much about Quick Books, but I did know Clint Eastwood starred in a three memorable spaghetti westerns-see I told you.

Another common question often posed was: Are you comfortable hiring and firing people? Something else you will be doing all the time. After owning a business for over twelve years, my answer is still, most certainly no! I had no problem hiring people. Before interviews, I would refer to a list of questions considered appropriate by Human Resource standards. I was smart enough to know I could not ask about marriage, kids, or sexual preference. Remember, "How old a man are you?". However, when it came to: "What would you consider your biggest strength, what is your biggest weakness?" I would often leave the script. I would tend to hire based on first impressions and no it was only based on looks-that would not be legal (I did learn something in twenty-five years). The truth was that I often hired the wrong people. I recruited friends, friends of friends, children of friends, misguided divorcees, desperate housewives, a sexist gay man, a Latino playboy, a petty thief, and a minibus full of inept veterinarians. Following twelve failing years of hiring comic book clichés, my veteran staff members would eventually forbid me from doing interviews-my hiring practices were just too damn dangerous for the rest of the hospital.

    I was terrible at hiring, but I was worse at firing. One of my valued ex-employees once joked about a terminated employee, "God, he finally fired her; she must have been awful. He doesn't fire anyone." Now that is not true. However, I anguished over every person I terminated. I was ending their job, removing their source of income, and if only for a moment, destroying their self-esteem. The person who coined the phrase, "Heavy lies the crown" must have owned a business. I always took it as hard as they did. I would run every fact through my head, look for reasons not to fire them. A local hospital administrator once reminded me, "You don't fire employees, employees fire themselves." I wish that were true. If they could just come into my office on a Friday afternoon in December and say, "Doc, I'm sorry I've got to do this, I know, I know it is Christmas and all, but I'm fired. You know why because you're just tired of all the bullshit, I come in late, I talk behind your back, and I'm the one who stole that money from the cash drawer. Oh, and I know this doesn't surprise you, but I come in high pretty much every morning. Believe me; I'm not even going to try for unemployment. As far as a recommendation, forget it, I wouldn't have the audacity to ask for one; honestly, I suck that bad." Now that would leave me with a clear conscience.

Almost A Real Doctor

The first employee I ever fired was a young receptionist who was very proud of her new art project; she was so proud, she wanted to show everyone in the hospital. Unfortunately, her latest masterpiece were two large butterflies on each butt cheek. She then allegedly showed these monarch butterflies to almost every employee-I guess butterflies are free and so was her exhibit. I felt terrible when I fired her-as she left the hospital sobbing. I questioned my decision. How could a butterfly be so offensive? Hell, she only tattooed it on her rear end. Even now, I still can't believe how foolish she was for showing the staff her bucolic cheeks and how clever she was for not showing me.

The second termination was much less emotional, at least for me. I had agreed to do a favor for a friend and hire her son as an entry-level veterinary assistant. Norman was a twenty-two year openly old gay man whose career in veterinary medicine spanned a full day and a half. He had two major faults: he refused to clean anything that even resembled any organic substance, like hair, urine, feces; and he referred to female staff members as his bitches. However, his final trait endeared even me; he would address female body parts in graphic slang that would make a longshoreman blush. On his second glorious day of employment, I witnessed a well-planned mutiny when I was surrounded in the lunchroom by five threatening female staff members and one man who stayed for moral support. I wasn't allowed to finish my chicken panini until I ejected good old Norm from the hospital; like the home plate umpire ejected Billy Martian from Yankee stadium. In his meeting of separation, he was truly surprised the women had taken offense to his frank language, "I meant affectionately," he stated. "Besides I don't need this job, I'm better than those bitches. I can do anything they can do and do it a hell of a lot better. Later Doc!" I should have asked him in his interview what he considers his best and worst trait. Oh. I didn't give him an interview because it was a favor for a friend!

Often, I have experienced the embarrassing condition known as premature termination. This moment happens when I am on the verge of firing an employee, even preparing a dramatic termination speech, and they conveniently go on a permanent lunch. One such technician went to lunch one Wednesday under a cloud of suspicion for stealing money from other employees. The week before three staff members noticed some of their cash in their wallets was missing-seven dollars here, nineteen dollars there. It was a brilliant scam. Who counts their money every day? However, because this person was the only employee working all those days in question, it made her the prime suspect. I was starting to realize her lunch hour was going on a little long when a week later we received a letter which stated, "Sorry I had to quit, but it was time for me to go… By the way, I wasn't the one who stole the money. I just thought you should know, so you stop talking about me." Damn, I guess we had the wrong suspect.

Some employees hung by their fingers, dangling on the edge of the precipice. Instead of trying to pull themselves up they decided to take an unauthorized hiatus-they didn't quit, they just enjoyed a well-deserved break. One gentleman, Enrico Sauvé, used his ponytail and Central American accent to lure innocent women into his den of iniquity. When he disappeared for ten days, we assumed one of those charmed virgins had finally ended him-hey, it happens. Then we received a query from the state unemployment office requesting verification of unemployment benefits. I wrote a brief response, "I didn't know he was unemployed." The following week we had a three-way phone interview and not the kind of three-way he enjoyed. Although the interviewer was a woman, I could see she was immune to his Latin charms.

"Doctor, could you tell me your last correspondence with Mr. Sauvé."

"Well, the last day he worked was Friday, February 8th. I hadn't spoken to him since. He disappeared for almost two weeks. I called his cell phone and left three messages, and he never returned my calls."

"Mr. Sauvé, is this true? Were you incognito for almost two weeks?"

"No, I wasn't incognito. I was in Jersey City at my dad's house."

"Why, didn't you show up at work? Why didn't you call?"

"I did call. I talked to the office manager. She told not to bother to come to work for ten days, so I just thought I was fired. I wasn't going to come in if I was fired."

"Is that true doctor, did the office manager tell Mr. Sauvé not to come in for ten days?"

"That is not true, we don't have an office manager, I would have taken all those types of calls personally, and I know I didn't take that call."

"Who did you speak too, Mr. Sauvé? What was her name?"

"Lucy, her name was Lucy. She told me I---

"Excuse me there's no Lucy who works here. However, we did have a Beagle named, Snoopy, who came in last week for an ear infection."

"Maybe it wasn't Lucy; maybe it was Laura or Tracey."

"OK, well I have all the information we need. You will both be getting a final judgment in about a week."

We did have a Beagle named Snoopy, but we didn't have a manager named Lucy, and we did not have to pay unemployment to Enrico Sauvé. He was shot down by a woman for the first time in his life.

He was the classic no show, no call ex-employee. Some were just lazy, and light-headed each hour they were at work. Some employees were bold enough to spend their workday seeking other employment opportunities on the hospital computers. Again, instead of firing, I chose to allow death by attrition, maybe if they got a good lead on a new job, they would fire themselves. Others played the classic bad apple, poisoning loyal employees and constantly seeking conflict where none existed. Those employees were adept at hating, for any reason, one employee after another. Those people harbored deeper issues which festered in places outside the four walls I had created- a truth they choose to ignore.

In twelve years, I have hired a full poker hand of veterinarians, and I have fired all but one-full disclosure-one was a premature termination she left during her lunch hour. I think that doctor is still at Taco Bell drive-thru waiting for her bean burrito. I believed when I started recruiting veterinarians that their technical skills, medical expertise, and professional ethics would be impeccable. Sadly, I was wrong again. I never guessed it would be so difficult to find a competent veterinarian who would mesh with my practice.

To illustrate a point and for the sake of brevity, I will use a literary trick called a composite characterization, I will combine the traits of multiple individuals into one character who goes by the name of Dr. Kill Patient. I will refer to this character, like older traditional meteorological nomenclature, in the feminine gender, but this may either refer to a woman or a man.

Four years into owning my practice with the apparent loss of reason and lack of common sense, I hired Dr. Kill A. Patient as an associate veterinarian. Dr. Kill Patient may have seemed impressive after one shallow interview but deeper down she harbored several regrettable traits. I should have suspected trouble from her colorful resume; she had almost a decade of experience and a different job every year; she changed positions faster than a kid with itchy pants. However, I wish she had provided me with her real transparent version, the one I believe describes her real professional talents-this is what I would have penned as her accurate curriculum vitae:

***

DR. KILL A. PATIENT

PROFESSIONAL SUMMARY: To obtain a position as a veterinarian where I can practice unrealistic medicine in a real practice. Using my lack of skills and my horrid personality to create a hostile work environment while pursuing my egocentric agenda in a manner which minimally benefits my patients.

EDUCATION: Ya think?

WORK SUMMARY: I came, I sat, I went home (usually early).

SKILLS AND ACCOMPLISHMENTS:

Degraded staff members with abusive criticism routinely using sexist, politically incorrect, and socially inappropriate insults.

Embellished accomplishments to increase my standing in the hospital while inventing fanciful stories to discredit the practice owner.

Ignored humane euthanasia protocols while practicing my own inhumane, painful, and disturbing methods which tortured pets and shocked clients.

Publicly shamed clients who had decided to put their pet to sleep to place my pious morals above theirs.

Increased practice revenue by badgering clients into performing unnecessary and repetitive lab testing, especially on animals which should have been euthanized.

Initiated a personal incentive program called, "My Friends and Family Plan." A covert after-hours program to supply free veterinary medical services to my friends and neighbors. This initiative allowed me to use hospital supplies at no cost to me while receiving personal kickbacks and alcohol driven benefits.

Reduced recordkeeping costs by refusing to complete, sign, or use patient records, this also minimized medical liability because of the absence of valid medical records.

Spent majority of workday focused on new puppies and kittens. Utilized Muppet-like voices to simulate childlike play, irritating pets, and bewildering pet owners.

REFERENCES: I can write any recommendation upon request

* * *

Dr. Kill Patient, over-diagnosed, misdiagnosed, mistreated, ignored hospital protocol, had fits of rage, antisocial behavior, and three-martini lunches. She damaged my reputation, alienated clients, and aggravated almost every staff member. It was my responsibility and my sincere pleasure to exorcize the many personalities of Dr. Kill Patient in all her grotesque forms. My clients, my patients, and my hospital deserved better. My dream was worth more than this "one" inadequately trained, undedicated, self-absorbed, diva or a prima donna. My chosen profession also deserved better. Dr. Kill Patient wasted her golden ticket of veterinary medicine. That ticket entitled the holder to a career as a veterinarian-a real doctor-a ride she did not deserve. Her presence cheapened the deep sacrifice I made to achieve that goal.

Veterinarians love lawyers and lawyers love lawsuits. Dr. Kill Patient believed her rants of immortality and self-worth. Following termination, her attorney penned her delusional fantasy very eloquently by attributing every success in the practice to her incapable hands. The lawsuit demanded severance and damages for mental anguish. It threatened my entire business, my professional reputation, and my personal life. I should have sued for mental anguish and lost business-that would have been justice. This case crawled forward slowly for months until my attorney snuffed her ridiculous claim like a misplayed slam dunk.

In the past, incompetence was reason enough for dismissal, and embarrassment was sufficient reason to disappear quietly into the sunset. However, now in the days of the entitlement generation, the fault and responsibility will always lie with someone else. This concept was bluntly illustrated by what I call the "letters of defamation." These letters were sent by terminated employees which contained harsh criticisms of my management style and medical expertise and were usually sharply critical of most employees. Some staff members even warranted whole paragraphs dedicated to their destruction. Those ex-employees with the most biting criticisms were often the people with the most considerable transgressions. When I started the business, I expected to make enemies of my competition but what I did not expect was to make enemies from the people I hired, especially if those people were initially called friends-like Fred, my technician in the first years of my practice-such cases cut deep wounds which will never heal. This world of failed friendships, threatening employees, self-righteous doctors, and creative lawyers with fantasy lawsuits grew into a force which placed a third crack in my perfect snow globe.

The fragile, imperfect glass which had insulated my perfect adolescent veterinary snow globe from reality for over three decades, was finally shattered on the morning of one of the most important milestones of my daughter's life. I received a summons from the bank who aggressively financed my renovations seven years before. Today an equally aggressive process server handed me a legal notice as I waited for the bus with my daughter on her first day of kindergarten. I refer to this bank as the D&C Savings & Loan because they performed a dilation and curettage procedure on my business; without sedation or even local anesthesia to alleviate the pain of a broken dream.

It was a different economy in 2007 but the same greedy baking system. The fifth-largest bank in the country offered $385,000 at a hefty 10% interest rate. This was the same bank which received $7.7 billion in bailout money under the Obama Administration's "Troubled Asset Relief Program" (TARP). This was the same bank which used a portion of those tax dollars to buy another banking franchise in 2008 shamelessly. This was the same bank I petitioned for my temporary relief following Hurricane Sandy in the fall of 2012. That day in early November I had asked for a simple two-month forbearance to lessen the financial loss suffered after the storm. Their answer was a resounding "no." Let's review: President Obama's answer in a banking crisis was-yes, D&C's answer in a natural disaster was-no. I called the Philadelphia office of a commercial banking representative a week after the storm; he expressed D&C banks sincere concern for the victims of superstorm Sandy, "We are eager to do anything to help those affected by Sandy, but a two-month forbearance is out of the question. However, I can reduce any late charges for November as a onetime courtesy. If you need anything else, let me know." Now that is the bank with a heart.

Now, two years later this bank filed suit for a final balloon payment of $60,000. In June of 2014, I had satisfied my eighty-four-month payment agreement, leaving the final balloon payment. Six months before I requested a refinance schedule; I offered to pay my regular monthly payment over the next twelve months. Again, D&C's answer was no. I had been paying almost $8,000 a month for seven years, I had spent over $640,000, they had made a profit of nearly three-hundred-thousand dollars, and now they refused to negotiate a timely settlement for $60,000. The problem; part of the note was an SBA loan. My attorney accurately stated that the federal government guarantees these loans for only part of the repayment period. The same government that advanced this bank $7.7 billion in 2008. The final two years of the SBA loan is the bank's responsibility; a responsibility they did not want any longer. They just wanted their money, and they didn't care if it destroyed my business. Donald Trump once referred to friendly bankers as not being very nice people. I now understood what he meant.

This loan was not bad. The bank just wanted it closed. I remember that angry redhead who threw that $132.00 check in my face the first year I opened, "Here's your money, I hope you choke on it," she said. Now I hoped my checks would get caught in the opposite end of the banker's GI tract. The head of this division probably gets bonuses based on how many of these accounts they close out before the end of the fiscal year. When I confronted the bank representative with those accusations, he could only answer, "I can't deny anything you are saying, but I can tell you the banking system allows us to default on any business loan overdue in as little as fifteen days. We are not obligated to make any concessions, and there is not a whole lot you can do about it."

"I know you are not making these decisions," I argued. "I know there is some community college, MBA above you who is pulling the strings. Some greedy, self-serving little kiss ass who drives his foreign hybrid up the Schuylkill Expressway to his North Philadelphia townhouse each night and kisses his mainline wife on the cheek as she hands him brandy to help him relax from his trying day. Tell me what does he say? What does he tell her when she asks him, 'How did your day go honey?' Does he say, 'I saved a life today?' Does he say, 'Today I performed a difficult surgery for the first time and sent the dog home in the arms of his happy owner, without once asking when she could pay her bill?' Does he say, 'I ended the suffering of someone's best friend and shared their tears in an emotional embrace?' No, of course, he doesn't. He uses someone else's money to put other people in debt. He spends his day destroying those dreams, tearing down things other people have built. Why does he do it? Fun, ego, or for the sake of his yearend bonus-a bonus taxpayers probably paid through TARP money. I have two words you can relay to him; you're welcome." Commercial banking can be a cesspool and bankers are the people who spend their day making gold bars out of the blood and sweat of struggling businesspeople. I had been negotiating with this man for months; he had a heart. I knew he wasn't the problem. So, I gave him one final heartfelt recommendation, "Get out of this business before it turns you into one of them."

My heart and my resolve sunk into the rising water of despair; this started with the recession of 2008, worsened with the hurricane of 2012, was soured by the personal attacks of ex-employees, and now was finally condemned by a merciless banking system. I had started my practice twelve years before to reinvent the compassionate veterinary hospital. I worked six days a week for almost four years and every Saturday for nearly ten years-time I could have spent with my wife and children. The year before I had struggled to squeeze out a total of four consecutive days of vacation. I worked over a decade fighting to pay off leases, satisfy loans, and make payroll. It was a daily battle, juggling debt to keep drugs stocked, insurance current, and utilities paid. I had grown weary dealing with aggressive bankers and debt collectors one minute and entering a room with an itchy poodle the next — the whole time acting every bit the caring professional. The problem was that I didn't care anymore.

In the play, *Camelot*, there is a scene near the climax where the kingdom of Camelot is crumbling. King Arthur, in desperation, asks Merlin the magician to turn him back into a hawk, like he did when he was a child, so that he could fly away from his painful reality. He was a reluctant king whose idealistic world was crumbling-his flame was burning out. I, a reluctant boss, wanted to fly away from my pain. Honestly, for the first time in my career, I was burnt out. Professional burn out is a frequent subject in veterinary trade magazines. One step farther, other articles speak of the plague of drug addiction in veterinary medicine. Still a step farther, an article in JAVMA highlighted a study: "1 in 6 veterinarians have considered suicide." I had reached the first stage, but desperation had yet to drive me to the last two. After eight years of school and twenty-five years of practice, I deserved to live a comfortable lifestyle, take family vacations, send my kids to college, and to earn a living wage without working eighty hours a week. It was no longer possible. Regret is like cancer, slowly destroying hope one dream at a time. Maybe, I should have charged more, paid less, and demanded perfection. Perhaps, I should have been greedy; callous. Maybe profit should have been my first goal, but for me, it began and ended with the animal-a naïve ideal in today's world. It may appear to some that I hate this profession; on the contrary, I love this profession; I only hate what it has become. Veterinary medicine has become a discretionary afterthought for disposable pets.

My friend John the owner of a local veterinary practice placed it into perspective, "Owning a practice is one constant headache after another," he said. "If it's not finding a decent doctor, it's getting clients to pay their bills. If it's not making payroll, it's keeping up with the fifty other bills to pay every month. I can't take vacations; it cost too much money to pay a reliable relief vet. I feel trapped, I can't sell, none of the new graduates want to own a practice, and they couldn't get a loan even if they wanted one. Some of these new vets are coming out with over two hundred thousand dollars of debt; they'll never make enough to pay it off, let alone afford their own practice. I don't see a way out."

Dr. Park, my original ticket to vet school, is still working six days a week after forty years in business. Dr. Klein would often say out of pure frustration, "Owning a practice is like a prison sentence without parole." Fortunately, I had been considering my options for over two years-I was granted a parole hearing.

Shortly after Superstorm Sandy, I started to investigate a proposition to sell my practice. I had my practice appraised and evaluated; I researched the advantages and considered my path. The most significant hurdle was, as my colleague stated so profoundly, few people had the resources to purchase a practice this size. I started to look towards the scourge Dr. Klein had spoken of fifteen years ago-corporate America. I had heard many horror stories about the dangers of corporate buyouts. They threatened employee's layoffs, changed policies, and compromised medicine. In September, I was approached by a corporation unlike those I had heard before, one that would allow me to practice my brand of medicine with fewer headaches. However, I still was conflicted, and for the first time since working as a janitor, unsure of my future. The strain of the last few years had drained my hope; my dreams were no more than a waning sunset.

Two weeks after being served with D&C banks love letter (the court summons), I was still nauseous from the last conversation I had with the bank representative. The following Friday I had a career day at one of the local elementary schools. As I drove my minivan ten minutes to my one o'clock class, I recalled the lecture I had attended in high school thirty-five years before. I remembered the nasty, little man who discouraged twenty-two students with a brief thirty-minute diatribe.

I now understood; the vision hit me in the face like a Steve Carlton fastball. I felt the truth behind that man's words like I was hearing them for the first time. The power struggle with bad employees, the conflict between the needs of selfish clients and the practice of good medicine. The scars of surgical failures and the lack of credit for medical triumphs. The cruel economic reality of merciless banks, government regulation, a weak economy, and natural disasters. The strain had been constant, even during the prosperous years it was still one valley after another.

In high school, I was discouraged by the honest words of a bitter veterinarian behind a fiberboard podium. Now I was disenchanted by twenty-five years of practice. My own demons haunted me; the slowing heartbeat of a dying bunny or the words of a vengeful client over the death of her dog: "I hope you can sleep at night knowing what you did." The advice of my pre-vet advisor warning me: "Not to screw it up for someone else." Dr. Klein's warning, "That's not what you want, I don't know if you have it in you to run your own practice." I recalled my own voice questioning God on a bridge in my third year of vet school: "Is this why you brought me here?" Finally, I remembered one more voice, my father's words to my mother: "I just don't think he's got what it takes."

Then I envisioned the naïve twelve-year-old boy delivering kittens in his mother's bathroom. I could see the vet school pamphlet slip from the pages of the *Merck Veterinary Manual*. I could again hear my mother read my veterinary school acceptance letter over a plastic corded phone, bathed in her maternal praise. I remembered reciting the veterinary oath in that auditorium on a scolding day in May twenty-five years before. I could recall discharging my first dog spay, alive and well; and the relief I felt as she bounced into her owner's arms, tail wagging as she pranced out the door. I saw the pets I had diagnosed, treated, and cured so they could continue to have years of life with their grateful owners like the little Yorkie saved by a hail Mary surgery to remove the stones from its urethra. I could still recite every word of Mr. Whitehead's sermon of praise-he preached it for so many years. I can recall the first time I saw my name stenciled in glass on the front door of my hospital and the article in the local paper that announced my grand opening.

    This mediocre student succeeded out of pure persistence. I created a highly successful, well-respected practice from nothing. However, now I was more a businessman than a doctor; I was just another practice owner struggling to succeed in an economy unkind to small business. A myth of the American dream; owning your own business, like being you own boss, had become a flawed fantasy. God, I was taught, will always open the next door when he closes the first. I am a firm believer in signs-signs that lead you through that next door. The problem was I didn't know if I should stand, like an obstinate German, with my foot in the threshold to prevent this door from slamming shut or start looking for another path. I had a brief conversation with my wife that morning before I left for that elementary classroom. "Have you made a decision? What do YOU want to do?" She asked.

I answered without hesitation, "I just want to be a doctor, that's all I ever wanted to be, A REAL DOCTOR."

I walk into the third-grade classroom with the same briefcase I carry to all my career days. Today it contains only a pack of small folded pamphlets published by the American Veterinary Medical Association, "Veterinarians-Protecting the Health of Animals and People." I usually carry more coloring books, souvenir AVMA pencils, and a lecture outline, but today I only have about thirty bright green brochures meant to seed the next generation of veterinarians. I have lost my focus and enthusiasm. I am to speak about a profession that has failed me. Should I read a fairy tale, glorifying the veterinary profession with words like respect, satisfaction, and limitless potential; or should I be honest and tell the truth with words like sacrifice, disappointment, and struggle. Isn't it my obligation to lead these young children into the future based on fact? Like I did when years before I had encouraged my oldest son to choose pediatrics over veterinary medicine. However, I also did not want to be a sour memory, that bitter man behind the podium, who would dissuade a third-grade boy or girl from pursuing his or her dream, who might by some great act of God make a difference in this profession-who might achieve pure happiness in veterinary medicine.

I stand at the podium and look out over twenty-four third graders, their fifty-five-year old teacher, and her young auburn-haired teaching assistant. There is the typical chaos of grade school students turning in their seats, giggling, as one boy throws a rolled-up paper at another across the aisle. The gray hair teacher raises her voice in disapproval and a with loud hush she scolds the two boys; they are more interested in tormenting each other than listening to my speech. Most see this half hour as a break from their next math lesson, not a call to duty. I think to myself; I wish I had that kind of carefree enthusiasm for anything. I look out over their heads and see a décor typical of a thousand third grade classrooms. A numbers line, a map of the world, and posters filled with quotes to stimulate thought and perseverance. Two posters catch my eye; one is a Holstein cow with the phrase: "Got milk?" The second, a red kitten hanging on a branch with the saying: "Hang in there, Baby!"

The teacher makes a brief introduction as a welcomed calm comes over the class. I quickly notice one girl with blonde pigtails sitting in the first row just in front of the podium; she has bright blue eyes framed by pink rimmed glasses. She transfixes her eyes on me; I think for a moment that I can see my reflection in her lenses. She holds up a small picture in her right hand, and next to a broad smile she proudly states, "This is my bunny, Flopsy. She lives in my bedroom." She reminds me of my daughter who is just a year younger in a second-grade class down the hall. This young girl seems oblivious to the bluster of her classmates behind her. Could she be interested in what I will say? I swallow the lump in my throat, take a deep breath and one last time I ponder why I am there; why I am anywhere. I whisper a quick, silent prayer and look directly into her eyes. Then I begin to speak…

BIBLIOGRAPHY

AVMA. One hundred and Fifty Years of Education, Science, and Service. AVMA Press. Schaumburg, Illinois, 2012.

AVMA/AAHA. Reversing the Decline of Veterinary Care Utilization: Progress Made, Challenges Remain. AVMA Press. Schaumburg, Illinois, 2014.

Bernard, Stephen. PNC Buying National City with Money Bailout. The Charlotte Observer, October 2008.

Fiala, Jennifer. Economic Downturn Hits Veterinary Practices. VIN News Service, March 2009.

Geller, Joy, DVM, ABVP, Dark Shadows, Drug Abuse and addiction in the Veterinary Workplace. DVM 360 Magazine, 47:7 (2016).

How to Stay Busy During Your Practice Recess. Veterinary Practice News, 21:6 (2009).

Knecht, Allen, Williams, Johnson. Fundamental Techniques in Veterinary Surgery. Philadelphia: W. B. Saunders Co., 1987.

Lim, Christine, DVM et al. Financial Expectations of First-Year Veterinary Students. JAVMA, 247:2 (2014), Pgs. 196-203.

Nett, Randall, et al. Risk Factors for Suicide, Attitudes Towards Mental Illness, and Practice Related Stressors Among US Veterinarians. JAVMA, 247:8 (2015). Pgs. 945-955.

What Happened to the Recession Proof Practice? Veterinary Forum Magazine, 26:8 (2009).

ABOUT THE AUTHOR

Dr. Robert Cimer was born in a small suburban town in Southern New Jersey. He received his Bachelor of Science degree from Rutgers University and earned a degree of Doctor of Veterinary Medicine from the University of Missouri-College of Veterinary Medicine in 1988. The first year following graduation he practiced farm animal medicine in a small town in Central Missouri then moved back to New Jersey to practice small animal medicine for the next thirty years. He founded a successful companion animal practice in Central New Jersey in 2003. He was an associate professor at a local community college teaching two veterinary medical courses, one geared for children, another for adults. He is married and has three children. He has owned everything from a white mouse to an Alaskan Malamute and continues to see new furry patients every day

Made in the USA
Middletown, DE
20 July 2019